Women and States

Momentous changes in the relation between women and the state have advanced women's status around the globe. Women were barred from public affairs a century ago, yet almost every state now recognizes equal voting rights and exhibits a national policy bureau for the advancement of women. Sex quotas for national legislatures are increasingly common. Ann E. Towns explains these changes by providing a novel account of how norms work in international society. She argues that norms don't just provide standards for states, they rank them, providing comparative judgments which place states in hierarchical social orders. This focus on the link between norms and ranking hierarchies helps to account better for how a new policy, such as equality for women in public life, is spread around the world. *Women and States* thus offers a new view of the relationship between women and the state, and of the influence of norms in international politics.

Ann E. Towns is Assistant Professor of Political Science and International Relations at the University of Delaware. Her research centers on gender in global governance and international society, with a focus on the status of women as a standard of rank in international politics.

Women and States

Norms and Hierarchies in International Society

ANN E. TOWNS

CAMBRIDGE
UNIVERSITY PRESS

CAMBRIDGE
UNIVERSITY PRESS

University Printing House, Cambridge CB2 8BS, United Kingdom

Cambridge University Press is part of the University of Cambridge.

It furthers the University's mission by disseminating knowledge in the pursuit of
education, learning and research at the highest international levels of excellence.

www.cambridge.org
Information on this title: www.cambridge.org/9780521745918

First published 2010

A catalogue record for this publication is available from the British Library

Library of Congress Cataloguing in Publication data
Towns, Ann E., 1970–
Women and states : norms and hierarchies in international society / Ann E. Towns.
    p.   cm.
Includes bibliographical references.
ISBN 978-0-521-76885-6 – ISBN 978-0-521-74591-8 (pbk.)
1. Women's rights – History.   2. Women – Social conditions.   I. Title.
HQ1236.T694 2010
305.42–dc22

                                                                2009054026

ISBN 978-0-521-76885-6 Hardback
ISBN 978-0-521-74591-8 Paperback

For my parents

Contents

Tables

Acknowledgments

This book is the product of many years of labor in multiple parts of the world. Many of the ideas I have tried to formulate here have had a long period of gestation and growth, being shaped by a number of different intellectual contexts. In the first stages, I was greatly aided by the lively intellectual environment of the graduate program in political science at the University of Minnesota. It is difficult to do justice to the value of the enthusiasm, generosity and support of my thesis adviser, Kathryn Sikkink, whose intellectual guidance and astute suggestions continue to pervade and shape this book. Raymond Duvall graciously served as an additional, if informal adviser, and I am eternally grateful for his intellectual direction and involvement in this project. Special thanks also go to Jeanine Anderson, Elizabeth Boyle, Petrice Flowers, Emilie Hafner-Burton, Roudy Hildreth, Amy Kaminsky, Johanna Kantola, Sally Kenney, Helen Kinsella, M. J. Maynes, Darel Paul, Richard Price, Naomi Scheman, Latha Varadarajan, and others who provided invaluable comments on this project during the dissertation period.

Many people at other universities and research institutions helped me think through various aspects of the thesis in order to develop it into a book. I would especially like to thank the faculty and graduate students of the Department of Political Science at Göteborg university, Sweden, where I spent three years on a post-doctoral fellowship. Hans E. Andersson, Mette Anthonsen, Monica Bauer, Ulf Bjereld, Marie Demker, Andreas Johansson, Johannes Lindvall, Helena Stensöta and Lena Wängnerud were particularly helpful. The revision process has also benefited from comments and suggestions in various contexts from Lisa Baldez, Drude Dahlerup, Mala Htun, Mona-Lena Krook, Iver Neumann, Mark Lynch, and Diane Sainsbury. Thanks as well to two anonymous reviewers who provided excellent comments and suggestions for revisions.

In the many years of working on this project, I have also acquired a substantial debt to a number of research assistants. For the assistance of

Javier Diez Canseco, Geun K. Joakim Sebring, Andrea Stiglich, Juliette Tolay-Sargnon, Margarita Velasco and Mayu Velasco – mil gracias, tusen tack. Numerous research centers, archives and libraries have opened their doors and offered their expertise on the location of crucial documents. The staff of the library of the University of Minnesota, CENDOC-Mujer (Peru), Biblioteca Nacional del Perú, Archivo Nacional de Perú, Centro de la Mujer Peruana Flora Tristán, the archives of the Peruvian Ministry of Justice, Riksdagsbiblioteket (Stockholm), the archives of the Swedish international development agency (Sida) and the Göteborg university library have been particularly helpful. I am very grateful to the many workers who went above and beyond their formal duties to locate obscure, forgotten or misplaced documents.

A number of organizations, foundations and individuals have facilitated the research financially and practically. During the thesis period, these included a William F. Stout Fellowship, a Max M. Kampelman Graduate Research Fellowship in Human Rights, and a University of Minnesota Doctoral Dissertation Fund Fellowship. The dissertation research was also funded through a MacArthur Doctoral Field Research Grant, University of Minnesota Grant for Research Abroad, and grants from Fredrika Bremer-Förbundet and Kjellbergska flickskolan. The post-thesis research and writing were greatly aided by a major three-year grant from the European Commission and a one-year fellowship at the Swedish Institute of International Affairs.

Finally, this project would have never come to fruition without the support of my family. Tusen tack to my farfar and farmor, Åke and Vivan Korner; my parents, Johnny and Franziska Korner; my sister, Sarah Korner; my aunt, Ulla Hoffmann; and last but not least, my husband and children, Reynolds, Inga-Lisa and Kajsa. My family has cheered me on while simultaneously reminding me to keep academics in a larger perspective. This book is their accomplishment as well as my own.

1 | *Introduction*

I can only answer the question "What am I to do?" if I can answer the prior question "Of what story or stories do I find myself a part?"

Alasdair MacIntyre[1]

This book has two aims, one empirical and the other theoretical. The empirical aspiration is to account for a development that has received insufficient attention within the field of international relations: [the worldwide emergence of state behaviors that expressly target women.] [The theoretical ambition is to propose a rethinking of the operation of norms in international society. Norms do not simply homogenize states, as is conventionally argued – norms rank and set up relations of hierarchy among states as well.] In short, to understand and explain the spread of certain state practices towards women, this book points to the importance of the status of women as a standard of rank in international society.

The spread of state institutions on women

The worldwide changes in the relation between women and the state are nothing short of revolutionary. A century ago, all polities that were organized as states rested on the exclusion of women from their formal [* Think "Founding Fathers"] institutions. With the exception of an occasional queen as head of state, women were shut out of the public roles of state representative, official or civil servant. In the emerging democracies of Europe, women became expressly prohibited from voting and in some cases even from joining political parties or attending political rallies. German political activist Clara Zetkin complained in 1895 that "prohibition after prohibition of women's assemblies takes place, the expulsion of women from public meetings are [*sic*] a daily occurrence and penalties for women for

---

[1] MacIntyre 1984: 216.

1

violating the Law for the Formation of Associations inundate the courts."[2] Women had no place in the formal affairs of state in the nineteenth century.

Today's situation is thoroughly different. Virtually every state has incorporated women in some manner, whether as voters, public officials or political representatives. The incorporation of women into state institutions around the world has taken place in sets of changes that developed neither simultaneously nor jointly. Women's suffrage emerged in the late nineteenth century and has now become virtually universal, institutionalized in all but a few states. Suffrage legislation emerged globally in four waves, following an interesting clustered path. The female vote was first conceded among states on the outskirts of what was then "civilized society" – New Zealand (1893), Australia (1902), Finland (1906), and Norway (1907) – to eventually include most of the remaining European and North American states by the end of the two World Wars. An overlapping though quicker second wave of transformations took place in the emerging socialist states of Eastern Europe and Central Asia, which institutionalized women's suffrage primarily between 1918 and 1924. Latin America passed suffrage laws in a third wave, mainly between the late 1930s and mid-1950s. Finally, whereas suffrage was extended to women in certain colonized areas, formal political roles were generally denied women under European colonial rule. Suffrage instead emerged in most of Africa and Asia when national independence was won, between 1945, in Indonesia, and 1975, when Portuguese colonies such as Angola and Mozambique finally became independent.

Over 90 percent of contemporary states have furthermore created a public bureau to handle women's issues, what is called in United Nations parlance a national women's machinery (NWM). These bureaus are charged with addressing the situation of women in public policy and thus bring women's issues (and women) into the formalized public policy planning and implementation processes. Whereas the more specific mandates of national machineries vary, they all share a directive of institutionalizing the situation of women into the formal political, fiscal or bureaucratic processes of the state.

Unlike suffrage, which developed in temporally distinct waves, these national policy machineries came into being rather swiftly. It took less

[2] Zetkin 1895: 61.

than two decades for these bureaus to become created in two thirds of the world's states. And unlike suffrage, their geographical trajectory was not clustered, emerging seemingly randomly across the world beginning with the USA (1961), Australia (1963), Argentina (1965), Malaysia (1965), West Germany (1965) and Nepal (1967). One set of states was notably absent in embracing this development, however: not one of the communist states created a national women's machinery. It would take the collapse of communism as a form of state before post-communist states came to create NWMs.

[handwritten margin note: interesting... why? contradictory to comunist values?]

We are now in the midst of another transformation in the relations between women and the state that may become global in scope: the incorporation of women into national legislatures through some form of quota legislation. Legislature sex quotas generally demand that a certain portion of candidates for national legislatures be slotted for women, ranging from 20 percent to 50 percent. They may also involve the less common action of reserving legislative seats specifically for women. Not only do most states now allow women to serve in legislative assemblies, in other words, but positive action is institutionalized to increase the number of female legislators.

[handwritten margin note: Quota vs. Merit good or bad?]

Nearly fifty states have adopted some form of quota legislation to increase the level of women in the national legislature since 1991. And this number is likely to increase, since there are presently campaigns in another fifty some states to pass such laws. Interestingly, the geographical path of these quota measures could hardly be more different than those of suffrage and national women's machinery. The present surge of national quota laws developed primarily out of Latin America in the 1990s, where the great majority of countries passed such laws during the past decade. African and Asian states are now following suit, including several Islamic states, such as Djibouti (2002), Pakistan (2002), Morocco (2002), Indonesia (2003) and Jordan (2003). The constitutional provisions for 25 percent women in the new national legislature of Afghanistan (2004) and the provisional constitution of Iraq (2004) have received a great deal of attention. Standing out against this trend, the use of quotas in Western Europe and North America is exceedingly rare and, by the end of 2009, includes only Belgium (1994), France (2000) and Spain (2007).

[handwritten margin note: What do these states have in common other than Islam?]

Considering the worldwide scope of adoption of these three measures, it is not an exaggeration to suggest that the relations between women and the state have changed in astonishing ways during the past century. Virtually all states have institutionalized female voting and now address the situation of women – however variably – through a national women's machinery. Legislation to augment the number of women in national legislature is increasingly being adopted around the world. In view of the evenness of these worldwide state transformations, they are clearly touched by international processes.

Despite their international character, these profound changes have received remarkably sparse attention by international relations (IR) scholars. There is, to be sure, a small and important body of work that has done so, and this scholarship will be addressed throughout the book. But the issue has certainly not given rise to anything akin to a debate in the discipline. From this, we can by and large conclude that the formal designation of half of the world's population as political agents has not yet been included in the "small number of big and important things" with which IR has been so preoccupied.[3] The worldwide emergence of female suffrage, national machinery for women and sex quota laws remain among the many subjects on women, gender and international politics that are still fundamentally under-explored within the field of IR.

The aim of this book is to help fill this gap by providing an account of the worldwide emergence of women's suffrage, national machinery for women and sex quota laws. However, as will become apparent throughout this book and as I shall illustrate briefly below, it is far from evident what these practices are all about, since the meaning of each practice is far from given. One of the most fundamental questions to ask is thus how to characterize and understand these developments. That is indeed my first question: *What* is going on here? In other words, what *are* these transformations? As we shall see below and throughout this book, the answer to this question is not straightforward and demands theoretical attention. Once these developments are characterized, a subsequent set of closely related questions can be posed, centering on *how* and *why* these transformations were brought about. How can we account for these changes, from an international relations perspective?

More similar states in a homogenized international society?

Even though the discipline of IR has not yet given much attention to the spread of women's suffrage, women's policy bureaus or sex quotas, the

[3] Waltz 1986: 329.

analytical tools of the field can help to characterize the transformations and provide answers to how and why the relations between women and the state have become restructured. The rich tradition of constructivism is particularly well positioned to do so. If we begin with the first and fundamental analytical question of how to characterize such developments, scholars who emphasize the role of norms and constitutive world culture scripts would contend that these developments are indications that the actors of international society are becoming increasingly similar. Centuries ago, the world was made up of a host of different kinds of polities, with heterogeneous forms of political organization around the globe. During the past one hundred years in particular, these scholars claim, we have witnessed the regulation and homogenization of political life worldwide, as the state has become the chief mode of political organization.

Along with the state, the individual citizen has also come into being globally, if still unevenly, with the help of international norms. Suffrage, state bureaus and quota measures would probably be characterized as instances not only of the victory of the state as the predominant polity but also of the individualization of humanity. Sexual differentiation and the exclusion of one sex from formal state affairs may be giving way to the treatment of men and women alike as individual citizens. Constructivists would likely assert that states are becoming more and more similar in their behavior towards increasingly de-gendered human beings who are more equally empowered politically.

[handwritten margin notes: media influence? how have we gone from citizens to global citizens; gender recognition but not homogenization?]

The spread of these institutions is often characterized not just as homogenization but as Westernization. In many contemporary contexts around the world, there are persistent presumptions that the empowerment of women is a particularly Western or European phenomenon with roots in the Enlightenment. Such views have even made it into the core of political science. For instance, Inglehart and Norris (2003) call gender equality the source of "the true clash of civilizations." Like many others, they attribute the empowerment of women unequivocally to Western values and traditions. Susan Okin's rhetorical question and essay title, *Is Multiculturalism Bad for Women?*,[4] likewise points to the anxiety that many in Europe and North America feel about the presumed conflict between non-European politico-cultural traditions and sexual equality. Western, liberal states are the

---

[4] Okin 1999.

best guarantors of female empowerment and dignity in this view. Other states are not.

These claims resonate in the field of international relations. As we shall see in Chapter 2, constructivists generally approach the homogeneous nature of international society as having its roots in the norms, values and ideas of the European Enlightenment. The international spread of suffrage, women's policy bureaus and sex quotas may appear to be a particularly clear case of Westernization, an indication that modern and liberal values and ideas on women have spread from the West across the world.

This portrayal, of the worldwide standardization and homogenization, is certainly plausible. There is a homogenizing dimension of norms. A measure such as women's suffrage is undoubtedly approached and discussed as the same kind of practice around the world, in the more narrow sense of involving women casting votes for political candidates. There is wide agreement that women should be allowed to vote to the same extent as men. In this sense, norms do make states more similar to one another. And yet there are crucial empirical challenges that should make us rethink the claims about international norms and state similarity, as we shall see below.

Women as a standard of rank in a hierarchical international society

The main empirical challenges presented in this book concern the understanding and meaning of suffrage, national machinery for women and sex quotas across the world. If, as constructivists must, one takes inter-subjective meaning seriously, one cannot set apart what state institutions *are* from the meanings through which they are constituted and reproduced. And if the worldwide emergence of these state institutions is really about homogenization, then the understandings of what these institutions are and do should point to a world of more similar states.

However, as this book will show, the rationales and motivations for these practices – the understandings of why such behavior is appropriate for a particular state – have consistently rested on identifying certain kinds of states as inferior to others. State behavior towards women has often provided an opportunity not only to differentiate among states but also to evaluate and rank states in a hierarchical manner. Let me take a moment to provide a few illustrations to make this point more clear.

In 1902, by the end of the Philippine–American War, Philippine patriot and feminist Clemencia López took her anti-imperialist advocacy to Boston. One of the groups she addressed was the New England Woman Suffrage Association. López took the opportunity to speak about the situation of women in the Philippines, making the following statement:

I am glad of this opportunity to address you, so that you who are kind enough to give me your courteous attention may have a better idea, and may form a different and more favorable opinion of the Filipinos, than the conception which the generality of the American people have formed, believing us to be savages without education or morals.

I believe that we are both striving for much the same object – you for the right to take part in national life; we for the right to have a national life to take part in. And I am sure that, if we understood each other better, the differences which now exist between your country and mine would soon disappear.

You will no doubt be surprised and pleased to learn that ... mentally, socially, and in almost all the relations of life, our women are regarded as the equals of our men. You will also be surprised to know that this equality of women in the Philippines is not a new thing. It was not introduced from Europe ... Long prior to the Spanish occupation, the people were already civilized, and this respect for and equality of women existed.[5]

López was clearly responding to what she considered a misrepresentation of the situation of women in the Philippines, that Filipinos were "savages without education or morals" who knew nothing of equality between men and women. Her challenge invoked a then predominant hierarchical classification scheme, namely that the world consisted of peoples and polities along a continuum from savagery to civilization. Americans had misunderstood the position of the Philippines in that hierarchy, she objected. Filipinos were civilized long before the Europeans arrived, and the equal standing of women and men was evidence of this.

López's statement is suggestive of the unequal status between what were then considered "civilized" and "barbarous" societies. Like many of her contemporaries, she discussed the situation of women in terms of this hierarchy. López used the situation of women as a standard of

[5] López 1902.

assessment, a criterion by means of which she could define and evaluate the Philippines and place it in the hierarchical order between civilization and barbarism.

López is far from alone in using the situation of women to assess and rank states. Amina Al Saied, the Egyptian representative in the African-Asian Solidarity Organization and secretary-general of the Arab Women's Union, was an important transnational activist for the political empowerment of women in Africa and Asia in the mid to late twentieth century. In 1958, she explained that "whenever I visit a foreign country for the first time … I compare between the status of women in it and the status of our women and then I work from this to extract … the place of the modern Egyptian woman in the pageant of world civilization." Compared to "advanced" societies such as France, the USA and Britain, she argued, Egypt was still "at the bottom of the ladder." However, matched up to most Asian and African women, Egyptian women were the "pinnacle of culture and advancement."[6]

In both of these examples, we can see a comparative and even competitive dynamic around the situation of women. States not engaged in proper behavior are identified as different and inferior – as barbarous, in the language of López and Al Saied. Importantly, as this book will show, even when states do engage in what is presumably the same behavior – enabling women's suffrage, for instance – the rationales and explanations for the appropriateness of this behavior still rank-order states. This simultaneous ranking and differentiating dynamic is not compatible with the portrayal of norms only as a homogenizing force.

A more adequate characterization of the worldwide spread of women's suffrage, policy bureaus and quota laws needs to take into account both the homogenizing and the stratifying dimensions of norms. What we need to understand and explain about the worldwide spread of state institutions is not simply increased similarity but rather what I claim to be an interconnected dynamic of simultaneous homogenization and stratification. This book takes to heart Roland Robertson's contention that the true challenge to the study of globalization is "spelling out the ways in which homogenizing and heterogenizing tendencies are mutually implicative."[7] To study norms is also to study social hierarchies.

[6] As cited in Bier 2004: 104.   [7] Robertson 1995: 27.

This book will show that an abstract and rather general norm about state practices towards women has been effective in international society at least since the early nineteenth century. In the abstract, the norm can be captured as "Better states exhibit appropriate practices towards women." State practices towards women have been and continue to be important standards of rank across the world. But what sorts of practices are deemed appropriate and, in turn, which states appear as superior to others are matters of perspective and subject to debate. In 1998, for instance, a young Afghan woman was given one hundred lashes at the Kabul Sports Stadium, for an alleged act of adultery. Her persecutor is reported to have cried out: "Thanks to the Taliban, the army of God, that we can protect the honor of our people ... thanks to God that we are followers of God and not the West," before the 30,000 spectators.[8] Like many others, Taliban clerics and rulers saw a close link between the empowerment of women and the West. The official and often violent subordination of women to men became one set of state measures held to differentiate Taliban Afghanistan from the despised West.

However, the prevalent idea that equality between women and men is an exclusively European invention or a particularly Western and liberal set of values has been far from unchallenged around the world. Indeed, this idea has been disputed ever since it developed. As an illustration of such a challenge, let us return for a moment to the address by Clemencia López before the New England Suffrage Association in 1902. Her claim could not be clearer: "Equality of women in the Philippines is not a new thing. It was not introduced from Europe." This book will show that like López, many activists, scholars, state representatives and other public officials have grappled with and then rejected the idea that the political empowerment of women is a practice stemming from Europe or North America. They have instead traced the appropriateness of the institutions that are the subject of this book to pre-colonial and non-Western polities and values. This book will also show that many others have objected that these practices are about communism rather than liberal, Western statehood. With such disagreements over the sources and rationales for suffrage, women's policy machinery and quotas, it is questionable whether the political empowerment of women is attributable only or primarily to the liberal West.

[8] Gentile 1999.

Norms, social hierarchies and change

Much of this book is concerned with the primary analytical question of how to characterize and understand the worldwide emergence of women's suffrage, national machinery for women and quota laws. Laying out the conceptual link between norms and social hierarchies is a major theoretical task of Chapter 3. Demonstrating, examining and dissecting the simultaneous stratifying and homogenizing nature of the international norms governing these state practices take up a large portion of the subsequent empirical chapters. However, the book also attempts to help to explain the origin and process of these worldwide changes. This moves us to the second aim identified above, addressing why and how these transformations came about.

Explaining how and why norms change (and homogeneity is brought about) is the primary task that much constructivist scholarship has set out for itself. Chapter 2 of this book shows that constructivist explanations vary more than the characterizations of international society – some explanations are structural and emphasize the importance of contradictions in world culture as a source of homogenizing change, whereas others are agent-oriented and trace these transformations to the work of social movements. What the explanations nonetheless share is an assumption that the worldwide adoption of new state practices is unrelated to states' "'class' position[s] in the system."[9] Social relations of hierarchy among states are assumed not to be part of the explanation for how and why new state behaviors emerge and spread. This book fundamentally challenges that assumption.

In short, I make three claims about the role international social hierarchies have in prompting change in state practices worldwide, relating to the *origin* and *process* of new behavior among states. The first claim is that social stratification helps to account for the origin in international society of new worldwide state behavior. New policies may originate with states that abide by norms and are high in rank, in order to maintain that standing. Whether admired or envied, their rank – being seen as superior to other states in some regard – then helps to prompt other states to follow suit.

But change does not exclusively emerge out of the so-called core of international society. States that are low in rank may also become the

---

[9] Meyer 1980: 115.

first to change their behavior, attempting to rise in rank within a given order or as a rejection of that order. Crucially, new state behavior towards women may develop "from below." The fact that a new behavior develops from below can generate a competitive dynamic among states higher in rank, who may feel a need to follow suit in order not to be outperformed. More prevalently with regard to the policies treated in this book, international hierarchies have served as barriers for subsequent adoption, barriers whose overcoming required effort. Once an institutional development became associated with what were considered less advanced states, it became possible to make the argument that it was not a policy appropriate for the more advanced. It has thus taken a considerable amount of effort to reinterpret and reframe such policies so that they become seen as appropriate and legitimate for states higher in rank. This reframing has largely been the work of actors identified as important in previous norms scholarship, such as transnational networks, social movements and international organizations.

Since change can emerge from states that are high or low in rank, my claim about social hierarchies and the origin of change obviously does not help us predict where new policies will develop and from where they will spread in a law-like manner. This book nonetheless helps us explain the origin of change in the sense of better understanding the causal dynamics at work. Ranking is an important and overlooked force for initiating change on a worldwide scale.

The second claim concerns the process of worldwide change and the role of stratification therein. The hierarchical nature of a normative order may have effects not just on the origin but on the subsequent pathway of policy change. This book will show that the global adoption trajectory of all three policies under examination has been clustered along major dimensions of normative stratification. States considered similar in kind and rank have tended to engage in a new behavior within similar time frames. Such clustered pathways of adoption are neither captured nor explained by existing constructivist approaches.

The third and final claim also concerns the process of change: social hierarchies shape how new policies are understood, advocated for and legitimated. This book shows that new state practices are continually framed in terms of the unequal standing of states generated by existing norms. When activists or political party officials try to make a state engage in a new behavior, they need to make clear why that state *as a*

being of a certain kind and rank should do so. In other words, they have
to invoke normative ranking orders in which a state is positioned.
Arguments must be developed to explain why, for instance, a "traditional" state should engage in "modern" behavior. Getting a state to
behave in ways considered typical of states seen as inferior is particularly difficult. In contemporary northern Europe, for instance, it would
be ludicrous to advocate for a new gender policy by suggesting that
the policy is emblematic of "traditional" or "developing" states.
Arguments about change have to take into consideration the rank of
the state in question in a particular interpretation of hierarchy.
Proponents of change must make clear how and why it makes sense
for a state of a certain rank to change its behavior towards women.

In sum, international social hierarchies help us understand why new
state behaviors may first emerge among states considered less advanced.
Stratification among states may pose a barrier for subsequent adoption,
and it often takes a considerable amount of effort to reframe the
behavior as appropriate for states considered superior or more
advanced. The original framing and the subsequent reframing of the
international norm necessarily invokes stratification and rank, pointing
to the inextricable relation between norms and social hierarchies.
Precisely how the reframing is done is historically contingent and the
subject of the empirical chapters of this book. Crucially, social hierarchies are part of the story, all the way, of how these institutions become
worldwide.

Plan of the book

The rest of this book is organized around its two main aims: the first
part is theoretical and links norms to stratification, and the second part
accounts for the worldwide spread of women's suffrage, women's
policy bureaus and national legislature sex quota laws. Chapter 2
begins the theoretical work by taking stock of constructivist claims
about worldwide changes of state behavior. Although it is common to
contend that constructivism is not "a theory" in the sense of offering
empirically falsifiable causal claims, I show that a careful examination
of constructivist empirical scholarship nonetheless reveals three strands
of inquiry with distinct explanatory accounts of norms and state behavior. This examination includes the small body of scholarship that
focuses on state policies toward women, scholarship that is better

understood when sorted within the three constructivist approaches than as an alternative "feminist" perspective. Most importantly, these current constructivist conceptualizations of norms largely discourage the identification of their connected homogenizing and stratifying dynamics. It is not surprising, then, that the importance of social hierarchies for how and why change occurs among states is overlooked.

Chapter 3 continues where Chapter 2 leaves off, with a conceptual discussion about the nature of norms. The main contribution is an attempt to show that norms necessarily both generate and draw upon social stratification, the process of ordering actors as superior and inferior. A discussion of the status of women and social hierarchies among states then follows, which sets out three ways in which norms about state behavior towards women are embroiled in the validation and ordering of states. The chapter ends with a discussion of how to think about social hierarchies and change and makes a call for approaching constitutive analyses as inherently dynamic rather than static.

The second part of the book consists of an attempt to understand and explain the operation of norms in worldwide changes of state policy towards women. The book centers on women's suffrage, national women's machinery and legislature sex quotas as three cases of worldwide changes in state behavior. Voting rights, state agencies and the composition of national legislatures are core concerns of political science. These policies have been and continue to be of great interest to a large number of transnational activists, politicians, international organizations and others. Understanding the international dimensions of these changes is clearly important, within political science as well as outside the academy. Curiously, there is nonetheless very little research grappling with the international aspects of these issues.

The three cases were selected for additional reasons. As I illustrated in the beginning of this chapter, they provide three enormously divergent historical and geographical trajectories of worldwide change. Women's suffrage was first adopted among newly established Anglo-European states at the end of the nineteenth century, and it would take over a century and several waves of activism until most states accepted equal voting rights for women and men. Women's policy agencies emerged much later, in the 1960s, almost simultaneously among a few North American, Latin American and Asian states and without much activism. Within a mere two decades, essentially all non-communist states had created a national policy agency focused on women's issues whereas no communist states had done so. The adoption of legislature sex quotas is a contemporary phenomenon subject to a lot of activism, emerging first among Latin American states in the 1990s and now primarily in Asia and Africa. To be convincing, my claims about norms, social hierarchies and changing state behavior should hold despite these variations in activism, timing and geographic origin.

Focusing on the inclusion of women should furthermore present particular difficulties for the claim that new state practices may emerge "from below" or from the margins of international society. Although there are challenging views of the world, Europe and the Anglo-European states are commonly seen as its powerful center. And the political empowerment of women is widely presumed to be of European or Western origin, possibly more so than other policy areas. These are thus hard cases for my proposition about the origins in international society of new state behavior and their relation to international norms.

The chapters in the second half of the book are organized around the empirical cases, in chronological order: women's suffrage (Chapter 5), national women's agencies (Chapter 6) and legislature sex quotas (Chapter 7). New state behaviors do not emerge in a normative vacuum, however, since new norms and behaviors have to transform prior norms and be accommodated within social hierarchy. Chapter 4 thus asks about developments that came prior to the adoption of women's suffrage, in what was called the European "society of civilized states" in the nineteenth and early twentieth centuries. That is where this book about the worldwide transformation of state policies towards women begins.

While situated within the constructivist IR literature, the book – the empirical chapters in particular – is heavily indebted to feminist scholarship from a range of disciplines. I thus end by addressing a theme that has received quite a bit of attention in the feminist IR literature: the gendered character of states. States are generally understood among feminist IR scholars to be masculinized constructions, crafted from understandings about appropriate male traits and behaviors as contrasted with femininity (and with devalued forms of masculinity). What are the implications of the worldwide incorporation of women for the gendered character of states? Have the masculine qualities of state institutions been transformed in order to accommodate the arrival of women? What, in turn, does the inclusion of women into formal politics mean for the potency of feminization as a means to devalue actors and behaviors in international politics?

Before turning to the issue of the gendered character of state institutions, the concluding chapter sums up the main insights and assesses the claims about norms and social hierarchies. One important part of this assessment is a comparison with alternative constructivist accounts. How well does the evidence support a focus on social hierarchy in the study of international norms and changing state behavior?

Three forms of evidence are used to draw conclusions about norms and stratification: (1) the worldwide pathway of change, (2) secondary sources and (3) the meanings and knowledge-structures constitutive of these state behaviors. I begin by tracing the spatial scope and temporal sequencing of the spread of both the state behavior in question and the activities of actors trying to bring that change about. Documenting when and where these activities and state policies emerged involves quite a deal of work. The Inter-Parliamentary Union (IPU) keeps records of the adoption of women's suffrage, and the Institute for Democracy and Electoral Assistance (IDEA) recently put together a web-page on quotas that continuously updates their adoption. I have compiled a listing of national machineries, relying primarily on various UN publications. The identification and sequencing of relevant actors involved in the promulgation of these measures are even more laborious. The tracing of the where-when-who of each state policy required the reading of an immense volume of published scholarship, conference papers and proceedings, publications by international organizations and NGOs, internet websites, conversations and interviews. I furthermore used my language skills to their limit in reading these sources.[10]

The pathway of change provides the first cues about norms and stratification. Without any attention to context and meaning, preliminary inferences can nonetheless be made about the order of international society. Even though this is a respectable beginning, more careful contextual analyses are absolutely necessary in order to avoid arguing for social hierarchies by assertion.

An extensive reading of secondary sources provides a skeletal and suggestive interpretive historical framework to characterize and explain the emergence of women's suffrage, women's bureaus and sex quota

---

[10] Fluency in English, Swedish (and thereby Danish and Norwegian) and Spanish, proficiency in French and Portuguese and limited comprehension of German.

laws worldwide. Such a reading pieces together and retheorizes the work of others, in light of the historical and geographical path of each policy. Milliken highlights that the "secondary sources" approach not only serves as a foundation for analysis, but also functions as a matter of external checks.[11] The scholar's own analysis can usefully be compared with the studies of other scholars and reflections by activists on the same issue, "to ascertain whether in this light [the] interpretation continues to work well."

The third form of evidence – meaning and knowledge – is the most important one for a constructivist analysis. As Kratochwil argues, "communicative structure among actors ought to constitute the referential framework for attempts to understand why actors do the things they do."[12] Constructivist analyses should rest heavily on making intelligible the utterances of social actors by placing them in broader structures of signification. It is important to stress this point of the broader communicative structures, as this is often overlooked or misunderstood in the discussions of such work: the goal is not simply to restate the understanding of the actors but rather to attain greater clarity than the immediate perception of the actors involved.[13] To have understood or explained a phenomenon thus means to place utterances about some phenomenon within a larger discursive context. To understand international norms, they must be seen within their broader contexts of meaning.

In sum, evidence is generated through a three-step analysis that begins with tracing the path of the worldwide changes in state behavior, then turns to relevant secondary sources, and ends with an analysis of the meanings of these state behaviors. Such a three-step analysis enables the cross-check of different sorts of evidence. The possibility of contradictory results helps us assess the viability of focusing on social hierarchies when studying international norms.

---

[11] Milliken 1999b: 235.   [12] Kratochwil 1988: 277.   [13] See Neufeld 1993.

2 | Constructivism and worldwide changes in state policy

Several heavyweights within the field of international relations, spanning the theoretical spectrum, have argued that constructivism is not "a theory" in the sense of offering explanations as empirically falsifiable causal claims. Kenneth Waltz recently argued that "constructivism is not a theory at all. If a so-called theory does not explain, it is not a theory."[1] Alexander Wendt likewise claims that "constructivism is not a theory of international politics ... it looks at how actors are socially constructed, but does not tell us which actors to study or where they are constructed."[2]

Many constructivists would likely agree – constructivism is a set of ontological commitments and an approach to understanding international politics.[3] If we look more closely at constructivist research in practice, however, a different picture emerges. On the question of changing state behavior on a worldwide scale, constructivist research does have explanatory aspirations. And these explanations do tell us which actors to study, where they are constructed, and even how and why change is brought about. In practice, there are constructivist theories, even in the narrow causal sense, about global changes in state policy.

In this chapter, I identify and address three theoretical strands of constructivism that offer distinctive accounts of norms and changing state practices: world polity institutionalism, the liberal international norms literature and post-structuralisms, which I refer to as "critical constructivist" approaches. The small body of existing IR scholarship that has dealt with changing state policies with regard to women is attended to in this discussion, as this scholarship can fruitfully be sorted as falling within one of these constructivist strands. Each section begins by addressing how the worldwide changes in state behavior are

---

[1] Waltz 2004: 5. [2] Wendt 1999: 7.
[3] See e.g. Adler 1997: 322; Checkel 1998: 325; Katzenstein 1996: 6.

characterized, and then discusses how the change is explained. While each strand provides important cues and insights for understanding the spread of suffrage, women's agencies and quotas, none of them approaches international society as a hierarchical society in which states are socially ranked and ordered. This, I argue, is related to the conceptual failure to capture the ranking effects of norms.

Three constructivist strands

1. World polity institutionalism

Characterizing the outcome: isomorphism and a rationalized world polity?

Scholarship within the so-called world polity institutionalist perspective of the Stanford school of sociology makes state structuration and what is presumed to be *structural isomorphism* among states and individuals the central object of study.[4] Of the three approaches under review, the institutionalist explanatory framework is the most ambitious and comprehensive, insisting on a global social structure with a specified substantive content which constitutes states' identity and aims. This form of integrated argument furthermore provides a clear alternative to systemic neorealist and neoliberal approaches,[5] an alternative of which Martha Finnemore has been the most ardent exponent within IR.[6] The primary challenge is to account for a phenomenon that neorealist, neoliberal and Marxian approaches would have difficulty explaining: "a world whose societies, organized as nation-states, are structurally similar in many unexpected dimensions."[7] Impressive efforts have been made to document the worldwide existence of a range of state institutions, and there is an important contribution in the focus on the puzzling global proliferation of a wide variety of state agencies, ministries, laws and social policies. In contrast to IR approaches, these sociologists have furthermore paid a substantial amount of attention to recording the global existence of state institutions on women, including women's

---

[4] This perspective is perhaps best laid out in Thomas *et al.* 1987. See also Boli and Thomas 1997 and 1999; Berkovitch 1999b; Finnemore 1996b and 1996c; Frank and McEneaney 1999; Meyer 1980; Meyer *et al.* 1997; Ramirez *et al.* 1997.
[5] Finnemore 1996a.   [6] See Finnemore 1993, 1996a, 1996b and 1996c.
[7] Meyer *et al.* 1997: 145.

suffrage,[8] reproductive rights,[9] same-sex sexual relations,[10] legislation prohibiting female genital cutting,[11] and state bureaucracies for women's affairs.[12]

World polity scholars embed these state bureaucracies and policies in a single global social structure, a *modern world culture*, which operates as a constitutive and directive exogenous environment for states. Set forth as universalistic scripts, the world polity is theorized as a Weberian rationalized culture of progress. World culture defines much of corporate action as *statehood* and human action as "*individuality*." As outcomes of this culture, states and individuals are constituted as instrumental beings, guided by the anticipated outcome of actions. ⌈The actors are culturally instructed to choose among actions as more or less efficient *means* to a further end – progress – rather than valuing these actions for themselves.⌋ Indeed, the pursuit of rationalized progress among states has become remarkably uniform. Whereas liberal, rationalist or choice-theoretic approaches assume instrumental rationality, the world polity scholars see this mode of being and action as a fundamentally cultural institution.

Allegedly arising out of Western Christianity, world culture began to crystallize organizationally in the second half of the nineteenth century and it has allegedly played a particularly forceful role in state structuration during the past fifty years.[13] The concrete bureaucracies and policies of states are understood to be standardized features of highly rationalized state actors that all exhibit "territorial boundaries and a demarcated population; sovereign authority, self-determination and responsibility; standardized purposes like collective development, social justice, and the protection of individual rights; authoritative, law-based control systems; clear possession of resources such as natural and mineral wealth and a labor force; and policy technologies for the rational means-ends accomplishment of goals."[14]

Explaining change: diffusion of world culture?
The question of how states come to incorporate new institutions and policies is a central component of the world polity approach. World culture functions as a generative structure that accounts for the creation

---

[8] Ramirez *et al.* 1997; Berkovitch 1999a.   [9] Ramirez and McEneaney 1997.
[10] Frank and McEneaney 1999.   [11] E.g. Boyle *et al.* 2001; Boyle *et al.* 2002.
[12] Berkovitch 1994.   [13] Meyer *et al.* 1997.   [14] Meyer *et al.* 1997: 153.

of everything from environmental ministries to abortion rights, and efficient causation is consequently not of great concern to world polity scholars. The most important organizational fields in which world culture takes form are identified as the immense collections of international associations, epistemic communities, NGOs and transnational social movements.[15] Indeed, world society is characterized as a *stateless* force *exogenous* to the state actors themselves: "The operation of world society through peculiarly cultural and associational processes depends heavily on its statelessness."[16]

After they form among international organizations, international NGOs or transnational social movements, scripts for particular institutional forms then diffuse among states. There is some, though very limited, elaboration on the diffusion process itself. A few world polity scholars claim that the mechanisms for early adoption of state organizational forms are different than for those of late adopters. Empirical research, DiMaggio holds, has demonstrated that "early adoption (that is, adoption of an innovation soon after its introduction, before a large portion of the population at risk has adopted it) of organizational innovations is strongly predicted by technical or political attributes of adopters but that later diffusion is more poorly predicted by technical or political measures."[17] In this vein, Ramirez, Soysal and Shanahan argue for the importance of political agitation in early, as opposed to later, cases of adopting women's suffrage. Initially, they claim, transnational mobilization was necessary for convincing core industrialized states to change, whereas a diffusion process took hold once a critical mass of these states had adopted the institution. Finnemore (1993: 592) in turn contends that the organs of world society may "pick up [a script] from successful and powerful states and popularize it."[18] She suggests that the technical effectiveness of a particular state form among some states coupled with what she calls the teaching efforts by international organizations provide the source for diffusion and thus change among the others. What is important for present purposes, and a claim that can be

---

[15] E.g. Boli and Thomas 1999: 1–12; Meyer *et al.* 1997; Ramirez *et al.* 1997.

[16] Meyer *et al.* 1997: 145.

[17] DiMaggio 1988: 6. For a similar argument, see also Finnemore 1993 and 1996b; Ramirez *et al.* 1997; Tolbert and Zucker 1983. See also Finnemore and Sikkink 1999.

[18] Finnemore 1993: 592.

empirically evaluated, is that change always takes place first among the so-called core Western states.

As a causal force that is *exogenous* to virtually all states, world culture serves as a single causal factor that exerts the same force on all states. Given that world polity institutionalism hinges all its explanatory force on world culture, it is a particularly serious problem that the approach has not accounted for what makes Western, rationalized culture such an allegedly successful candidate for diffusion. Marxian-inspired arguments about modes of production and exchange as funda-mental social processes along with functional rationality arguments based on a liberal ontology of a universal drive for satisfaction of interests are dismissed in favor of a thoroughly culturalist understand-ing of state structuration. But what, then, accounts for the dynamism of this apparently unstoppable cultural force? What makes states such allegedly willing students of the teachings of world cultural scripts? The stasis of the framework is indeed its Achilles' heel and has given rise to several unsuccessful attempts at rectification. In my view, the brief attempts at addressing the dynamism issue raise more questions about the viability of the world polity model than they put to rest. It should be noted, furthermore, that these scholars have spoken to the issue of dynamism essentially in passing, with no empirical work to substantiate the claims. Let me nonetheless tackle the line of reasoning briefly.[19]

One major contention for what Meyer *et al.* call the "intense dyna-mism" of world culture points to the competitive effects of having multiple actors in a common world frame. The authors argue that *"given actors' common identity and ultimate similarity*, competition is not only the prevailing theory of interaction but a source of collective moral meaning ... The greater the number of entities, whether indivi-duals, organizations, or nation-states, that pursue similar interests

---

[19] One of the features identified as providing dynamism is the lack of an overarching world state authority. This point is argued simply by claiming that "a powerfully organized and authoritative worldwide actor would obviously lower the dynamism of world society" Meyer *et al.* 1997: 169. While one could question the assumption that a world state would necessarily reduce dynamism, the point is moot in my view: a successful argument that a future world state would reduce dynamism does not in itself serve to show the source of dynamism of today's stateless world society. Such a mode of argument simply presumes that which it attempts to explain.

requiring similar resources, the more the entities will come into conflict with each other and develop theories of one another as sources of social ills."[20] Competition is not identified as an inherent aspect of world culture, here or elsewhere, but rather as one of its effects. As Wendt (1992) has so effectively argued, however, similar entities with similar goals do *not* automatically engage in competitive behavior. As he suggests, we have to understand competition as a social (i.e. cultural) practice. Doing so would give us some leverage on world culture's dynamism, as I shall attempt to elaborate below.

This line of reasoning raises a related question of crucial concern to this book. If we presume that states and individuals come into conflict with one another and "develop theories of one another as sources of social ills," are the effects still a world culture of similarity and conflict-free diffusion? Are we not then forced to come to terms with a world polity whose culture also entails difference and contestation? What is more, competition hardly helps to account for the alleged isomorphism and the conflict-free mimicry by so-called peripheral states of rational state scripts. One is left with the suspicion that world polity theorizing relies heavily on modernization theory's notions of "culture contact" and natural selection – the mere exposure to rational (modern) scripts leads states to abandon the "old," as the anticipated benefits of Western rationality somehow automatically triumph over alternatives. If this is the case, then in the end, although world polity scholars place heavy weight on "rationalization" as an *effect* of world culture, the approach simultaneously imputes a high degree of a certain kind of rationality as a *cause* of change.

A more promising source of dynamism is briefly developed under the heading of "cultural contradictions." In contrast with most norms scholars and some other noted constructivists such as Wendt, the world polity approach rejects notions of culture as internally consistent, closed and thereby static and in demand of a non-cultural source of agency for change. Instead, Western, rational world culture is held to entail

rampant inconsistencies and conflicts ... inherent in widely valued cultural goods: equality versus liberty, progress versus justice, standardization versus diversity, efficiency versus individuality ... All of these priesthoods preach in

---

[20] Meyer *et al.* 1997: 169–70, my emphasis.

terms of ultimate values and with considerable authority, reflecting and reproducing a remarkably dynamic culture ... The cultural construction of rational actorhood endows individuals and groups with exalted spiritual properties that justify and motivate mobilization, innovation and protest.[21]

Finnemore similarly contends that "tensions and contradictions among normative principles in international life mean that there is no set of ideal political and economic arrangements toward which we are converging. There is no stable equilibrium, no end of history."[22] The explanatory challenge that remains, of course, is how uniformity and homogeneity – isomorphism – is produced out of contradictions and inconsistencies. I shall attempt to develop such notions of normative tensions and inconsistencies to account for the homogenizing and heterogenizing processes entailed in the worldwide proliferation of state institutions on women, which will be further elaborated below.

The concept of cultural contradiction *still* does not get to the bottom of the causal force that produces diffusion of (contradictory) *Western* culture and the seemingly automatic displacement of non-Western political practice and organization. Briefly discussing the simple diffusion and modeling processes of the contemporary world, Meyer *et al.* suggest that "obviously, much of this reflects the main dimensions of world stratification – the poor and weak and peripheral copy the rich and strong and central ... [any new state] would undoubtedly turn first to American, Japanese, or European models for much of their social restructuring."[23] Again, the approach turns to theoretically exogenous factors, factors that largely rest on assumptions of rationality, to account for the diffusion and mimicry. Curiously, whereas the "economy" and "power politics" are carefully separated from "political culture," it is the former two that are granted not only the status as main dimensions of world stratification but also the explanatory power for the mimicry by the periphery.

To resolve some of the problems of the world polity approach, we need at a minimum to have a theory of power that encompasses the social processes we identify as "power politics" and the "economy." There is no mention of world culture itself as a form of social power that produces and structures the social *relations* among states and other actors, relations that entail social roles, domination and an unequal distribution of resources. In fact, world polity theorists approach states

[21] Meyer *et al.* 1997: 172.   [22] Finnemore 1996b: 135.
[23] Meyer *et al.* 1997: 164.

as discrete entities with no relation to one another (dependent variables) that are all similarly exposed to the exogenous force of world culture (independent variable). Meyer makes the argument that the adoption of institutions is unrelated to a state's "'class' position in the system." To do so, he reasons that "in the face of enormous and continuing world economic inequalities ... peripheral societies shift to ... all the institutional apparatus of modern social organization."[24] What is taken to be similarity in *outcome* is then erroneously presumed to indicate similarity in *cause*. As we shall see in coming chapters, not only have social relations of hierarchy in international society generated different dispositions in the world, so that some states are subjected to more extensive pressures for change than others, but stratification provides much of the impetus and arguments for change.

Leaving elaboration to the discussion below, this book furthermore rejects the notion that world culture should be conceptualized solely as ever-expanding Western customs and the presumption that so-called peripheral states "obviously" turn to the USA and Europe as models for state institutions on women. As we shall see in the chapters to come, this is simply not borne out in practice. It is furthermore far from obvious that Western Christian culture should somehow be particularly well suited for the formal political incorporation of women. This leads me to the final point with regard to world polity institutionalism, a point that will also be developed below: we need to rethink whether worldwide developments of state institutions, such as those of suffrage, national machinery and quotas, are really simply or only cases of isomorphism.

2. *Liberal international norms scholarship*

Characterizing the outcome: a society of liberal norms?

In the past decade, we have seen the ascendance of an enormous body of scholarship on international norms. The relations of international norms to sex/gender institutions have unfortunately not been granted much attention or significance by these scholars, but analyses to date nonetheless speak directly to the question of the worldwide incorporation of women into formal state institutions.[25] Unlike the world polity

[24] Meyer 1980: 115.
[25] Finnemore and Sikkink 1999, Keck and Sikkink 1998, and Meyer (1999) are some of the rare exceptions to this statement.

institutionalists described above, norms scholars do not expressly present a comprehensive theory of the international. There is furthermore no grand theorist akin to John Meyer who has attempted to pull these studies together as a self-identified and more unified approach. This notwithstanding, I contend that much of the now enormous norms literature shares certain assumptions about the world that make it legitimate to treat it as an approach.[26] We can therefore ask the same questions that were posed to the world polity institutionalists: What would the world look like if we read only the literature on international norms? How is the world – its components, relations and dynamics – theorized? How does change come about in international society? Does such an account adequately characterize the world in terms of the emergence of suffrage, national machinery and sex quotas?

Most norms scholars draw on one of the oldest streams of scholarship within IR that investigate the production of state forms – the so-called English School.[27] The international is approached as a "society" in which states, as a condition of their participation, conform to shared norms and rules.[28] An array of international norms and institutions makes possible and structures inherently social international actors, relations and practices within this society. Like world polity institutionalists, the English School investigates what is taken to be the expansion of a single, Western international society. Indeed, as Bull claims in a statement representative of the approach, "Contemporary international society ... is the culture of the dominant Western powers."[29] Here,

---

[26] To be clear, the characterization is based on the following specific works: Checkel 1998 and 2001; Cortell and Davis 1996; Crawford 2002; Florini 1996; Flowers 2009; Gurowitz 1999 and 2000; Hawkins 1997; Keck and Sikkink 1998; Klotz 1995a, 1995b, 1996 and 2002; Legro 1997; Meyer 1999; Risse 2000; Risse *et al.* 1999; Sikkink 1993a and 1993b; Thomas 2001; Thomson 1990. Finnemore and Sikkink 1999 could also be included here, although the article pulls towards the world polity approach. Likewise, whereas his work generally falls within the critical constructivist camp, Price 1998 could possibly also be included.

[27] E.g. Bull and Watson 1977 and 1984: 1–9; Gong 1984; Watson 1992; Wight 1966.

[28] Bull and Watson (1984: 1) define international society as "a group of states ... which not merely form a system, in the sense that the behaviour of each is a necessary factor in the calculations of the others, but also have established by dialogue and consent common rules and institutions for the conduct of their relations, and recognise their common interest in maintaining these arrangements."

[29] Bull and Watson 1977: 39.

however, the boundaries and content of international society are understood as contingent and open-ended, and the seeming determinism of
world culture is rejected. English School analyses are furthermore historical, with rich detailed accounts of how Europe incorporated non-
European areas into international society by means of conquest and
colonial relations. Coercive power is thus very much a part of the
narrative of the emergence of present-day international society, resol-
ving some of the problems of the world polity approach in accounting
for how this society allegedly came to be Western. However, once
established, coercive power no longer forms the core of its maintenance.
Instead, international society is thought to rest on the legitimacy of its
fundamental norms and social institutions, including international law,
diplomacy, and the responsible leadership by major powers. Rather
than being coercively induced, states are thought to generally *consent*
to such institutions as an essential aspect of social membership. These
social institutions, again, are not fixed or immutable across time and
place but are historically produced and variable.

Norms scholars importantly part ways with the English School on
viewing international society not primarily as a society of states but rather
as a heterogeneous society of multiple and changing actors, including
states, international organizations, transnational social movements,
international NGOs and so on. Yet, much of the recent norms literature
uses the English School notion of the establishment of an international
society as a background context within which the contemporary emergence and spread of more narrowly conceived "norms" take place.
Norms, according to Katzenstein's widely used definition, are the "collective expectations for the proper behavior of actors with a given identity."[30] The given identity studied is so far exclusively that of states, as
the approach accounts for state behavior and provides a theory of state
interest-formation. Norms are used to indicate rule-guided behavior and
they are primarily held to entail a *moral* mode of interaction based on a
"logic of appropriateness."[31] Within this logic, state actors behave
as they are instructed to do, as being of a certain identity and as the
context calls for. This mode of interaction is often presented as the norms
alternative to strategic, rational behavior that seeks *material* gain – the
"logic of consequentialism" – which is left as the terrain of realist and
liberal approaches. To be sure, many scholars argue that the way to the

---

[30] Katzenstein 1996: 5.   [31] See March and Olsen 1989 and 1998.

norms-governed logic of appropriateness is via the logic of consequentialism, so that appeals need first be made to the benefits of conforming with a norm before it becomes a taken-for-granted social institution. In either case, to most norms scholars "defining the system to include constitutive norms is an important conceptual shift, yet it creates neither an insurmountable disciplinary divide nor a rival paradigm" to realism and liberalism.[32] Instead, norms have largely come to function as an important "value added" to rationalist analyses, to use Risse's formulation.[33] The relationship to predominant approaches is thus expressly less ambitious than that of world polity scholars, who try to displace these with thoroughly constructivist premises.

Like the world culture of world polity institutionalism, norms are theorized as productive of state *isomorphism*, the creation of a more homogeneous international society of similar states. The isomorphic nature of international society is likewise thought to have its roots in the European Enlightenment and Western Christianity, so that "virtually all of the norms that are now identified as essential ingredients of international law and global society have their roots in the jurisprudence of European scholars of international law and in the notions and patterns of acceptable behavior established by the more powerful Western European states."[34] In other words, international society is theorized by norms scholars as a single Western society into which new members are induced, although the *liberal* nature is emphasized over the *rational* aspects that are at the center of the world polity analyses. Expectations for states to respect principles such as racial non-discrimination, human rights, women's suffrage, and asylum rights are interpreted as testimony of the liberal nature of international society. This society is furthermore a slightly more open one than the world polity, in the sense that Europeans and North Americans do not have complete monopoly on introducing new norms.[35] However, even if they are no longer solely introduced by European actors, norms are nonetheless understood to be framed in what were originally Western and liberal terms and concepts. What used to be an exclusive and discriminatory society of "civilized states" has now expanded into a liberal

---

[32] Klotz 1995b: 17.   [33] Risse 2000: 5.   [34] Nadelman 1990: 484.
[35] On the importance of Latin American activists for the institutionalization and activation of human rights norms in international society, see Sikkink 2004. See also Meyer 1999.

international community that incorporates essentially all those who wish to belong and are willing to make the necessary adjustments.

Explaining change: activism and persuasion?

The question of how norms change – and thereby state practices – is central to the norms agenda. There is a shared assumption among these scholars of general social or normative stability that is interrupted by episodes of change. It is indeed these episodes of change that are the center of analysis. The thicker social contents of international society, its boundaries and the sociopolitical construction of its various agents are all approached as stable and function as largely exogenous background conditions for strategic action and intentional change by various actors. Like world polity scholars, the norms literature points to immense associations and networks of international organizations, epistemic communities, NGOs and transnational social movements as important for norms transformation. In contrast with the world polity approach, which emphasizes the statelessness of the initiation of world cultural change, Western state agencies, departments and individual representatives are also identified as important collaborative agents.[36]

Whereas the world polity approach understands these actors as non-agentic "organizational fields" within which world culture percolates, norms scholars impute much more causal force to them as *inventors* and promoters of new principles for behavior, often making an analogy to *entrepreneurs*.[37] If cultural structuralism characterizes the world polity approach, then norms scholarship can be said to place activism, expressly understood as agency, in the limelight. Indeed, in a largely choice-theoretic framework and although other factors are added to the analysis to account for the actual outcomes, essentially all the *impetus for change* is hinged on the deliberate efforts of activists. A basic assumption shared among virtually all norms scholars is that change is an outcome of actors (activists as well as states and others) choosing between alternatives in order to satisfy their goals. Norms shape action initially by becoming integrated into state interests and possibly later by taking on a taken-for-granted logic of appropriateness.[38] In either case,

---

[36] See e.g. Keck and Sikkink 1998; Risse and Sikkink 1999; Thomas 2001, among others.
[37] E.g. Florini 1996; Keck and Sikkink 1998; Nadelman 1990.
[38] On this point, see especially Risse and Sikkink 1999.

were it not for the goal-oriented struggles of norms promoters, there would be no normative change in international society. The analyses of change almost exclusively begin with a few key individuals, social movements or networks with a novel vision and then trace out how these were able to make such a vision a more general condition for international politics.

The basic causal process by which activists get states to enact a norm is that of *persuasion*, also referred to as socialization.[39] In other words, enactment does not spring forth automatically, as in the case of the diffusion and imitation of world polity theory. It instead takes coaxing, strategic framing, and persuasion by various actors to convince and pressure states into complying with a norm. These non-state actors are generally not powerful enough in a conventional sense to be able to effect change coercively. Networks of non-European and European/North American activists may therefore link up transnationally in collaboration with certain Western states, placing pressure from within and without on other states for change. It is the often contentious processes and strategies of generating the consent first of some Western states and then of remaining states by manipulating the moral aspects of international society that lie at the center of the analyses.

Change is imputed to two primary factors: rhetorical and non-rhetorical activist strategies. *Practical reasoning* as rhetorical strategy has been identified as an absolutely central resource for the activists. The societal and moral nature of the international is the conventionally overlooked factor that provides an opening for such reasoning. By appealing to existing moral principles of international society, activists make the case that the prescription of a new norm is the logical extension of an accepted principle. The choice of a proper "frame" and of appropriate metaphors and analogies is crucial, though not sufficient, for the triumph of a new norm. When a norm is successfully related to an already authoritative liberal moral principle, states are more likely to comply with the prescribed practice. In this vein, a number of scholars have successfully demonstrated how transnational activists strategically link a norm with an already authoritative moral principle that enjoys

---

[39] The process has been described as the "induction of new members ... into the ways of behavior that are preferred in a society": Finnemore and Sikkink (1999: note 62); Risse and Sikkink 1999: 11. On state socialization, see also Alderson 2001; Checkel 2001.

widespread legitimacy in international society or in the domestic context of a powerful Western state.[40] In addition to framing, a few scholars hold that activists making more internally consistent arguments within a particular frame are more successful.[41] The importance of non-rhetorical, meaningful strategies has also been granted attention in the literature, including not only the use of visual symbolism but also the importance of organizational savvy and the generation of financial leverage (e.g. sanctions and boycotts) through Western states to "get the message out" to the rest.[42]

As Florini has pointed out, "Deliberate efforts to promote particular norms may work – or they may not."[43] Whereas the world polity approach is interested in permissive causation/constitution with world culture as a generative structure productive of all kinds of actors, interests and practices, norms scholarship is much more concerned with the identification of effective causation: Under what circumstances does the promotion of a norm succeed?[44] What accounts for variation in outcome? There have therefore been numerous and increasing calls for and attempts at "theoretical specification," understood as enhancing the predictive capacity of norms hypotheses (in a Mid-Range Theory framework) by developing the scope conditions that stipulate expectations of (a) *when* a norm, (b) *which* of many norms, and (c) the *extent* to which a norm becomes effective.[45] Additional factors have therefore been suggested in addition to the importance of the activist strategies discussed above. Some of the more prevalent supplementary variables include the nature of domestic formal institutions and rules, the objective fit between international and domestic norms,[46] the objective fit between the international norm and the broader normative

---

[40] E.g. Florini 1996; Keck and Sikkink 1998; Klotz 1995a; Nadelmann 1990; Price 1998.

[41] E.g. Crawford 2002; Franck 1990; Risse 2000.

[42] Crawford and Klotz 1999 and Keck and Sikkink 1998 are but two excellent examples of this line of work.

[43] Florini 1996: 375.

[44] This shows that the norms literature has discarded some of the fundamental ontological premises of constructivism, pressing towards a "thin" constructivist variant.

[45] An illustrative but far from exhaustive list of such calls and attempts include Checkel 1998, 1999 and 2001; Cortell and Davis 1996; Crawford 2002; Florini 1996; Keck and Sikkink 1998; Klotz 1995b; Legro 1997; Thomas 2001.

[46] E.g. Checkel 1999; Thomas 2001.

context,[47] and what is understood as the intrinsic qualities of the inter-national norm itself.[48] Such calls are of course possible only if one assumes the meaning and form of social conditions to be stable (at least in the Mid-Range), allowing for bounded generalization. As stable conditions, these factors are furthermore inert – whereas they may shape outcomes, they are not theorized as providing *impetus* for change on their own.

In these attempts to develop scope conditions to account for the variation in norm effectiveness among states, some norms scholars have importantly begun to turn to a largely neglected aspect of interna-tional norms – state identity. Whether there is "norm effectiveness depends upon the identity of the state actor in question," it is argued, and some states are thereby more receptive to international norms than others.[49] Similar propositions have been put forth regarding the relation of a state's identity to international society and the effectiveness of norms. Pointing to the varying desire among states to belong to inter-national society, Keck and Sikkink argue that "countries that are most susceptible to network pressures are those that aspire to belong to a normative community of nations."[50] Risse and Sikkink make an analo-gous argument, stating that leaders who "want to belong to the 'civi-lized community' of states" are more easily persuaded to adapt to international norms.[51] Thomas likewise contends that "the more salient the identity specified by an international norm, the more the actor will seek to fulfill its obligations under that norm."[52]

Given that international society is presumed to be liberal and Western, the suggested global trajectory of institutions such as suffrage, national machinery and quotas is thus similar to that proposed by the world polity scholars: Western, liberal states should be the first to adopt

---

[47] E.g. Crawford 2002. Keck and Sikkink (1998: 27) argue that norms that involve bodily harm and legal equality of opportunity are universally more likely to be an effective tool for activists.

[48] Franck (1990), Keck and Sikkink (1998), Legro (1997), and Thomas (2001), among others, point to the importance of the objective (non-interpreted) clarity of the norm, that it clearly distinguishes between compliant and non-compliant behavior.

[49] The quotation is from Thomas 2001: 15. See also Eyre and Suchman 1996; Finnemore and Sikkink 1998; Flowers 2009; Gurowitz 1999 and 2000; Keck and Sikkink 1998; Risse and Sikkink 1999.

[50] Keck and Sikkink 1998: 29.   [51] Risse and Sikkink 1999: 15.

[52] Thomas 2001: 15.

such practices, as these allegedly correspond with their identities, and these states form the foundational core of international society. Their emergence in the rest of the world should be largely predicated on the extent to which the state in question is trying to raise its status in relation to the Western core (and the presence of activists and supplementary variables).[53] Whether such a rendering of international society is adequate is evaluated empirically in this book.

The important implications of introducing identity notions such as "aspirations to belong to a community of states" have not yet been theorized. Even though identity is tied to norms in the very definition provided by Katzenstein, identity is conceptually and empirically underdeveloped in the norms approach. This in turn has implications for the analysis of how state institutions become worldwide in scope. Along with the world polity institutionalists, norms scholars have tended to treat states as formally equal and (to one another) unrelated entities, although with varying desires to belong to international society. The society of states thus seems at odds with any other known human society, as it is portrayed as devoid of patterned relations of social hierarchy and the norms productive of such relations. This is particularly curious given that one of the most central questions within the sociological study of society – from which constructivist IR borrows rather heavily – has been that of social stratification.

Such a treatment furthermore overlooks one of the central conceptual premises of constructivism, namely that identity is a *relational* concept that is established through processes of differentiation (as will be further elaborated below in the section on critical constructivism). In other words, we cannot know what an object or actor *is* without knowing what it is *not*, and the processes by which categorical identity distinctions are made are inherently political. In the case of suffrage, for instance, Keck and Sikkink characterize the given identity of European and Anglo-American states as a *liberal* one: "The issue lent itself to framing and action that appealed to the most basic values of the liberal state – equality, liberty and democracy,"[54] key for belonging to the then restricted

---

[53] Agreeing with this premise, Gurowitz (1999) has also added that since core Western states are more secure in their international standing, they are more capable of resisting the (rare) norms that may not correspond to domestic circumstances than are those with a more "insecure" status in international society.

[54] Keck and Sikkink 1998: 53.

international society. As we shall see in Chapter 5, an essential component of establishing that suffrage was a matter of liberal identity (or what I shall insist on as "civilization") consisted of demonstrating that it *was not* a polity of a different and less valued kind, namely "barbarous." The creation and maintenance of liberal society thus rested on the simultaneous articulation of and relation to the "barbarous" and "savage" world.

In characterizing international society as an increasingly isomorphic one, norms scholarship thus faces the same dilemma as world polity scholars in its failure to contend with identity and difference. As I shall argue throughout this book, norms not only unify – they also entail processes of differentiation and stratification. These processes are absolutely central to the worldwide emergence of state behaviors. Much of the intensity of the struggles and debates around suffrage, national machineries and legislature quotas derived not only from the fact that predominant international hierarchies were challenged and redefined but also from the fact that they called into question the placement of particular states within those hierarchies – their identities. Rather than seeing them as "given," we must therefore take seriously the fact that *identities are neither fixed nor given a priori* in the development of norms.

Finally, whereas I do not discard the importance of human inventiveness for the transformation of international society, norms analyses' conceptualization of change is unduly restricted in their exclusive focus on agent-level intentional and goal-oriented action. In the next chapter, I shall make the case for approaching social structures[55] not as stable and inert but as potentially dynamic and thus a source of change. Let it suffice for now to point out that even if we approached international norms as part of a closed and consistent cultural system, this culture could be dynamic. "Progress" indeed *demands* constant change in the identities of states and other actors. Failure to keep up with progress may have dire consequences for a state's identity, as the fate of Argentina in its regression from "civilized" to "developing" over the past century illustrates. Adjacent identities entailed in the major epics of progress of our time – those within Civilization, Development, Industrialization, Liberation – should indeed be characterized as

---

[55] By "social structure" I am referring broadly to social institutions, norms, culture or inter-subjective meaning, all as materially expressed.

processes of becoming rather than as stable, acquired attributes. As products of these discourses, norms promoters are not necessarily the starting point (and thus cause) of the transformation of norms and identities but rather themselves an effect of a dynamic world culture.

3. Critical constructivist approaches

Characterizing the outcome: an idiosyncratic world of multitude?
Although far from a unitary school, the various approaches within critical constructivism[56] (or post-structuralism, loosely defined) also investigate the constitution of the state.[57] Characterizing this literature is difficult. As Brown points out, it is "peculiarly resistant to sentences which begin 'Post-structuralism (or intertextuality or whatever) is …': to complete such sentences is to subvert the project."[58] Most of the interventions have furthermore been meta-theoretical in nature, directed at the conceptualization of international politics within the discipline in ambitious attempts to fundamentally displace conventional approaches. Since there is now an admittedly small but growing body of empirical scholarship that shares enough theoretical commitments to warrant categorization under the single, broad label of critical constructivism, and with no intention to "subvert the project," I shall nonetheless attempt such a characterization and ask the same questions that were posed to the world polity institutionalists and norms scholars: What would the world look like if we read only the critical constructivist literature on states? How is the world – its components, relations and dynamics – theorized? How does change come about in international politics? Does such an account adequately characterize the world

---

[56] Weldes *et al.* (1999: 13) suggest three loose analytic commitments of critical constructivism: "(1) What is understood as reality is socially constructed. (2) Constructions of reality reflect, enact, and reify relations of power. In turn, certain agents or groups of agents play a privileged role in the production and reproduction of these realities. (3) A critical constructivist approach denaturalizes dominant constructions, offers guidelines for the transformation of common sense, and facilitates the imagining of alternative life-worlds. It also problematizes the conditions of its own claims; that is, a critical constructivism is also reflexive."

[57] To be clear, the discussion is based on the following specific works: Ashley 1987a and 1987b; Campbell 1998; Doty 1996; Fierke 2000; Inayatullah and Blaney 1996; Milliken 1999a; Neumann 1996a, 1998 and 1999; Price 1997; Ringmar 1996; Rumelili 2003; Shapiro 1988; C. Weber 1995; Weldes 1999; Weldes *et al.* 1999.

[58] Brown 1994: 222–3.

in terms of the emergence of suffrage, national machinery and sex quotas?

The main empirical focus of post-structural IR analyses of the state has been the condition of general statehood, investigating states as unitary and territorial sovereigns that are "not only *categorically* distinct from other classes of subjects or objects, but also *numerically* distinct from each other, and therefore ordinally separable."[59] There has been little if any analysis of the state as bureaucratic authority or much in terms of the state as legal authority. Instead, sovereignty as the production of inside/outside boundaries has been analyzed and conceptualized both as a categorical and as a numerical form of state identity.

The concept of identity is central to these scholars. Identity is understood as a relational concept that denotes the social meanings and practices through which an actor becomes distinctively recognizable or known as such. In stark contrast to world polity and norms scholarship, *difference* is held to be intrinsically involved in the construction of an identity, including that of the state. It is only through contrast and differentiation from that which is unlike that the like can be identified and known as such. As Connolly emphasizes, "The definition of difference is a requirement built into the logic of identity."[60] The discursive production of subject positions and identities is furthermore conceptualized as expressions of power. By contrast with direct and intentional control of other actors, such productive power rests on diffuse social relations and defines the very parameters of possibility for acting and being in the world.[61] In dramatic contrast with world polity and norms scholarship, which largely adopts realist understandings of power, discursive power is understood very broadly as *productive* social practices and structures of meaning that create the conditions of possibility of various important international actors and modes of behavior.

Unlike in norms scholarship, which presumes the state to be stable unless there are identifiable and intentional episodes of change, the state is theorized as an ongoing process of constitution. If the state appears stable, that should be understood as an effect of a "regulated process of repetition" rather than as an ontological status of inertia.[62] Drawing heavily on Butler, David Campbell (the perhaps most influential representative of this line of scholarship) contends that

---

[59] Bartelson 1998: 298.   [60] Connolly 1991: 9.
[61] Barnett and Duvall 2005.   [62] Campbell 1998: 10.

the problematic of identity/difference contains, therefore, no foundations that are prior to, or outside of, its operation. Whether we are talking of "the body" or "the state," or of particular bodies and states, the identity of each is performatively constituted. Moreover, the constitution of identity is achieved through the inscription of boundaries that serve to demarcate an "inside" from an "outside," a "self" from an "other," a "domestic" from a "foreign."[63]

Indeed, as Ashley had expressed previously, foreign policy functions as "a specific sort of *boundary producing political performance*" constitutive of the state.[64] The identity/difference nexus, the ongoing establishment of the boundaries that constitute states, is thus the main locus of inquiry.

  To expose the discursive contingency of the state, most of the scholarship has employed deconstruction, "pointing to the binary oppositions that constitute the state as essentially continuous, indivisible and distinct from other forms of political life."[65] These analyses have primarily conceptualized and deconstructed the state as an effect of self/other binaries. Anarchy is not seen as a natural absence of meaning and authority but is instead conceptualized as a meaning-laden and constitutive discourse for states, productive of self/other distinctions based largely on threat and danger. Threat has indeed been a central concept for these studies. Ashley (1987a) argues that the very anarchy problematic (the alleged absence of authority) becomes the threatening Other that gives identity to the state as the presence of authority. Campbell agrees and adds that "the constant articulation of danger through foreign policy is thus not a threat to a state's identity or existence: it is its condition of possibility."[66] A series of studies has investigated the constitution of the state self through the identification of others as threatening and dangerous.[67] Within Realist discourses of security under conditions of anarchy, other actors become defined on a scale of level of threat to the survival of state identity: as friends, rivals or enemies.[68] Self/other differentiations are thereby not only or necessarily maintained through threat, a notion which Connolly (1991),

---

[63] Campbell 1998: 9.   [64] Ashley 1987a: 51.
[65] Bartelson 1998: 313.   [66] Campbell 1998: 13.
[67] E.g. Campbell 1998; Rumelili 2003; Shapiro 1988; Weldes *et al.* 1999.
[68] See Wendt 1999 on this point, although he expressly distances himself from the critical or post-structural approaches.

Inayatullah and Blaney's (e.g. 1996), and Rumelili (2004) have elaborated by drawing on the work of Tzvetan Todorov.[69]

Collective identity-formation among the states of Europe through the differentiation from primarily Eastern Others has also been granted a fair amount of attention.[70] There is presently a flurry of research activity on European boundary-production and differentiation processes. It is important to note that the connection of multiple states as *similar* "Europeans" who share a common identity is maintained without these states being fully collapsed into a single Self, processes these studies unfortunately do not show empirically. The simultaneous maintenance of differences among them – generally not through discourses of threat – is a crucial if under-explored dimension of European states as categorical *and* numerical beings.

It is difficult to infer how these scholars would approach the worldwide emergence of suffrage, national machinery and quotas. Given the aversion to authoritative truth-claims and singular generalities about the world, trying to tease this out may indeed threaten to subvert the project. I surmise two possibilities, however, neither of which is fully satisfying, for reasons that will be further elaborated below. First, among those concerned with anarchy/sovereignty, the international is approached as general discursive structures with the same mutually constitutive relationship with all states. An essential *homogeneity* is thereby emphasized in the analyses of what makes states categorically distinct from other beings. Theoretical claims about the nature of numerical or state–state differentiation are also made in general terms, suggesting a common conundrum of difference as an ontological premise for community and being. Since the empirical studies from which those general claims emanate are almost exclusively of European and Anglo-American states, we could draw the conclusion that the world of states is presented as a Western one.[71] Neumann defends the application of allegedly Eurocentric self/other notions by expressly confirming the view of the world as Western: "Due to the continued pertinence of its European cultural roots to international society and the continued pertinence of international society to world politics, a 'Western'

[69] Their elaboration on the types of relations that may develop between Self and Other has focused on first-encounter situations, wherein already constituted actors meet and develop notions of differentiation.

[70] See particularly Neumann 1999; Rumelili 2003 and 2004.

[71] E.g. Doty 1996; Campbell 1998; C. Weber 1995.

conception of the person [and the state] continues to exert its influence on world politics everywhere, for better or worse."[72] One could imagine a line of argument akin to that of the world polity approach but with the crucial additions of discursive power and difference: the discursive scripts for what makes states categorically different from other beings demand the incorporation of suffrage, national machinery and quotas. The production of the state as a subject is inherently and profoundly power-laden, disabling other forms of being as it enables the state to be.

There is a second option, and one I find more amenable to the gist of this approach, namely the characterization of the world as multiply interpreted, consisting of multiple structures of meaning. Although she concentrates her study on Europe and the USA, Weber nonetheless argues that

> international relations was and is an arena for the contestation of meaning ... the meanings attached to sovereignty and the practices which follow from them are historically and geographically variable. And, if this is the case, then the state – that seemingly foundational entity in global politics "essentially" described by the term sovereignty – is historically and geographically variable as well.[73]

Interpreted in this way, critical constructivism parts the way with world polity and liberal norms scholarship by opening the possibility of approaching the world as a differentiated and contested space of multiple interpretation. An additional source of change is thereby introduced in addition to the contradictory scripts within Western world culture and intentional action: non-Western interpretations and practices.

Explaining change?
Critical constructivists have shown little interest in analyzing change in state constitution or international politics more generally. Walker's (1993) and Bartelson's (1995) genealogical analyses of state sovereignty come to mind as two notable exceptions, demonstrating changes in the discourses constitutive of states. Genealogies importantly contrast with world polity and norms scholarship in their focus on historical

---

[72] Neumann 1996b: 140–1. For the critique of Eurocentrism to which he responds, see Geertz 1979: 229.
[73] C. Weber 1995: 13, 16.

specificity and the adjacent shunning of causal generalization even of the Mid-Range variety. Indeed, as Price illustrates,

the point of departure for the genealogy is the insight that institutions are contingent structures "fabricated in piecemeal fashion" out of the vicissitudes of history. As a result of the marriage of chance occurrences, fortuitous connections, and reinterpretations, the purposes and forms of moral structures often change to embody values different from those that animated their origins.[74]

The question of change does pose a challenge for many critical constructivists, however. Even critical practitioners such as Milliken charge that these investigations tell "not so much about how discourses of International Relations have been discontinuous, with heterogeneous conditions of emergence and spaces for dissent, but how dominating discourses have been largely *continuous*."[75] Laffey similarly makes the case that "post-structural scholars (and many others) claim that we live in a period of dramatic and profound change. But performative accounts of subjectivity often emphasize the reproduction of the self."[76] Presuming a world of flux, many post-structural scholars have asked: "How is the meaning of state sovereignty fixed in theory and practice?"[77] With the question largely reversed from that posed by norms scholars (who presume stability and analyze change), the empirical identity analyses indeed problematically appear as transhistorically constant reiterations and reproductions of self/other binaries in many of the deconstructive works. Stasis and continuity are not inherent in constitutive analyses, however, as I shall argue in the next chapter.

If the question of change has posed a problem to much constitutive scholarship, so does the issue of identity/difference. As was noted previously, scholars interested in sovereignty have generally studied states as an undifferentiated category of beings in the sense that all are treated as like – sovereign – units. Studies of specific states, on the other hand, suffer from a built-in particularism or subjectivism. As the analyses of particular states have not been situated in anything akin to an international society or world culture, state identity appears as if it were unique to each state actor. In many cases, foreign policy representations come

---

[74] Price 1997: 7–8.   [75] Milliken 1999b: 246.
[76] Laffey 2000: 434.   [77] C. Weber 1995: 3.

into view entirely as a function of US and British policy-makers' imaginations both of the Self and of the Other.[78]

There is furthermore a general tendency to overemphasize the role of discourses within that which becomes bounded as a state (i.e. the "self") in the production of identity, and particularly the role of US and European selves. The importance of *inter*-subjectivity and relationality is lost and the broader social truth conditions for state identity claims are overlooked. The international from such an angle would emerge as utterly idiosyncratic. Like the world polity and norms literatures, these scholars would benefit from connecting particular state identities to some notion of *international society* of inter-subjective norms (though possibly multiply interpreted and contested), putting to work their conceptual tools of power, discourse and subjectivity. Furthermore, and as these scholars would undoubtedly agree, the various states that function as others of Europe and the USA also operate as selves and engage in meaning-construction and othering practices.[79] With regard to my research question, leaving out these other practices and a more systematic theorizing of an international society are serious shortcomings.

Conclusion

The constructivist tradition provides important insights that take us some distance in understanding the spread of suffrage, women's agencies and quotas. World polity institutionalism and norms scholarship have elucidated the homogenizing force of norms. The importance of normative contradictions and human agency as sources of change is significant and will be reaffirmed in the empirical analyses in this book. The critical constructivist focus on hierarchical relations of difference will likewise prove crucial for understanding the worldwide changes in state behavior towards women. This book draws upon these central insights and thus falls within the constructivist tradition.

However, the importance of social hierarchies as a core feature of international society has been neglected in the constructivist literature

[78] E.g. Campbell 1998; Doty 1996; Milliken 1999; Neumann 1996a and 1999; Weber 1995; Weldes 1999.
[79] Inayatullah and Blaney 1996: 66. Critical constructivist scholars influenced by post-colonial theory are a notable exception here; e.g. Biswas 2001; Muppidi 1999; Niva 1999.

to date. None of these strands approaches international society as a stratifying society in which states are socially ranked and ordered. A central aim of this book is to draw our attention to the significance of social hierarchy, both as a constitutive element of international society and as a source of change. To do so, the next chapter lays out a framework for understanding norms as inextricably linked with inequality. The role of social rank in the generation of normative change is then discussed.

3 | *A complex society of norms and social hierarchies*

This book starts with the premise that the international should be approached as a society in the sense of being *social* – constituted by inter-subjective knowledge and meaningful practices, and composed of arrangements of social relations among actors. International society, as patterns of organization of relations, is discursively constituted, structured and regulated by a multiplicity of norms, values and causal claims. I have no presumptions about international society being a singular and coherent system of meaning and relations within which all actors share certain common values. Instead, I leave the question about the complexity and diversity of international society open, to be investigated in the empirical analyses.

Norms are central components of international society. We may agree with the contention that "society *means* that norms regulate human conduct."[1] Adapting Katzenstein's widely used definition, I use norms to connote *social standards for the proper behavior of actors of a stipulated identity* (with identity never being given but always in-the-making). A norm is thus not a mere generalization of regular practices but rather refers to recognition or knowledge of relations between specified behaviors and a stated identity. In other words, norms help set the terms for what can be said and done as a certain kind of actor. They also set out what has to be said and done in order to be regarded as a certain kind of actor. This process of connecting behavior with identity is inter-subjective, or socially shared. And the inter-subjective character of norms in turn means that the analysis of norms is not about seemingly subjective or private beliefs inside people's heads. Like many other constructivists, I take an agnostic stance on private mental beliefs and motivations and let these remain outside the scope of analysis.[2]

---

[1] Dahrendorf 1968: 173.
[2] On this point, see Cancian 1975; Laffey and Weldes 1997.

Identity/difference

As the definition of a norm suggests, norms and identity are closely linked; indeed, they stand in a mutually constitutive relationship. We have to engage the question of identity to understand the operation of norms. Like critical constructivists, I define an identity as *the social meanings and practices through which an actor becomes distinctively recognizable or known as such*, enabling the becoming of an acting "self." Stated differently, an identity or subject position demarcates the possibilities for a particular actor to *be* and *act* in the world.

Whereas norms and identity are closely related, they are not one and the same: *norms communicate the relation between behavior and being (identity)*. Norms help us establish what kind of behavior is appropriate for and indicative of a particular type of being. To know norms, to paraphrase Giddens, is to know how to go on as a certain kind of actor, something that generally involves a great deal of tacit knowledge and often takes on a routine character.[3] To know norms is also to know how to become a different kind of actor. For instance, the successful transformation from a "traditional" to a "modern" state demands an understanding of the criteria that define these state varieties. As we shall see throughout this book, norms provide crucial guides for transformations in beings, away from undesirable and towards desirable conditions. The institutionalized behavior towards women has become one important set of criteria for the process of change.

Thanks to the work of critical scholars, it is now generally accepted that identities are established through ongoing processes of differentiation. The logic of identity demands differentiation, since it is only by drawing distinctions that it is possible to identify a being as distinctive from another. We have to know what something is *not* in order to know what it *is*. Such distinctions do not have to be set up between contemporaneously existing identities. The existence of democratic states, to use an important example, presupposes and demands simply the hypothetical definition of undemocratic states. Historical modes of being are often used to give meaning to present identities. The construction of post-war European identity has largely rested on depictions of Europe's own past, interpreting the new Europe as peaceful and humane against a history of warfare, genocide and colonialism.[4] A hypothesized future state of affairs

---

[3] Giddens 1979: 67.   [4] E.g. Diez 2004.

can likewise also function as a point of comparison and self-definition, such as visions of an approaching state of justice. However, many of the important differentiations among states in contemporary international society draw boundaries between states as they are now, such as between developing and developed, Western and Islamic, democratic and un-democratic, or European and North American states.

It is important not to conflate difference and hierarchy conceptually, since each relation of difference is not necessarily one of social rank. There is certainly a possibility of understanding distinctive categories of being as simply different, neither better nor worse. Such is the case when social beings are governed by different norms, providing no shared standard of evaluation or assessing comparison. This would also be the effect of indifference, in the absence of evaluative assessments. Advocates of intercultural communication sometimes emphasize the importance of abstaining from judgment, of telling oneself that "our culture is not superior, it is just different," in the interactions between peoples understood as culturally distinct.[5] In short, it is crucial to keep in mind that "the notion of differentiation does not in itself imply any distinctions of rank or value among the differentiated elements."[6]

Norms/hierarchies

Norms are not simply about setting out the relationship between beha-vior and being and thereby helping to differentiate between different kinds of beings. Norms are also essentially about *value*, as they validate certain kinds of behavior for specific sorts of actors and devalue other sorts of behavior. The assignation of value is key to understanding the operation and effectiveness of norms – indeed, the assignation of value gives norms much of their force. In contrast with prior studies of norms in international society, this book draws on sociological traditions of analyzing society as relational stratification processes. More specifi-cally, I make use of scholars who have elucidated the role of norms in generating and drawing upon social hierarchies.[7]

Social hierarchy, a term I use synonymously with social inequality, stratification or rank, concerns *the ordering of actors as superior or*

---

[5] Triandis 1994: 3. See also Inayatullah and Blaney's work (e.g. 1996).
[6] Dahrendorf 1968: 167.
[7] Particularly Dahrendorf 1968, but also Cancian 1975; Giddens 1979.

inferior to one another in socially important respects.[8] German social theorist Ralf Dahrendorf is a particularly helpful source for thinking through the concepts of social hierarchy and norms.[9] A wide array of scholars, he argues, presume an original state of equality and ascribe to property, mode of production or division of labor the crucial role in destroying this equality. Positing a period of equality, whether a state of nature or primitive communism, it is possible for thinkers as different as Rousseau and Marx to approach inequality as a historical phenomenon whose elimination is conceivable.

Dahrendorf, in contrast, traces the origin of inequality to the very nature of societies as value-laden communities. Although it is possible to eliminate particular kinds of inequality, such as class, the eradication of social inequality as such is unachievable unless there is a full state of indifference and absence of assessment. In short, his argument runs as follows. He begins with Durkheim's famous premise that every society is a moral community, constituted and regulated by established and inescapable evaluative expectations – norms – which are "always related to concrete social positions."[10] Societal norms, in turn, neces- sarily entail some sort of tacit or overt sanctioning of behavior accord- ing to the level of conformity to the norms for that identity. Norms assess better and worse practices, desirable and undesirable behavior, what is normal and abnormal, for a particular kind of actor. Given that norms always entail sanctioning evaluative criteria, Dahrendorf con- cludes that in any given historical society,

whatever symbols they may declare to be outward signs of inequality, and whatever may be the precise content of their social norms, the hard core of social inequality can always be found in the fact that men as the incumbents of social roles are subject, according to how their roles relate to the dominant expectational principles of society, to sanctions designed to enforce these principles.[11]

In other words, whereas norms change contextually and over time, all societies are characterized by some form of social hierarchy. Such inequalities are built into the very fabric of society and are an inescap- able effect of the existence of norms. Norms do not simply generate a

---

[8] Paraphrased from Parsons 1951: 69.
[9] The discussion that follows draws in particular on his 1968 essay "On the Origin of Inequality among Men."
[10] Dahrendorf 1968: 167.   [11] Ibid.

more homogeneous society of like units, in other words. They simultaneously help to differentiate and hierarchically order actors. Homogenizing and heterogenizing tendencies are mutually implicated in norms.

Again, the discussion so far is not to suggest that international society is best conceptualized as a single, coherent whole with one view of the nature and order of international society shared by all. Far from it. Differing worldviews and perspectives abound, providing different standards of assessment and bases for stratification. Norms are thereby not only contested but also often contextually reinterpreted. Kratochwil (1988) has cautioned against narrow interpretations of the meaning of norms and the identities they delineate. Taking this caution seriously, I attempt to show some of the broader discursive conditions for understanding what norms are and do. As an example, the claim that "civilized states grant women the vote" is minimally premised upon the existence of beings identifiable as "states" in the world, that these states are categorized as "civilized" and "uncivilized" and that they are characterized by certain kinds of relations. The utterance furthermore presumes that there are beings categorically identifiable as "women" (rather than "men," "hermaphrodites," "states" and so on), and that there is a set of institutional practices known as "the vote" that could connect these women to the civilized state. One of the most interesting implications of this broader notion of a norm is that challenges to any one of these components – the conceptualization of the actors or the relations between them – might lead to change. What is more, the meanings and rationales of what may appear as a simple and single norm may vary substantially. One of the core contentions of this book is that different interpretations of a norm may generate dissimilar standards of assessment and thus different interpretations of hierarchies among states.

In sum, inequality is a requisite component built into the logic of norms, a component that should not be conceptually conflated with difference. Norms inevitably generate comparative judgment, often among actors rather than simply against an abstract standard. As actors take on meaning by being ranked and assessed in relation to other actors, norms help to constitute actors relationally and hierarchically. Since norms function as standards of assessment, norms should be conceptualized in conjunction with stratification. Over forty years ago, Dahrendorf concluded that "*the origin of inequality is thus to be*

found in the existence in all human societies of norms of behavior."[12]
This book concurs, and contends that we may think of norms/hierarchy
as a nexus parallel and related to the identity/difference connection.

The status of women and social hierarchies among states

Norms on women are embroiled in the validation and ordering of states
or categories of states.[13] Exactly how certain institutional behaviors
help to make states social beings of a certain kind and standing is a more
complicated question. Three alternatives emerge in this book. First, the
political status of women may function as a rather straightforward
definitional and ranking criterion. By behaving appropriately towards
women, a state counts as a certain kind rather than another and is
assessed accordingly. Women's suffrage is presently among the predominant absolute criteria for differentiating between democratic and
undemocratic states, for instance, and the absence of female voting
helps to define and devalue states such as Saudi Arabia as undemocratic
and patriarchal.

State practices towards women can help to define and assess states in
a second manner. The official status of women is often seen as an *effect*
of prior economic, political or cultural processes and conditions. The
status of women thus becomes an indication of prior conditions, rather
than a simple defining standard. For instance, whether women have
access to legal abortion is presently often interpreted as an effect of
cultural values. The legalization of abortion has thus come to indicate
whether a state rests on conservative/religious or liberal/secular values,
which are understood as a temporally prior cause of the abortion
legislation. When change is understood to take place in progression,
such as in levels of civilization or development, the status of women can
come to function as a shorthand gauge of where in the process a state is
located. By suggesting that certain kinds of broader changes have taken
place beforehand, practices towards women thus help to assess what
kind of being a state has become.

---

[12] Dahrendorf 1968: 169–70, my emphasis.
[13] Scholars of nationalism have shown the symbolic and material functions of
women and gender for national identity and national self/other relations. While
this literature is too large to review here, Yuval-Davis 1997 is an excellent
representative of this line of scholarship. The literature on gender and nation has
had little to say about the state, however.

Behavior towards women can help to define and rank states in a third manner. Behavior towards women is often understood to be a *cause* of the condition and standing of a state over time. An institutional relation to women may thereby be considered appropriate in order to become or to keep being a certain kind of state in the future. In other words, norms regarding women can come to serve as a road map (for development, democratization, transparency and so on). For instance, while instituting a high ratio of female parliamentarians may certainly immediately mark out a state as modern and progressive or suggest that the state has undergone prior modernizing changes, a large proportion of women is widely understood to be helpful to future national economic development by allegedly countering political corruption. Instituting a larger proportion of women legislators can thus presumably help to reconstruct and develop a state in the longer term. In other words, there are institutional relations to women considered appropriate for becoming a better kind of state in the longer term.

The status of women defines and ranks states as

1. a simple definitional criterion
2. an indicator of prior conditions
3. a cause of future conditions

There are, then, at least three ways in which norms regarding women are mired in international ranking by defining and assessing states. The institutional treatment of women may be entailed in intensely competitive comparisons among states, particularly when the rank is understood in relative terms among categorically differentiated states. State behavior towards women is rarely free of assessment. Whether women may vote, stand for office, control their reproduction, initiate divorce or are required or forbidden to veil themselves seldom involves questions of simple differentiation among states. These are highly value-laden practices whose official regulation involves a great deal of debate and judgment.

Constitution, hierarchy and change

Like all constructivists, this book shares the assumption that intersubjective meaning structures are constitutive of our social world. The remaining conceptual question concerns how, more specifically, to think about constitutive analyses and change. Constitutive analyses are often portrayed as static. Wendt characterizes constitutive analyses as *"property" theories* which "account for the properties of things by reference to the structures in virtue of which they exist." Like others, he contrasts them with causal ones, characterized as *"transition" theories* whose central objective is "to explain *changes.*"[14] A purely constitutive analysis, Wendt alleges, "is inherently static."[15]

There are better ways to conceptualize constitution and change, however. To elucidate the notion of constitution, it is common to use the analogy of the game of chess.[16] The game of chess, as a set of institutional rules, is constitutive of the game pieces, their relations and player practices – these take on their meaning and being *solely* by the contextual factors of the game of chess. "Threatening the king in a chess game by announcing 'check' means something *only* with reference to the underlying rules of the game. Thus, the meaning of the move and its explanation crucially depend upon the knowledge of the rule-structure."[17] In using the analogy of chess, football or other such games, constitution is made to appear as something that takes place at a foundational moment and then remains static as a single set of fixed rules whose meaning is identically interpreted and apparent to all.

The problem for students of international politics is that social rules and norms rarely function that way. I shall quote Giddens at some length here; he contends that

we have to be very careful about using the rules of games – like chess – as illustrative of the characteristics of social rules in general. Only certain features of "knowing a rule" are best exemplified in this way, because games like chess have clearly fixed, formalized rules that are established in a lexicon, as well as because the rules of chess are not generally subject to chronic disputes of legitimacy, as social rules may be.[18]

---

[14] Wendt 1998: 105. See also Fearon and Wendt 2002.   [15] Wendt 1999: 181.
[16] E.g. Kratochwil 1989; Wendt 1999. Wendt 1999: 172 also uses the analogy of cashing a check at a bank: "In order to perform this action, teller and patron must both understand what a check is and what their roles are, and this shared knowledge must be backed up by the institutional context of a bank and banking system."
[17] Kratochwil 1989: 269.   [18] Giddens 1979: 67.

Giddens suggests a better analogy to illustrate the constitutive nature of rules of discourse, that of *children's games*. Here, there may be no lexicon of formal rules, "and it may be an essential characteristic of those rules which do exist that they cannot be strictly defined."[19] Without a strict definition, the children may not all have the same understanding of the rules of the game, a game which they nonetheless play. In this view, constitution is not limited to a primary stage but is rather an ongoing process of iteration and reinterpretation of norms. The interpretation of norms in the continuity of practice – "chronically involved in the instantiation of rules [and] not separate from what those rules 'are'"[20] – in turn continuously subject norms to gradual and often unintentional change. If we furthermore allow for the possibility that children may bring different pre-understandings to the game, thus relaxing the assumption of cultural holism that is the basis of Wendt's reasoning, then there is even less conceptual reason to presume that constitutive analyses are inherently static. The dynamism of inter-subjective structures of meaning means that we do not necessarily have to look to non-discursive sources for change. *A purely constitutive analysis is inherently dynamic.*

This book makes three general claims about the role of social hier-archies in normative change, relating to the origin, process and effect of normative transformation. The first claim is that social ranking is a crucial source of dynamism in international society, one that has been overlooked and under-theorized in previous constructivist work. Dahrendorf contends that social hierarchy "becomes the dynamic impulse that serves to keep social structures alive. Inequality always implies the gain of one group at the expense of others; thus every system of social stratification generates protest against its principles and bears the seeds of its own suppression."[21] The social rankings generated by norms impel normative transformation, in short.

The actors that are constituted as disadvantaged in a social order may become agents of change. Indeed, as we shall see in this book, new state practices may first develop among states considered peripheral or lesser in some regard. States that are devalued in some respect, identified as less developed or less civilized than other states, may be under more pressure to initiate change than those validated through their perfor-mance. Devalued social agents may attempt to rise in rank within the

---

[19] Giddens 1979: 68.   [20] Ibid.   [21] Dahrendorf 1968: 177.

existing order, they may challenge the belittling interpretation of their behavior or they may reject the normative context that debases their performance more fundamentally. Indeed, what the core *is* may be a question of perspective as well as a matter of contestation. Crucially, new institutional behavior towards women can develop "from below" and may function as a challenge to international stratification or to a particular state's position therein.

This claim is an important addition to a constructivist literature that presumes that new institutional forms always develop in the so-called core of international society. Ranking among states is furthermore not the only form of social inequality centrally at stake in the spread of state institutions on women. Women are also constituted and hierarchically ordered through norms. Indeed, the identification of women as a unified and devalued category of being has been a crucial source of institutional change, among states of high and low standing alike. This further strengthens the contention about stratification as a source of change.

New state practices may clearly also emerge first among validated states of high standing, however. As is further elaborated in the discussion on the process of change, social rank is important in these cases as well, since new state practices must be interpreted in light of the identity and standing of the state in question. It is important not to approach social hierarchies and change in a mechanistic or deterministic manner. Incorporating social stratification into an analysis of international norms does not help us predict more precisely where and when change will emerge. Which particular actors will challenge a social order and the form that challenge will take remain historically open questions rather than generalized regularities. However, it is absolutely crucial to recognize the possibility that those who experience themselves as disadvantaged in a normative order will search for ways to reinterpret and challenge that social order (or to advance their position therein while reproducing it).

The second general claim about stratification and change concerns the *how* of change, the process by which new institutional norms spread among states. This book argues that the process is always and necessarily shaped by social ranking. When they develop, new institutional practices must be interpreted in terms of the unequal validation and standing of state forms generated by existing norms. It must be clear why a state *of a certain kind and standing* should adopt certain behaviors or institutions. The appropriateness of the new practices must be accounted for – explained as a question of justice, Islam, development, national independence, progress, democracy, gender equality, civilization, or what the case might be. As we shall see, activists have had to interpret and frame their claims in light of predominant norms, the social hierarchy these are understood to entail, and a particular state's position within that normative order. Whereas these orders may be challenged and reinterpreted in the process, new institutional practices must make sense for a state in terms of the normative order of which that state is understood to be a part.

Once a practice has taken hold in one or a few states, their identity and standing among other states becomes important for the subsequent process of change. The institutionalization of a practice held to be emblematic of states considered lesser must be explained and justified – it had to make sense for a Western state to adopt an institution considered characteristic of communist states during the Cold War, for instance, or vice versa. In some cases, it may seem unimaginable to adopt an institution considered typical of a differing and devalued state form. Legislation mandating veiling in public places is presently not likely to spread to Western states, for instance. Social hierarchies among states may then function as boundaries, setting the terms for how far a practice will spread internationally. In other cases, it may seem imperative to adopt an institution of a devalued rival, in order not to fall behind.

The third and final general claim about stratification and change concerns the effects of international norms. World polity and norms scholars alike presume that the international spread of a state practice should be seen as a case of increasing isomorphism, a process by which states become more similar. This book disagrees and claims that norms simultaneously make similar and stratify the states of international society, for reasons discussed earlier in this chapter. The possibility of multiple interpretations of a norm gives further reason to dispute the presumption of simple homogenization in the emergence of international norms.

A note on human agency and change

So far, the discussion of change has made the argument that constitutive inter-subjective meaning structures should be approached as dynamic, and that norms and stratification are centrally implicated in change in international society. The question remains of what to make of the fact that suffrage, national machinery and sex quotas were all subject to intense and intentional mobilization, primarily by female activists. Should this activism be interpreted as discursively produced, or is transnational mobilization indication of non-discursive sources of change?

As world polity scholars have elucidated, the notion that the world may be alterable and subject to rational human manipulation is a form of culture or discourse that instructs actors to seek change. The improvability of humankind as progress, however that progress is interpreted, generates and indeed *demands* transformation of states. The discourses of civilization, development, modern democracy and neoliberalism, all central to this book, have been progressive in this sense of commanding change. They often extend the promise that those unfavorably constituted and positioned may alter their categorization or rank. Those favorably constituted, on the other hand, are often instructed to keep up with transformations in order not to fall behind.

From this perspective, progressive scripts constitute agents as strategizing and mobilizing beings and provide the justifications and reasons for their activism. Mobilization and rational strategizing are thereby matters of cultural instruction and cannot simply be equated with agency, if by "agency" we mean some form of human intervention that generates something creatively new.

I still grant some independent status to agency as human ingenuity, however, finding myself uneasily situated between the dynamic cultural structuralism of critical constructivists and the agentic norms approach. This stance is perhaps best expressed in Giddens's structurationism, once the source of great interest in IR. Giddens writes:

The concept of structuration involves that of the *duality of structure*, which relates to the *fundamentally recursive character of social life, and expresses the mutual dependence of structure and agency* ... According to this conception, the same structural characteristics participate in the subject (the actor) as in the object (society). Structure forms "personality" and "society" simultaneously – but in neither case exhaustively ... every process of action is a production of something new, a fresh act; but at the same time all action exists in continuity with the past, which supplies the means of its initiation.[22]

---

[22] Giddens 1979: 69–70.

history as the foundation of the political emancipation of women, this discovery is astounding. What is more, European history itself further places in question the notion that "tradition" is the culprit for keeping women out of politics. During the European Middle Ages, women of the estates often had the formal ability to influence decision-making in the negotiations between the estates and the monarch. As an example, English abbesses were called to the first parliaments and women land-owners could influence elections to the parliament on a par with men.[1] To make the argument that the liberal, constitutional state of "civilized" Europe developed by excluding women from the polity, this chapter will analyze the transformation in the construction of women and the state in Europe from absolutism to the nineteenth century.

The state of the past several centuries is a contextually variant polity, held together through structures of rule that position the "state" as a certain kind of being, with certain aims and capacities for action. In the most abstract sense, these structures of rule include materially mani-fested norms, prescriptive rules and social institutions. Approaches to the state have largely moved away from a search for *the* fundamental structure of rule that holds the state together, whether mode of produc-tion, patriarchy or anarchy/sovereignty. Instead, understanding the state as the site of multiple interactive and sometimes conflicting struc-tures, we can appreciate multiple, fruitful approaches to the state. The state then also emerges as a less coherent being.

The thrust of this chapter deploys a constitutive analysis that largely leaves out causal questions. My main contention is that sex/gender systems and state-formation are intimately connected with interna-tional social hierarchies. As this chapter will show, the nineteenth-century European state developed as an entity congruent with the articulation of women as a separate category, as well as within the development of a society of so-called "civilized" states. The simulta-neous formation or construction of these three entities – women, state, civilization – and the regulation of their relations is at the center of the analysis. Importantly, the formation of all three entities was permeated by similar systems of rule. During the period of unitary state rule under absolutism, Europe also saw a unitary notion of sexual being – a one-sex model. During the period of absolutist rule, there were female sovereign monarchs across Europe, and women of the estates had access

[1] Styrkársdóttir 1998: 48.

to state office. Between the late seventeenth and the nineteenth century, in the transformations of absolutism that accompanied the rise in science, secularism and processes of industrialization, the notion of what a "person" and a "state" are, how these beings are unified, also altered dramatically. There was a two-fold bifurcation: state–society, male–female. Rather than serving as a simple source of the inclusion of women into the state, the secular sciences, liberalism and the emergence of parliamentary democracy in the core of the developing "European civilization" helped to give rise to the creation of what was understood as an ontologically separate category of women and the exclusion of that category from the emergent "political" realm.[2] As we shall see, the exclusion of women from formal state institutions expressly became a practice of the "civilized" world. Before women could be politically empowered in Europe, they had been differentiated as ontologically separate beings from men and politically disempowered as such.

The rest of the chapter is organized into three sections. It begins with a cursory discussion of the development of the European state from the age of absolutism to the nineteenth-century constitutional state. The section is brief, not primarily because the discussion is likely familiar to IR scholars but because it is only by bringing in an analysis of "woman" and "civilization" that we can really understand the nature of and analyze the nineteenth-century European state in its concrete manifestations. The second section is more extensive in its analysis of the co-determination of "woman" and the "state" and the changes in their relation between absolutism and the nineteenth century. Here, I bring the work of feminist political theorists and historians into conversation with the conventional IR treatments of the state. The final section is given most elaboration, as it brings in "civilization" as a third crucial element for understanding the relation between women and the nineteenth-century state. That analysis is based on primary sources.

From absolutism to the nineteenth-century constitutional state

From the late sixteenth to the eighteenth century – often referred to as the age of absolutism – the territorial state was consolidated at the expense of other polities and was under the increasingly unitary rule of a monarch or council of state. The essential sociality of this

[2] See e.g. Bock 2002; Fauré 1991; Jónasdóttir 1994; Pateman 1989.

development has been widely noted, as ideologies and social practice moved across Europe and as each state came to exist in the recognized presence of and competition with other states. Concurrently, internal political institutions and forms of rule developed that enabled absolutist rule. The period of absolutism initiated what we could cautiously refer to as the simultaneous outward and inward developments of the state, separating state from state territorially in the "international" sphere, and "state" from "society" in what came to be the "domestic" sphere. A new form of rule emerged – law as an instrument of expressed sovereign will – displacing the previous negotiated understandings between the estates and the monarch.[3]

In contrast with later forms of state rule, law as sovereign will rested explicitly and expressly on coercive rule. Domestically, penal codes relying on the physical body as a target of punishment and on torture as public spectacle were in force all over Europe.[4] Succession battles over the throne and struggles with the estates over state rule regularly involved assassinations of monarchs (or monarchs-to-be) and of portions of the nobility. In the emerging "international" sphere, since each state's commitment to self-aggrandizement was legitimated, there was "the continuous and inescapable presence of other states bounding that 'will to sovereignty.' Over and over again, each state came up against *limits* to its sovereignty in the form of competing states striving to satisfy their own self-defined interests. Hence in this system … every claim was ultimately enforceable only through coercion – if necessary on the field of battle."[5] The pervasiveness and frequency of warfare only underscored this.

Unitary arrangements for the creation and execution of state-wide policies developed, operating in the name of the sovereign ruler. Courts and other institutions that created and executed law became not only more pervasive but also *public*; that is, physically and visibly distinctive as official organizations of the state. Around Europe, uniforms for functionaries of the state were assumed, akin to those of the military, and denoting the public nature of the inhabitants of state office.[6] The state thus became distinct from (and derived its meaning in relation to) the new sphere of "society," creating a realm where specifically "political" or "public" functionaries and personnel were located. At the same time, the absolutist state was empowered to rule *over* "society."

---

[3] Poggi 1978: 72–7.   [4] Foucault 1977.
[5] Poggi 1978: 90.   [6] Poggi 1978: 77–8.

That society, from the height of the state's level, appeared to be peopled exclusively by a multitude of *particuleurs*, of private (though sometimes privileged) individuals. The state addressed them in their capacity as subjects, taxpayers, potential military draftees, etc.; but it considered them unqualified to take an active part in its own business. It contemplated the civil society exclusively as a suitable object of rule.[7]

The whole of the state – the public functionaries, offices and organs – were permeated by and understood as an expression of the will of the sovereign in the rule over society. There was thus an ideal of an essential, hierarchical unity of the state.

Early nineteenth-century Europe had, roughly speaking, arrived at being composed of territorially bounded states in which each maintained a single currency and unified fiscal and legal systems, increasingly making claims to a national language and people. The structures of state power were to be profoundly reshaped, however. Another form of state rule emerged that was increasingly depersonalized, no longer understood as having been bestowed upon their populations primarily by the will of God by means of the actions of the sovereign monarch. Law, no longer primarily granted from above, became understood as founded on popular sovereignty and was deliberated in elected national assemblies. The state to a larger or lesser degree became conceptualized as a deliberate construction, a conscious, willful human creation that was often both represented and bounded by a written constitution.[8] Constitutional parliaments had emerged well before 1848 in Belgium, Great Britain, the Netherlands, Norway (in its union with Sweden), Sweden, and Switzerland, and they formed in Austria in the 1860s, France in the 1870s and Italy in the 1880s.[9]

There are a number of characteristic aspects of this transformation. First, although the state–society distinction was still central, the relation between the entities changed: the sovereign state no longer ruled *over* society, but increasingly a national community was thought to rule itself through the state. The relation between the state and the national citizenry was of great concern not only to many nineteenth-century

---

[7] Poggi 1978: 78.

[8] Most European states of the nineteenth century were to take the form of constitutional monarchies, combining the non-elective rule of the monarch with legislatures that were elected by restricted suffrage; see e.g. Haupt and Langewiesche 2001: 17; Therborn 1977: 9.

[9] Haupt and Langewiesche 2001: 17.

thinkers but also to the emerging mass political movements that demanded popular forms of government on a national scale.[10] "Except for Tsarist Russia, the prerogatives of the rulers were greatly restricted by constitutions in the decades after 1848 and opportunities for parliaments to participate in the legislative process were codified."[11]

Although the state became understood as man-made and thus lost some of its previous religious purpose, it continued operating "with reference to some idea of an end or function to which it is instrumental."[12] The second key aspect of the transformation in state rule is well expressed by Poggi's suggestion that "the moral ideal that ultimately legitimizes the modern state is the taming of power through the depersonalization of its exercise."[13] As the state expressly becomes an artifact of human reason, the law *itself* becomes both a source of legitimacy and the state's "standard mode of expression, its very language, the essential medium of its activity."[14] Law thus became self-referential: having been reasoned into being in accordance with set rules (themselves man-made), the state came to rest partially on *procedural legitimacy* rather than the will of the sovereign. Law, as an expression of reason, was importantly conceptualized as a limit on, rather than expression of, power, assuring that brute force and unbound passions could not reign. Representative institutions such as legislatures and executives took over the centrality previously accorded to the sovereign monarch, providing the fora for more "civil" and bounded controversy, debate, and law-formation.[15]

The law placed tenuous bounds on brute force, however, and was never thought to *remove* power as the essence of politics. Instead, the organizations and form of state rule bifurcated, so that the "political"

---

[10] E.g. Haupt and Langewiesche 2001; Hinsley 1966: 226–7; Rueschemeyer, Stephens and Stephens 1992.

[11] Haupt and Langewiesche 2001: 18.   [12] Poggi 1978: 96.

[13] Poggi 1978: 101.   [14] Poggi 1978: 102.

[15] To be sure, procedural legitimacy may have been particularly predominant in more liberal states such as the United Kingdom and the USA. The other form of depersonalization of state rule took its expression in the state's becoming a being of and to itself, operating on the basis of rational, scientific principles of *raison d'état*. In states such as Germany or Sweden, the role of government was not solely to represent interests of societal groups but rather, in the words of Uppsala political science professor Carl Axel Reuterskiöld (1911: 19) to "secure the undisturbed development of state life." On this logic, the state was not a humanly manufactured article but a being that operated according to its own logic.

nature of the state became separated from, though internally related to, its "civil" functions. A mutually constitutive political/civil division thus emerged within the state. Politics continued being understood largely as a matter of potentially power-laden conflict, connected with coercive rule, even if rules and legal procedures were in place to organize, regulate and bound dissent and thus "civilize" and tame brute power to the extent possible. Regardless of the rules and procedures, politics were still an arena of conflicting interests and competitive struggle, where combative passions ran high and cool reason did not always prevail. Moreover, it was the executive and legislative political organs that made the decisions about the financing and organization of the military and police. Those in control of the representative institutions formally controlled the state's coercive organs. Equally importantly, the political institutions of the state formally directed international politics, where war was still considered the extension of politics. Public functionaries and civil servants, on the other hand, became seen as the antithesis of the political – impersonal, non-political bureaucrats, the very embodiment and executioners of legal-rational authority. These were the technically specialized administrators who were to ensure the rational, functionally efficient pursuit of whatever goals were set up in the "political" sphere.[16]

Although the taming of power was important, there are other metaphysical ends or functions that are equally crucial in the ongoing generation and legitimation of the state. When Europe moved away from a teleology of divine providence, it moved into what Blumenberg (1983) refers to as an "unfinished world" of rationality and manipulability. This "unfinished world" becomes the teleology of the nineteenth-century state, a necessary condition for man's rational action. Were the world complete, there would be no possibility for man's reasoning or willing anything into being. Poggi hints at something analogous in a brief discussion of what he calls the *open-endedness* of the modern state: the state has "become oriented to abstract, ever-receding targets – be they the promotion of the state's power in the comity of nations, the people's welfare, or the individual's pursuit of happiness." Operating "in the name of these targets (as they are defined and mutually adjusted through the political contest) ... such a political system *must of necessity*

---

[16] See Silberman 1993; Torstendahl 1991; M. Weber 1947.

*always be generating new themes for public concern and for authorita-
tive action.*"[17]

Such themes – whether of "progress," "national security," "social
justice," "economic growth," "development" or "individual liberty" –
have since structured and given direction to the state, giving rise to
particular kinds of complex organizations, sets of organs and offices
with specified spheres of competence, resources and modalities of
operation, and providing legitimacy for their action. Paradoxically,
the legitimacy and urgency of these themes often find their source not
simply in mere arguments of procedural correctness (e.g. having been
arrived at through the proper democratic process) but in appeals to
principles and commitments thought to exist outside of human invention or reason. The source and scope of these discourses were always
transnational, as will become more apparent in the chapters to come.
European states therefore not only came to share similar aims and take
on comparable institutional forms, but they came to identify themselves
as similar in relation to polities and peoples deemed different. Before we
turn to those processes, however, we must examine the emergence of
women as a constitutive other of the nineteenth-century European state.

The consolidation of woman and her relation to the state

The total exclusion of women from state institutions in the nineteenth
century was preceded by centuries of access by landed women of the
estates into the state apparatus as well as state rule by sovereign queens.
This access was, importantly, enabled by the unitary ideal of being and
rule characterizing not only the state but also sex/gender conceptualizations during the era of absolutism. "One-sex models" of sexual being
were pervasive throughout the sixteenth and seventeenth centuries,
reviving and reinterpreting ancient Greek teachings that conceived
of all humans as of essentially a single sex.[18] One version understood
woman as simply *lesser man*, an inferior variant of a single male
anatomy.[19] More prevalent were notions that as one-sex bodies, all
human beings contained both "male" and "female" elements,

---

[17] Poggi 1978: 111, emphasis added. See also Meyer 1980: 117.

[18] E.g. Bock 2002; Laqueur 1990; Riley 1988.

[19] Aristotle had notoriously stated that "the woman is as it were an impotent male,
for it is through a certain incapacity that the female is female, being incapable of
concocting the nutriment in the last stage into semen" – as cited in Lange 1983: 9.

providing no clear biological boundaries productive of sexual difference. The male elements were generative (e.g. semen, which infused new
individuals with a soul) and involved vigor, physical strength, courage
and thus a predisposition for creation and domination. The female
elements, unsurprisingly, were inert and involved gentility, physical
weakness, cowardice and thus a tendency for submission. However,
and this is crucial, it was the "predominance, rather than the exclusion,
of one or the other ... [that] helped to determine sexual identity," as
Stephen Greenblatt argues.[20]

Men and women were thus not conceived as mutually exclusive
categories defined by their essential difference. Even though male attributes were valued over female, and the male elements led to rule, this
did not necessarily translate into those labeled *men* dominating
women. Someone identified as a woman could also rule, generally in
the absence of a man alternative and if she exhibited appropriate male
characteristics.

Among those speaking as and on behalf of women in the seventeenth
century, conceptualizations of women as a fully distinct category from
men, sharing certain essential features across religious, estate, or other
important divides, were extremely rare.[21] Contemporary interpretations of Christian theology underscored the one-sex model, as the soul
was relatively unscathed by its sex and man and woman were unified as
in essence similar beings with a God-given, desexed soul.[22] Appeals to
the unsexed soul were in fact an effective platform for those who began
speaking on behalf of women in the seventeenth and eighteenth
centuries.[23]

Although one-sex models were pervasive around Europe, they
offered a range of routes for conceiving the relationship between ruler
and polity. Women's position in the relationship between the ruler and
state-society complexes, while hotly debated, thus remained quite divergent even as the more unitary absolutist state developed. There were
several attempts to deal with what appeared as a fundamental paradox:
monarchs died, but the state survived. In fifteenth-century France,
scholars came to espouse a polity, or body politic, of *the king's one
body* (that did not die) which was regenerated over time through for-
mative male seed.[24] A system of rule that centered on monarchic

[20] Greenblatt 1986: 35.   [21] Henderson and McManus 1985; H. Smith 1982.
[22] Riley 1988: 18.   [23] Riley 1988: 42.   [24] Hanley 1997: 133.

replication through male reproductive capacity, connecting male virility with French kingship and state, could not accommodate direct female succession, which was prohibited.[25] However, as guardians of young regent sons, queen mothers did direct the council of state and France experienced three such regencies from 1560 to 1651 alone.[26] In addition to a history of military alliances with France, eighteenth-century Sweden was profoundly influenced by the French Enlightenment and French cultural practices.[27] With the Swedish state also becoming an explicitly male body politic, the constitution of 1720 prohibited female succession to the Swedish throne.[28] Until then, women had not only ruled as monarchs but had also served as state officials. As an example, two of the royal postmasters in the seventeenth century were women, presiding over the entire national postal service.[29]

In most of the rest of Europe, generally in the absence of acceptable male alternatives, women rulers were tolerated.[30] This is supported not only by succession rules but by the absence of written works systematically or consistently hostile to women rulers writ large.[31] In England, the notorious assault on female rule expressed in *The First Blast of the Trumpet against the Monstrous Regiment of Women* (1558) by Protestant John Knox was "idiosyncratic" and ultimately ineffective.[32] In contrast with France, English political axioms of *the monarch's two bodies* developed, distinguishing mortal individual monarchs from the immortal public office.[33] English common law had endowed the queen with two bodies: "a *body natural* and a *body politic* ... The body politic was supposed to be *contained within the natural body of the Queen*."[34] Female rule was thus accommodated.

English high-born women could furthermore inherit important state office with their property, and in 1711 Queen Ann decreed that unmarried women could vote for the English parliament.[35] The Russian and Habsburg empires similarly embraced female succession, seeing monarchs such as Catherine the Great and Maria Teresa of the 1740s. Female rule was always a source of anxiety, however, and narratives of the inherent dangers abounded, particularly in France. The voluminous French commentary in response to the rule of the Russian

---

[25] Cosandey 1997.   [26] Lightman 1981.   [27] Weibull 1997: 69.
[28] Weibull 1997: 58.   [29] Ohlander 2000: 118.   [30] Richards 1997: 119.
[31] Richards 1997: 102.   [32] Richards 1997: 115.   [33] Hanley 1997: 133.
[34] Axton 1977: 12.   [35] Styrkarsdóttir 1998: 48.

Catherine the Great centers on allegedly general problems of female rule, deriding her female characteristics to a degree unheard of in discussions in Russia, where she actually ruled.[36]

Between the late seventeenth and the nineteenth centuries, the notion of what a "person" is, how a being is unified, altered dramatically. "Woman" as a collective became conceptualized and voiced in new ways by the developing secular sciences that became such an important source of knowledge.[37] As will be further discussed in the next section, the broad field of evolutionary theory became central for thinking about all sorts of phenomena and processes of change, including women and the state. There was a general escalation in efforts to create clearly bounded and mutually exclusive scientific categories. In this context, new understandings of woman as essentially *different* from – as well as complementary and/or inferior to – man emerged. Two-sex models of separate spheres and being for men and women thus came to compete with and in many cases predominate over the previous one-sex models.[38] Liberal scholars' exclusion of women from the category of "individuals" who could make claims on the state is well documented. Mass mobilization among nineteenth-century workers to alter the standards of recognition in the state polity similarly contributed to the consolidation of separate spheres and the exclusion of women from politics.[39] As Steinberg and others have shown, "these struggles in the 1830s and 1840s served as the terrain for solidifying discourses and practices of masculine control and feminine quiescence among working people."[40]

Woman's becoming a distinct sex, always embodied and defined by her affections, gave rise to at least two possibilities for that which was *not*, and those who were *not*, woman. First, "man" became voiced as woman's carnal, biological opposite, so that each of the now two distinct sexes became the embodiment of *either* male or female elements. The nature of the "political" sphere of the state and "man" thus overlapped more tightly than before, while still espousing a form of rule that ultimately legitimized physical strength and coercion as vested in the military and police. To some, the state was therefore explicitly understood as being, in nineteenth-century German historian von Treitschke's words, of "male gender," of "purely male essence."[41]

---

[36] Meehan-Waters 1975.   [37] Hubbard 1983; Riley 1988: 14.   [38] Bock 2002: 84.
[39] Colley 1986 and 1992; Steinberg 1995; Vernon 1993 and 1994.
[40] Steinberg 1995: 43.   [41] Bock 2002: 133.

Second, generic "humans" or "persons" in possession of *reason* could emerge.[42] Such unsexed "individuals" (by definition not "woman") could deliberate and reason law into existence in the political sphere, speaking on behalf of the "common" good and "general" interests of the nation-state and placing bounds on brute force.[43] Such unsexed individuals could also occupy the new, impersonal bureaucracies of the "civil" domain of the state. Nineteenth-century "woman" was thus consolidated as a being with characteristics and capacities for action that were in direct opposition to those of the state itself: as the state became characterized by reason and force, woman became entrenched with emotion and weakness; as the state became characterized by science, woman became infused with faith and religion; as the state became modern, woman became understood as traditional; as the state turned self-interested, woman was cast as selfless.

In the bifurcation of rule of the nineteenth century – depersonalized rational-legal authority and coercive power – woman became the object of both forms of rule. And with the new species differentiation, it was possible for women *as such* to become excluded from all formal organizations of the state. Although formal participation in state affairs was still restricted for most men as well, their exclusion was not premised on a presumed sexual unity of being *men* but rather on a combination of wealth requirements, estate-belonging and what we can loosely refer to as religious and "ethnic" preconditions.

While shut out of deliberation and decision-making, women became an important object of the targets of the new, open-ended state. In the profuse scholarly deliberations on the state and the role of representative government leading up to the nineteenth century, arguments abounded on the need for woman to subordinate herself to man and abandon dominion over her body for the sake of public utility.[44] By the nineteenth century, such conceptualizations of politically inactive women as a resource for the public good had taken hold as predominant, though they were never unchallenged, in the emergent European national states.

---

[42] On reason and passions, see e.g. Elshtain 1981: 117–19.

[43] Jónasdóttir 1994; Okin 1979; Pateman 1989.

[44] Locke appealed to nature to legitimize women's exclusion from the state polity and their subordination to men (Okin 1979: 200). Other early liberal thinkers such as Hobbes, Hume and James Mill rejected the nature argument and used expressly utilitarian lines of reasoning that invoked the "common good" and its rights and needs (Jónasdóttir 1994: 141; Okin 1979: 197–9).

The practice of strictly separating politics from woman's sphere spread in the face of immediate and sustained debate and contestation throughout Europe in the nineteenth century. The foundation of the two-sex model became a largely unquestioned premise. On this ground, however, the woman question was an open and hotly debated issue.[45] That woman's difference necessarily dictated her exclusion from the state never became a simple taken for granted, unquestioned premise and it faced growing resistance as the space around women contracted throughout the century, as will be further discussed in the following chapter.

The standards of "civilization" and the exclusion of woman from the state polity

The analysis thus far has examined changes in female rule between the sixteenth and nineteenth centuries in Europe, drawing on existing scholarship to show that "woman" had emerged as a distinctive sexual category in ways that made her a constitutive other of the constitutional state. This process was intimately linked with the changing nature of international society and its social hierarchies. The European conceptualization of "civilization" – understood roughly as the process of transcending the presumed givens of "natural" existence[46] – emerged simultaneously with the constitutional state and consolidated woman from the broad currents of eighteenth-century Enlightenment thought. Deliberated law, the product of reason, was thought to tame brute power not only domestically, but increasingly among states. Of the late eighteenth century, Bartelson contends that although "European states pride[d] themselves on their internal legislation, their external relations [were thought to be] governed by the same set of uncivilized principles that organize[d] the savages of the new world, to whom legislation [was] unknown."[47]

The threat of war always lurked in the background. And yet the rise of international law and its institutions – highly professionalized and fairly secret diplomacy, third-party arbitration and mediation – provided a sense of rule-following order that allegedly assured that outcomes were not simply guided by military might.[48] The nineteenth

---

[45] Bock 2002. [46] Ortner 1972: 10.
[47] Bartelson 1995: 197–8. [48] Bartelson 1995: 18–25; Poggi 1978: 48.

century also saw one hundred years without a general European war, the "hundred years peace" (1815–1914), which further underscored that law could indeed move Europe away from the "barbarism" of war toward the civility of peace. This law-bound, "peaceful" group of states, which had earlier shared some sense of unity in Christendom in interactions with non-Christians, came slowly but surely to characterize its domestic legislation and international relations as "civilized."[49]

The large and amorphous field of evolutionary theory was central to how civilization was understood, as progressive, temporal *levels* of achievement. Civilization thus became articulated together with less advanced or backward groups of humans or polities on a single scale of development and success. The comparative method became central for analyzing these classifications and the relations between them, a method that was refined by scholars such as influential US anthropologist Lewis Morgan. One crucial aspect of the comparative method was spatial. A range of places and peoples across the globe were pulled together under the primitive/savage/barbarous/civilized labels, accompanied by collections of data to demonstrate that groupings such as "primitives" shared certain key characteristics. Another key aspect was temporal, using the primitive – civilized classifications to make sense of historical developments largely understood as "evolution" and "progress."

The groundbreaking work of Gustave Klemm in the 1850s and Morgan's mammoth, 560-page *Ancient Society, or Researches in the Lines of Human Progress from Savagery through Barbarism* (1877) are but two examples of the use of anthropological observation to understand historical change. The "primitive" and "barbarous" areas of the world were generally connected with a European past, stages beyond which Europe had allegedly progressed. One of the fundamental puzzles thus became how a society would move along the stages – what brought about change? A wealth of interpretations approached change as a competitive *struggle for existence* that brought about movement along the social stages.[50]

---

[49] Gong 1984: 5; Neumann 1999: 56–8.

[50] The nature of this struggle was up for debate and ranged between those who saw the struggle in aggressive, zero-sum terms (e.g. Count Gobenau in *The Inequality of Human Races*) and others who understood the struggle to entail active adaptation and man's advancing by acquiring experiential knowledge (e.g. Lewis Morgan).

European colonialism was clearly embedded in understandings of the stages of civilization. As Puchala and Hopkins have argued, from the vantage point of European capitals,

the world was perceived as divided into two classes of states and peoples, civilized and uncivilized ... inequality was an appropriate principle of international organization and standards and modes of behavior displayed toward other international actors depended upon which category those others fell into. Toward the "uncivilized," it was reasonable to behave paternalistically, patronizingly, and dictatorially, and acceptable to behave brutally if the situation demanded. Toward "civilized" countries normal behavior had to demonstrate restraint and respect: bargaining was an accepted mode of interaction, concession did not necessarily imply loss of face, humiliation was out of the question, and conquest for subjugation was not legitimate.[51]

International law was one important site for the articulation of inequality between Europe and non-European peoples and polities, expressing the acceptability of "civilized" rule over the "uncivilized."[52] The final conquest of Africa is telling: European statesmen deliberated and discussed the partition in Berlin in 1884–5 and produced a piece of international law – the General Act – that set out the rights and obligations that were to guide relations among the colonial powers.

The use of force was simultaneously legitimated in the relations between each European power and its colonial subjects.[53] The acquisition of civilization itself became a prerequisite set by Europe for the recognition of sovereign statehood and the privileged treatment that came along. The capacity for self-rule (which paradoxically was negated by the very fact of having been colonized) and the establishment of a domestic system of state structures resting on law were some of the criteria spelled out for achieving civilization.[54] However, since civilization was defined in relative terms together with barbarity, the criteria were ever changing and elusive and provided slim chances for advancement into the "civilized" fold of official statehood.

By the end of the eighteenth century, the status of women had also become intimately implicated in states' and other polities' advancement along the stages of civilization. French Utopian Socialist Charles Fourier (1772–1837) is generally credited with being the first to explicitly

[51] Puchala and Hopkins 1983: 70.
[52] E.g. Gong 1984; Jackson 1993; Price 1995 and 1997; Puchala and Hopkins 1983.
[53] Jackson 1993: 116.   [54] Gong 1984.

connect the position of women with a state's level of civilization, in 1808. However, it seems that this connection was made simultaneously or independently by a series of thinkers. Enlightenment theorist John Millar had included women as an indicator of level of civilization in 1771, in the first edition of his *Origin of the Distinction of Ranks*,[55] and Fourier's contemporary socialist Flora Tristán had done so as well.[56] Comparative debate on woman, her position within the political sphere, and civilization was in full force by the mid-nineteenth century, agreeing that "it matters not whether we regard the history of the remotest past or the diverse civilizations of the present, the emancipation and exaltation of women are the synonym of progress."[57] Woman as a category could itself be measured on the hierarchical scale of civilization, as the more or less "civilized" or "backward" of the sexes. Measured on such a scale, in crude terms, women turned into a physical resource whose use would help or hinder the state's progress.

The political status of women was conceptualized as causally related to the advancement of a state in three primary ways. First, narratives identifying general domestic progress towards civilization as a *cause* of the exclusion of women from the state were prevalent. The "level of civilization" of a state was then understood to be productive of the status of women. A second set of often complementary accounts conversely saw the level of civilization as an *effect* of the status of women. Whether as a cause or as an effect of progress, the status of women, thirdly, came to function as an indicator to gauge a state's advancement. As such, "the status of women" itself became constitutive of the very civilized – barbarian categorization, independent of whatever other forms of progress it was supposed to indicate. As we shall see in coming chapters, statesmen often became aware of the symbolic importance of woman, manipulating various indicators for the sake of demonstrating civilizational allegiance or belonging. Before we can proceed to those chapters, however, the relations identified above between women, the state and civilization in nineteenth-century Europe must be fleshed out.

Civilization as the cause of the status of woman

As one observer noted, "Civilization is the composite result of progress from the purely natural life of the animal to the purely artificial life of

---

[55] Riley 1988.   [56] Nimtz 2000: 201.   [57] Mason 1895: 276.

the most enlightened individuals and peoples."[58] Transforming the previous, absolutist expressions of the male *elements* as creative force, the inventive genius generative of progress came to rest conclusively with *men* in the nineteenth century, whereas women were articulated as vestigial. Evolutionary biology drew on examples from the natural world to develop a science of sexual selection, a form of progress that depended, in the words of Darwin, "not on a struggle for existence in relation to other organic beings or to external conditions, but on a struggle of individuals of one sex, generally males, for the possession of the other sex."[59] The physical strength and intelligence of men were allegedly constantly improved and developed by means of sexual competition for women, while women's capacities remained quiescent:

The chief distinction in the intellectual powers of the two sexes is shown by man's attaining to a higher eminence, in whatever he takes up, than can women – whether requiring deep thought, reason, or imagination, or merely the use of the senses and hands. If two lists were made of the most eminent men and women in poetry, painting, sculpture, music (inclusive both of composition and performance), history, science and philosophy, with half-a-dozen names under each subject, the two lists would not bear comparison. We may also infer ... that if men are capable of a decided pre-eminence over women in many subjects, the average of mental power in man must be above that of woman ... [Men have had] to defend their females, as well as their young, from enemies of all kinds, and to hunt for their joint subsistence. But to avoid enemies or to attack them with success, to capture wild animals, and to fashion weapons, requires the aid of the higher mental faculties, namely observation, reason, invention, or imagination. These various faculties will thus have been continually put to the test and selected during manhood.[60]

The social sciences of anthropology, geography and ethnology helped connect the notion of sexual selection with the stages of civilization by adding studies from the human world. Women, it became clear through plain observation, did not generate progress:

One has only to look around him in traveling through countries lately touched by civilization to notice that men have to drop their old occupations for new ones. In fact, not five men in a hundred in the most favored lands are at this moment pursuing the calling for which they were educated. But in transitions from savagery to civilization, and in the vicissitudes of life, women go on housekeeping, spinning, demanding if no longer making pottery, using the

[58] Mason 1895: 272.   [59] Darwin 1936: 69.   [60] Darwin 1936: 873–4.

same vocabulary, conning the same propositions, reproducing the same forms of ornaments, believing as of old, only making use of modified and better appliances. In this they are conservative, indeed, and the blood coursing through the brain tissue carries on the same commerce that has been familiar to women during many thousands of years.

The savage man in his normal life is ever changing ... On the other hand, the women of a savage tribe, and the ordinary run of women in any civilized land, who change slightly the duties they have to perform, or their manner of doing them, need to modify their conception and their opinions very little. The constant doing the same things and thinking the same thoughts from generation to generation pass the bodily activity and the mental processes on to a semiautomatic habit. Very few men are doing what their fathers did, so their opinions have to be made up by study and precedents. Nearly all women, whether in savagery or in civilization, are doing what their mothers and grandmothers did, and their opinions are therefore born in them or into them.[61]

In their explorations and comparative analyses of the world outside Europe, these scholars and travelers connected women across the geographical divides as a conservative rather than progressive force. Women, as more conservative, were thus simultaneously spatially and temporally located as backward and closer to the savage state of nature. Prevailing evidence clearly came to demonstrate that women simply could not advance on their own.

However, it was evident that women would prosper once advancement had been achieved by men. If law truly placed bounds on and civilized brute force, then women, as the weak sex, could only stand to gain – in an environment of might-is-right rule, women were thought to surely succumb. As vestigial beings of passions and little reason, it was critical that women not be entrusted with deliberating law and other forms of civilization into existence. If they did, the state of civilization and their own well-being would be jeopardized. Women were thus most in need of civilization, in order to be raised out of degradation and protected from sheer force, and yet simultaneously they posed a challenge to civilization's creation and maintenance.

If civilization was thought to protect women, it conversely became a matter of established fact that "the condition of woman has always been the most degraded the nearer we approach to a state of nature, or,

[61] Mason 1895: 274–5.

rather, the less we are raised above the level and mere animal characteristics of the brute creation."[62] The brute subjugation of women was by
the early to mid-nineteenth century widely represented as an effect of
savage society, an "oriental, and semi-barbarous delusion," a sign of
"Turkish contempt of females, as subordinate and inferior beings."[63] If
woman was brought into the fold of primitive society, the non-civilized
world was likewise simultaneously feminized. Indeed, the uncivilized
subordination of women paradoxically presented a form of "*unmanly
barbarism.*"[64] As we shall see in chapters to come, such representations
have remained surprisingly resilient and pervasive.

By the end of the nineteenth century, a number of social scientists had
attempted to dispel the truisms about the "savage" treatment of
women, but to little avail. In 1892, geographer Campbell explained
that with his stay in Korea, "the subjection of women, which is probably the commonest of accepted theories on the East, received a fresh
blow, in my mind ... Women in these parts of the world, if the truth
were known, fill a higher place and wield greater influence than they are
credited with."[65] Anthropologist E. H. Man similarly states of the
Andamanese islanders that "one of the striking features of their social
relation is the marked equality and affection which subsists [*sic*]
between husband and wife. Careful observations extended over many
years prove that not only is the husband's authority more or less
nominal, but that it is not at all an uncommon occurrence for
Andamanese Benedicts to be considerably at the beck and call of their
better halves."[66]

Rather than disrupting the prevailing view that the level of civilization was productive of the condition of woman, such reports were
reined in, and made sense of, through the notion that "woman in
politics" was an "antiquated idea" and that her non-involvement in
politics insured her protection as well as elevation. Indeed, subjecting
women to politics was widely seen as a barbaric form of mistreatment of
women. Noted US historian Francis Parkman contended that

---

[62] Fullom 1855: 149.   [63] Young 1837: 17.
[64] Young 1837: 20, my emphasis.   [65] Campbell 1892: 145.
[66] Man 1883: 791. For additional examples of social scientists marveling over the
level of equality between men and women in "savage" and "primitive" society,
see also Livingstone 1858; Pike 1892; and the observations of British Governor
and High Commissioner for the Western Pacific, Everard im Thurn (1883). For a
rendering in terms of "primitive communism," see e.g. Engels 1972.

the social power of women has grown with the growth of civilization, but their political power has diminished. In former times and under low social conditions, women have occasionally had a degree of power in public affairs unknown in the foremost nations of the modern world. The most savage tribes on [the North American] continent, the Six Nations of New York, listened, in solemn assembly, to the counsels of its matrons, with a deference that has no parallel among its civilized successors. The people of ancient Lycia, at a time when they were semi-barbarians, gave such power to their women that they were reported to live under a gynecocracy, or female government. The word gynecocracy, by the way, belongs to antiquity. It has no application in modern life; and, in the past, its applications were found, not in the higher developments of ancient society, but in the lower. Four hundred years before Christ, the question of giving political power to women was agitated among the most civilized of the ancient peoples, the Athenians, and they would not follow the example of their barbarian neighbors.[67]

The exclusion of women from the political sphere was widely represented as an elevation of woman and a characteristic effect of a state having reached an advanced stage.

In light of the discussion above, it may be tempting to simply equate civilization with men as essentially synonymous. However, man's relation to civilization was also a tenuous one, even if less so than that of woman. Herbert Spencer and others had divided the history of civilization into periods of militancy and industrialism. The period of militancy was characterized by savagery and barbarism, of warring between man and man so distinctive of the state of nature. After this period, Europe and some of its colonies were thought to have progressed to a civilized phase of industrialism and advancement.

Civilization could not entirely constrain man's natural passions, as Darwin pointed out: "Man is the rival of other men; he delights in competition, and this leads to ambition which passes too easily into selfishness. These latter qualities seem to be his natural and unfortunate birthright."[68] Mason, like many others, began arguing that "instead of an *age*, we should rather say a *sex* of militancy and a *sex* of industrialism. Certainly there was never an age in which there was a more active armament, larger battle ships, more destructive explosives and cannons, and vaster establishments for the creation of engines and implements of death than in our own."[69] And if there was a sex of militancy, there was

[67] Parkman 1884: 10–11.   [68] Darwin 1936: 873.   [69] Mason 1895: 2.

a sex of the savagery and barbarism it brought along. As the generative force, men were not solely responsible for *elevating* Europe but also for the savage *destruction* of civilization, a point not lost on the European suffragists, as we shall see in the next chapter.

The political status of woman as a cause of civilization

Far from everyone, and particularly not those who took on the new subject position "women," agreed that women had no essential role to play in the generation of civilization. The nineteenth century also saw prevalent identifications of woman as a crucial civilizing agent. Women were often claimed to have a distinct mission in the conversion of nature into culture, especially with reference to the socialization of children. "No universal agent of civilization exists but our mothers," argued Louis-Aimé Martin in his enormously influential *The Education of Mothers; or, The Civilization of Mankind by Women*[70] which had won French Academy acclaim and reached an impressive eleven editions in French by 1883, three in English and translations into Swedish, German and Italian.[71]

Many of those speaking as and on behalf of women objected not to the characterization of woman as a selfless, conservative, peaceful and religious being defined by her affections but rather to the devaluation of such qualities and the domination of one sphere over the other. Women's fundamental value as a good for public benefit and national betterment was furthermore rarely publicly questioned. "The one quality on which woman's value and influence depends is the renunciation of self," Sarah Lewis claimed in 1839, in the bestselling *Woman's Mission* that was to reach seventeen British and five American editions by 1854. She extended Martin's discussion and argued that "the fundamental principle is right – 'that women were to live for others' – and therefore all that we have to do is to carry out this fundamentally right principle into wider application."[72] To Lewis, Martin and others, that wider application absolutely did not include state organizations and the political sphere. Instead, "the greatest benefit which [women] can confer upon society is to be what they ought to be in all their domestic relations."[73] Women should demonstrate "devotion to an ideal good,

[70] Aimé-Martin 1843: 228.   [71] Bock 2002: 89.
[72] S. Lewis 1840: 54.   [73] S. Lewis 1840: 54–5.

self-sacrifice and subjugation of selfish feelings," so that they could be set aside from men, who had been ruined by the "selfish and groveling utilitarianism" of the state.[74]

In the domestic sphere, women furthermore fulfilled a vital function in relation to the Godless state, as "women may be the prime agents of God in the regeneration of mankind."[75] If women were to enter the public sphere of the state, they would risk succumbing to selfishness. With their nature ruined, they would thus cease to be the "potent agent for the amelioration of mankind," leading to the degeneration of civilization.[76] Unless properly nurtured in the domestic sphere, in Young's words, woman was "destined to be the mother of savages and barbarians, who in every age have been immersed in ignorance, blackened with crime and stained with blood."[77]

The answer to the question that sets up Lewis's book and which concerned so many statesmen of the time – "Would the greatest possible good be procured by bringing [woman] out of her present sphere into the arena of public life?" – was thus a resounding NO! Women's "empire is that of their affections," and the essential influence women exercise in the home is "the cultivation of the moral portion of [mankind's] nature, which cultivation no government has yet attempted, over which, in fact, governments and public institutions have little or no control."[78] "The beneficial influence of woman is nullified if once her motives, or her personal character, come to be the subject of attack; and this fact alone ought to induce her patiently to acquiesce in the plan of seclusion from public affairs."[79] The separation of woman from state institutions was furthermore in accordance with God's will, as "the principle of divided labour seems to be a maxim of the divine government."[80]

French utopian socialist Charles Fourier had turned the causal relation between the status of women and the level of a state's civilization into an explicit, general thesis that would continue to have effects for two centuries (though in contrast with most others of nineteenth-century civilization, he often argued against the separate spheres). Due to the importance of Fourier's thought, he is cited at some length. Using the comparative method characteristic of evolutionary theory, Fourier had stated in 1808 that

[74] S. Lewis 1840: 44 and 23 respectively.   [75] S. Lewis 1840: 24.
[76] S. Lewis 1840: 43, 48–9.   [77] Young 1837: 8.   [78] S. Lewis 1840: 23.
[79] S. Lewis 1840: 57.   [80] S. Lewis 1840: 49.

among the signs that promise the happy results to come from the extension of women's privileges, we must cite the experiences of other countries. We have seen that the best nations are always those that accord women the greatest amount of liberty; this can be seen as much among the Barbarians and Savages as among the Civilized. The Japanese, who are the most industrious, the bravest, and the most honorable of the Barbarians, are also the least jealous and the most indulgent toward women; this is so true that the Magots of China travel to Japan to deliver themselves up to the love that is forbidden them by their own hypocritical customs. Likewise the Tahitians were the best among the Savages; given their relative lack of natural resources, no other people have developed their industry to such an extent. Among the Civilized, the French, who are the least inclined to persecute women, are the best in that they are the most flexible nation, the one from which a skillful ruler can get the best result in any sort of task. Despite a few defects such as frivolity, individual presumptuousness, and uncleanliness, however, the French are the foremost civilized nation owing to this single fact of adaptability, the trait most alien to the barbarian character ... Likewise it can be seen that the most corrupt nations have always been those in which women were most completely subjugated ...

As a general thesis: *Social progress and historic changes occur by virtue of the progress of women toward liberty, and decadence of the social order occurs as the result of a decrease in the liberty of women.* Other events influence these political changes, but there is no cause that produces social progress or decline as rapidly as change in the condition of women. I have already said that the mere adoption of closed harems would speedily turn us into Barbarians, and the mere opening of the harems would suffice to transport the Barbarians into Civilization. In summary, *the extension of women's privileges is the general principle for all social progress.*"[81]

Arguing *against* bringing women into the state polity as this would be a degradation of woman, Lewis echoes such sentiments, stating that "this, then, is the law of eternal justice – man cannot degrade woman without himself falling into degradation: he cannot elevate her without at the same time elevating himself."[82] Lewis was far from alone in wanting to elevate civilization by keeping woman out of politics. Arguing for the *exclusion* of women from state office, New York State senator and gubernatorial candidate Samuel Young proclaimed: "Let man, when he feels inclined to boast of his advancement, look at the condition of the other sex; and, whilst he finds woman deprived of any

[81] Fourier 1846: 145–50.   [82] S. Lewis 1840: 41.

of the rights and privileges, which he enjoys, let him lay his hand on his mouth and cry, 'uncivilized'."[83]

With regard to the practice of voting to the more empowered legislatures, Kraditor states of the nineteenth-century sentiments that it is "therefore wrong to say that woman did not have the right to vote; rather, she had the right *not* to vote ... [woman] was exempt from the burden of it. She was exempt so that she could devote her mind and her energies to those vocations which most benefited society."[84] The anthropologists perhaps expressed the relation between the status of woman and civilization most starkly, declaring that "according to the law of survival of the fittest, a tribe or stock of human beings in which brutality of this sort has place simply chooses the downward road and disappears."[85]

Whereas there had previously been no European-wide formal barriers to women's political participation, exclusion was formalized into law in most of Europe in the late eighteenth to early twentieth centuries. In 1778, the English House of Commons prohibited women from attending and listening to its debates from the floor or gallery of the House.[86] In 1832, women were expressly prohibited from voting in the House of Commons through the introduction of the language of "male person" instead of the previous "person" in suffrage law.[87] In France in 1793, women's political organizations were dissolved and prohibited from reappearing,[88] and in 1848 new laws prohibited women from creating or belonging to political clubs and associations.[89] In Colombia in 1843, citizenship was similarly defined as exclusively for "*men* of means."[90] An 1851 Prussian law stripped women of all political rights and forbade them to attend political meetings;[91] the 1868 fourteenth amendment to the US constitution specified suffrage for the "male citizen" for the first time; and the reformed electoral law in New Jersey also disenfranchised all women. Similar legal changes explicitly barring women from participation in the state polity were made in the Netherlands (1887), Germany (1900), Austria (1907), Italy (1912) and Portugal (1913).[92]

---

[83] Young 1837: 23.   [84] Kraditor 1971: 19.   [85] Mason 1895: 6.
[86] Styrkársdóttir 1998: 48.   [87] Reuterskiöld 1911: 70.   [88] Zetkin 1906.
[89] Reuterskiöld 1911: 79.   [90] Gonzalez 2000: 690.
[91] Styrkársdóttir 1998: 48.   [92] Bock 2002: 133.

By the end of the nineteenth century, the following norm was evidently in place: *civilized states exclude women from politics.* Developments within Europe bear testimony to this norm. Perhaps even more telling are the legal shifts in states formally entering the society of civilized states, as well as the practices of European colonial powers in Africa and Asia. Concurrently with formal entry into civilized society at the end of the nineteenth century, Japan for the first time codified a total ban on women's political activities, such as attending political meetings and joining political parties.[93] The Chinese constitution of 1912, attempting to introduce Anglo-Saxon democratic practice into this first of Asian republics, explicitly excluded women from participating in electoral politics.[94] The elimination of matrilinear kinship systems and female political authority was carried out in the name of "progress" all over the territories under colonial rule.[95] Conquering the Sudan in 1899, the British regulated and codified politics as an exclusively non-female sphere. Reflecting the chauvinism of "civilization," el-Bakri *et al.* argue, the British "regarded those areas where relations between the sexes were relatively egalitarian as 'uncivilized' ... In situations where women shared relatively equal status with men, they lost this status under the pretext of 'civilization'."[96] The construction of colonial political institutions systematically enshrined the exclusion of women, displacing prior forms of institutionalized female political authority which were in existence in many places.[97]

Conclusion

By the turn of the century, "European civilization" had successfully purged women from its political realm. An international norm was in place: civilized states were not to cede political authority to women. The rationale supporting the norm was dual. On the one hand, it was an indication of advancement that women had been exempt from politics.

---

[93] Mackie 1997. [94] Edwards 2000: 622.
[95] On the systematic colonial elimination of matrilinear kinship systems in Africa, see Sacks 1982.
[96] El-Bakri *et al.* 1987: 177.
[97] E.g. Palau (Salvador 1995), the Andean region (Silverblatt 1987), the Sudan (el-Bakri *et al.* 1987; Hale 1996), and Ghana (Okonjo 1994). In writing the constitutions of Lebanon and Syria in the 1920s and 1930s, France similarly granted political agency to men but not women (Thompson 2000: 126).

After all, only "savage" societies were thought to accept such a practice. On the other hand, the maintenance of separate spheres was thought to assure further advancement, with each sex devoting its energies to appropriate tasks. International hierarchy was clearly built into this norm, which differentiated between civilized, barbarous and savage polities.

The importance of male rule for progress was always in potential crisis as a result of the destructive capacities of man, however. The shakiness of the norm that called on civilized states to expel women from the state polity stemmed from this tension, along with the unacknowledged circular causal claims about the relations between the political status of women and progress. The construction of women as a unified sex not only allowed for barring women from the state; it also set the stage for women *as such* to demand inclusion. In the words of Lévi-Strauss, and as we shall see in the chapters to come, "woman could never become just a sign and nothing more, since even in a man's world she is still a person, and since insofar as she is defined as a sign she must [still] be recognized as a generator of signs."[98] Contradictions in the arguments about the political role of women and state progress spoke to women in their quest for suffrage, as we shall see in the next chapter.

[98] As cited in Ortner 1972.

5 | Women's suffrage and the standards of civilization

In the last chapter, we saw that prohibiting women from state office and political activity became a standard of behavior among states in the nineteenth and early twentieth centuries. Whereas the ability of women to be part of formal state affairs had previously varied considerably across Europe, uniform expectations developed and barring women became standard policy. We also saw how such prohibitions became linked with European civilization and turned into a standard expressly for societies that had moved away from the so-called savage stage. Keeping women out of the formal political sphere had become a norm for civilized states.

In this context, one of the first book-length historical analyses of the then contemporary woman's rights movement stated that "woman's suffrage is the most radical demand made by organized women, and is hence advocated in all countries by the 'radical' woman's rights advocates."[1] Claiming suffrage to be radical was no exaggeration at a time when only four countries had granted women the right to vote.[2] This was about to change. In the coming century, almost every state introduced women's suffrage, making the measure global in scope and hardly extreme. In fact, to most, radicalism today is found in the extremely rare denial of women's suffrage, such as in the case of Saudi Arabia.

How should we portray this rather dramatic worldwide change in the relation between women and the state? And how were these changes brought about? This chapter contends that the new norm developed in, and became a constituent part of, a highly stratified international society. Women's suffrage initially became the expected behavior of so-called "civilized" states, around the end of World War I. Suffrage became indicative of having reached a more advanced level of

---

[1] Schirmacher 1912.
[2] New Zealand (1893), Australia (1902), Finland (1906) and Norway (1907).

81

civilization and thus helped to set these states apart from presumably inferior societies. Social hierarchy was part of the suffrage norm from the very beginning.

The political exclusion of women operated as one of many fixed but informal benchmarks to gauge the level of civilization of a state. Since far from all societies were regarded as civilized (nor did they desire to be), it was not clear what this new standard of civilization suggested for them, however. It was a formidable task of non-European activists to justify why their states should also pass suffrage laws. After all, as the Europeans claimed, this was behavior proper for "civilized" states rather than the "less advanced" or non-civilized. Creative reinterpretation of the initial norm was needed to explain why it was appropriate for states not part of the core of Western civilization to approve the vote for women. Crucially, as we shall see, whereas these explanations often challenged the hierarchy that located Western civilization at the apex of progress, they nevertheless also rank-ordered states.

Suffrage proponents around the world had to invoke the social hierarchies in which their target states were positioned. Rank was brought into play not only in the rationales for suffrage, however. International stratification was at work in the very ways in which suffrage advocates organized. Indeed, transnational suffragism developed in at least four overlapping waves, with distinctive membership, geographical scope and suffrage arguments rooted in international social hierarchies. The first wave emerged in the society of civilized states, from the turn of the twentieth century until the 1920s. Transnational suffrage mobilization in the socialist East constitutes a second, closely overlapping wave, from approximately 1907 until the 1920s. The third wave developed in the pan-American context, from the 1920s until the 1940s. Although much less research and evidence is provided, a fourth wave of transnational suffragism appears to have developed in the Afro-Asian postcolonial context in the 1950s.

Activist organizations and networks were the primary associational arena promoting women's suffrage, rather than international organizations or state actors. Transnational suffrage advocacy supplies a good empirical entry point to study the international suffrage norm. The rest of this chapter is therefore organized around demonstrating the existence of no fewer than four waves of transnational suffragism and analyzing how they invoked the international suffrage norm. Before delving into these waves of transnational activism and their understandings of suffrage, however, the chapter begins by looking at the global route of suffrage law adoption for potential cues about norms and stratification. The chapter ends with an assessment of prior attempts to account for the global emergence of women's suffrage.

The suffrage adoption trajectory

Potential patterns in the adoption path are a good first indicator of the feasibility of claims about how policies become worldwide in scope. Markoff has observed, but does not try to explain, that "women's suffrage was pioneered in lesser places in the geography of wealth and power and then advanced to more central locations" of the world.[3] This observation about the breakthrough of women's suffrage is interesting. As is clear from Table 5.1 below, women first won the vote in new states on the outskirts of the core – New Zealand (1893), Australia (1902), Finland (1906) and Norway (1907) – rather than in, say, France and Great Britain. By 1919, another twenty European states had passed suffrage legislation. It would nevertheless take many decades for a few European states, like Switzerland (1971) and Lichtenstein (1984), to allow women voting rights. Markoff is correct in noting that the measure moved "from the margins to the center" in the European "geocultural region."[4] Suffrage did nevertheless first become standardized among European and European settler states rather than elsewhere.

Like previous research on the worldwide emergence of women's suffrage, Markoff's observation about the location of the breakthrough says little about the subsequent adoption trajectory. One striking and overlooked aspect is that the ensuing path was clustered, as is evident in Table 5.1. The timing of adoption seems to cluster around four intersecting and rank-ordered transnational contexts in international society: European civilization, socialism, pan-Americanism and Afro-Asian post-colonialism. After suffrage had successfully won ground in a handful of "civilized" states, an overlapping though more concise second cluster of adoption took place in the emerging socialist states of Eastern Europe and Central Asia. These states recognized women's suffrage primarily between 1918 and 1924, simultaneously with many states of Western Europe. The so-called new world of the Americas passed suffrage laws in a third cluster, mainly between the late 1930s

---

[3] Markoff 2003: 90.   [4] Markoff 2003: 104.

Table 5.1 *Women's suffrage adoption (year and transnational context)*

Year	European civilization	Socialism	Pan-Americanism	(Post)-colonialism	Other/Unclear
1893	New Zealand				
1902	Australia				
1906	Finland				
1913	Norway				
1915	Denmark Iceland				
1917	Canada	Russian Federation			
1918	Austria Germany Hungary Ireland United Kingdom	Estonia Georgia Latvia Lithuania Poland			
1919	Belgium Luxemburg Netherlands Sweden	Belarus Ukraine			
1920	Czechoslovakia United States	Albania			
1921		Armenia Azerbaijan			

Table 5.1 (*cont.*)

Year	European civilization	Socialism	Pan-Americanism	(Post)-colonialism	Other/Unclear
1924		Kazakhstan Mongolia Tajikistan Turkmenistan			St. Lucia (UK)
1927					
1929	Romania		Ecuador		
1930	South Africa ("whites")				
1931	Portugal Spain		Chile		
1932			Brazil Uruguay		Thailand (Siam)
1934			Cuba		Turkey
1935				Myanmar (UK)	
1937					Philippines
1938		Uzbekistan	Bolivia		
1939			El Salvador		
1941			Panama		
1942			Dominican Republic		
1944	Bulgaria France				Jamaica (UK)
1945	Croatia Slovenia Italy			Indonesia Senegal (FR) Togo (FR)	Japan

Table 5.1 (*cont.*)

Year	European civilization	Socialism	Pan-Americanism	(Post)-colonialism	Other/Unclear
1946	Romania Yugoslavia	DPR of Korea	Guatemala Venezuela	Vietnam Djibouti (FR) Cameroon (FR)	Liberia Trinidad and Tobago (UK)
1947		China	Argentina Mexico	Pakistan Singapore (UK)	
1948	Israel			Niger (FR) Seychelles (UK) Surinam (NL)	Republic of Korea
1949	Bosnia and Herzegovina				Syria
1950			Costa Rica	India	Haiti Barbados (UK) Antigua and Barbuda (UK)
1951				Nepal	Dominica (UK) Grenada (UK) St. Kitts and Nevis (UK)
1952				Ivory Coast (FR)	Lebanon
1953	Greece			Bhutan	Guyana (UK)
1954			Colombia Honduras Nicaragua Peru	Ghana (UK) Eritrea Ethiopia Cambodia	Belize (UK)
1955					

Table 5.1 (*cont.*)

Year	European civilization	Socialism	Pan-Americanism	(Post)-colonialism	Other/Unclear
1956				Benin (FR)	
				Gabon (FR)	
				Comoros (FR)	
				Egypt	
				Mali (FR)	
				Mauritius (UK)	
				Somalia (UK/IT)	
1957				Malaysia	
1958		Laos		Nigeria (south – UK)	
				Burkina Faso (FR)	
				Chad (FR)	
				Guinea	
1959	San Marino			Madagascar	
				Tunisia	
1960	Cyprus			Tanzania (UK)	
				Tonga (UK)	
				Gambia (UK)	
1961			El Salvador	Malawi (UK)	Bahamas (UK)
			Paraguay	Burundi	
				Rwanda	
				Mauritania	
				Sierra Leone	
1962	Monaco			Algeria	
				Uganda	
				Zambia (UK)	

Table 5.1 (*cont.*)

Year	European civilization	Socialism	Pan-Americanism	(Post)-colonialism	Other/Unclear
1963				Kenya Fiji (UK) Kenya Congo (FR) Morocco	Afghanistan Iran
1964				Sudan	Libya
1965				Botswana Lesotho	
1967					
1968				Swaziland	
1970	Andorra	Yemen			
1971	Switzerland				
1972				Bangladesh	
1973					Bahrain
1974					Jordan
1975				Angola Cape Verde* Mozambique	
1977					
1978		Moldova			
1979					
1980					Iraq
1984	Lichtenstein				
1986					Central African Republic
1989				Namibia	

Table assembled from data provided in IPU (2002), Arat (2000), Edwards (2000).

and mid-1950s. The fourth cluster consists of the post-colonial states of Africa and Asia, where suffrage was extended to women primarily when national independence was won, between 1945 in Indonesia and 1975.

The clustered timing of adoption corresponds roughly with the timing of the four waves of transnational suffrage activism. The breakthrough for women's right to vote in the European West and the socialist East followed a period of sustained transnational activism that peaked during the decade preceding World War I. The adoption of suffrage in the Americas followed a longer period of transnational suffrage activism in the pan-American context from the 1920s until the 1940s. This chapter has not been able to focus as extensively on the Afro-Asian (post-)colonial context, but there is evidence of transnational suffragism developing in the 1950s to demand the vote for women among the liberating societies. To learn more about the international suffrage norm, we shall now turn our attention to each of these transnational movements.

Four waves of suffragism in a stratified international society

Suffragism in the society of civilized states

Nineteenth-century Europe was characterized by tremendously intense struggles over the nature of sexual difference and the implications of that difference for women in terms of participation in political life. The norm that civilized states keep women out of politics was thus always contested and had to be justified and bolstered in an ongoing manner. It is interesting to note that parliamentary calls for women's inclusion into the political sphere were made at the same time as women's political activities were prohibited throughout Europe. The demand for voting rights began already in the 1840s, not long after women were expressly barred from state affairs.[5] The first domestic suffrage organizations were also formed at this time, more or less simultaneously across Europe and some of its former colonies.

---

[5] E.g. France in 1848 (Bebel 1910: 285), England in 1867 (Zetkin 1906), Italy in 1867, Spain in 1877, Sweden in 1884, the Netherlands in 1887, (Bock 2002: 129) and Brazil in 1891 (Hahner 1990: 73).

The first push to connect some of this domestic activism across borders was made by British and US women in 1883, though without much initial success. The well-known International Woman Suffrage Alliance (IWSA) was instead founded in Berlin in 1904. Although there were a number of transnational women's organizations that worked for suffrage, such as the International Council of Women, few were as important as the IWSA. And the scope and character of transnational suffragism were part and parcel of the hierarchical international society within which this activism developed.

The phenomenon of transnational suffragism and the IWSA emerged in an era of new imperialism, with colonial conquests accelerating at a rapid pace. European powers such as Great Britain, France and the recently created Germany competed aggressively for territorial conquests, freshly joined by a USA with international aspirations. As we saw in the last chapter, the international society of the early twentieth century was deeply divided and, from the vantage point of Europe, roughly consisted of two classes of people and societies: the civilized and the uncivilized. Doctrines of racial and cultural superiority abounded, legitimating the superiority of the so-called civilized and their domination of the uncivilized.

Colonialism and the relations of inequality it entailed fundamentally shaped transnational suffrage activism. This was activism primarily by and for the "civilized" parts of the world. The nationality of the IWSA officers, the congress locations and the official languages of the association – English and French – were exclusively European until the 1930s. The member affiliations (organized as country sections) suggest a slightly larger circle, including Australia, white South Africa, and Argentina and Uruguay as the most European of the young Americas, as well as Russia and China, considered to be at the outskirts of civilization.[6] Tellingly, once most of Europe and the Anglo states had enfranchised women in the early 1920s, the IWSA moved to work on other issues.[7] This decision was made even though there were by then suffrage movements in Asia and Latin America that had still not

---

[6] Gong 1984: 19.

[7] Rupp 1997; Stites 1978: 94. Although suffrage was still officially on the Alliance's agenda, it was no longer considered one of "the more important resolutions" and it subsequently fell into the background.

attained their objective. The core of the organization and its activities matched the core of the society of civilized states.

The IWSA did make extraordinary efforts to extend its activities outside of Europe and North America, however. A lot of energy was expended on building suffrage organizations in places with colonial relations to Britain, such as Palestine and Egypt.[8] US suffragist Carrie Chapman Catt, perhaps the most assiduous traveler, made a grand suffrage tour together with Dutch suffragist Aletta Jacobs in 1911–12, and visited South Africa, Egypt, Israel, Palestine, Sri Lanka, India, Indonesia, the Philippines, Hong Kong, China and Japan.[9] Since they were traveling by boat, the scope of their travels is remarkable. And the attempt to reach out to non-European women is noteworthy at a time when many Europeans considered the subjugation of the "uncivilized" both necessary and legitimate.

These should nevertheless not be seen as attempts to build up a transnational network, if by a network we mean a non-hierarchical form of organization.[10] Instead, as will be developed further below, the suffragists presumed themselves to be more advanced, and their travels were undertaken as civilizing missions to help elevate Asian and African women.[11] When Catt and Jacobs's tour yielded meager results, it only strengthened their conviction that suffrage required a certain level of civilization in order to take hold.[12]

The suffragists were not alone in approaching the female vote as a matter of civilization. The expectation of the day was that civilized states keep women out of formal state affairs, as we saw in the previous chapter. Those in favor of the status quo could contend that "the propaganda of woman suffrage is part and parcel of the world-wide movement for the overthrow of the present order of civilized society."[13] The suffragists naturally had to meet such arguments in order to change the existing norm.

Presenting themselves as vanguard agents of civilization, the suffragists argued that human progress and women's suffrage sympathies

---

[8] Bosch 1999.　　[9] Ibid.　　[10] E.g. Keck and Sikkink 1998.
[11] Bosch 1999; Rupp 1997; Whittick 1979: 51.
[12] Bosch 1999: 17. Few suffrage organizations were created, except for the Philippines (where suffrage organizing had already been present for a decade) and the Dutch East Indies.
[13] Illinois Association Opposed to the Extension of Suffrage to Women 1900: 2.

went hand in hand.[14] As the International Congress of Women proclaimed, women's rights concerned "Our Common Cause,
Civilization."[15] J. S. Mill was frequently invoked, as the most influential
and best-known proponent of this view.[16] Whatever justice claims had
been made in the early nineteenth century came to give way almost
entirely to expediency arguments that centered on the benefit of women
as voters or non-voters.[17] And it was as a distinctive sex that women
needed to be included as voters for the advancement of the civilized
state.

In their attempts to show the benefits of women as voters for the
civilized state, the suffragists forged a specific subject position – "civilized women" – which differentiated them from men (civilized and
uncivilized) as well as from less civilized or non-civilized women. On
the one hand, the travel reports and descriptions of the Oriental, the
Negro, the Hindu and the Savage helped the suffragists distance themselves from the "less civilized" with which they were often associated
and compared. In relation to the non-European, they were now *civilized*
women, free beings, able to awaken less civilized women to demand
their rights. As such, the suffragists had ample voice in the mainstream
media. Writing in a US magazine in 1912, Catt credited the incipient
women's mobilizing in Egypt to British colonial tutelage: "Great Britain
has created a new Egypt," she announced. "It has awakened a sleeping
race and held before it the dazzling achievements of Western
progress."[18]

On the other hand, the suffragists also articulated women as the more
civilized of the sexes within Europe. Military service had provided
working-class men with a potent argument in their contention for the
vote, an argument which did little to bring women suffrage, as they were
barred from the military.[19] The suffragists instead pointed to the allegedly destructive and selfish capacity of men and the male state, which

---

[14] Bosch 1999: 17.
[15] This was the title of the mammoth official report of the 1933 International
Congress of Women, convened by the US National Council of Women in
Chicago, July 16–22.
[16] E.g Bosch 1999; Newman 1999; Rendall 1994; Rupp 1997.
[17] Kraditor 1971: 39.
[18] As quoted in Burton 1994: 191. See also Bosch's (1999) excellent discussion of
Jacobs's travel letters from the world suffrage tour that were published regularly
in the progressive Dutch daily paper *De Telegraaf.*
[19] E.g. Steinberg 1995.

rested on coercive power and resulted in the menace of war. States solely in the hands of men threatened the advances of European civilization, a civilization that, in turn, provided protection and elevation for its women. The portrayal of men as a threat to civilization had been made for some time, as we saw in Chapter 4. Particularly around times of war, interpretations of other cultures were used metaphorically to give meaning to the savagery and barbarism of male power and masculine politics. At the onset of the 1871 Franco–Prussian War, British suffragists roared that "the franchise is needed as a protection for women from the uncontrolled dominion of the savage passions of men." The female forces of civilization were needed to overpower the "savage instinct in men" and to save Europe from the destruction of war.[20]

In most cases, the extension of women's suffrage was not simply a matter of argumentative savvy and ability to mobilize great numbers of suffrage supporters. And by the 1910s, the fact that three states on the outskirts of civilized society had enfranchised women also failed to impress most state representatives in the core of civilized society. The behavior of New Zealand, Australia and Finland towards women did not set a standard for other states to follow. Indeed, the social hierarchies among civilized states erected barriers to emulation.

The fact that suffrage was granted in three *new* states gave rise to doubt among those of the *old* world of the desirability of this measure. The implications had to be pondered, however – while new and peripheral, these were nonetheless "civilized" states whose behavior had a bearing on the old world. "When other civilized nations begin to grant the franchise to women, it might be time for the most civilized nation in the world to see whether it would be well to follow their example," argued Conservative member of the British House of Commons C. W. Radcliffe Cooke in 1897.[21]

The Swedish government created a public commission which produced the report *On the Development and Application in Foreign Lands of the Idea of Women's Political Suffrage* in 1911. While principally open on the issue, the author questioned the propriety of bringing suffrage to old civilized states. Although New Zealand had enfranchised women "expressly to make New Zealand a model and precursor state for the New and the Old world," its example simply was not relevant

[20] As cited in Rendall 1994: 143–4.   [21] Quoted in Dalziel 1994: 42–3.

for Europe.[22] What is more, the newly created state of Finland (which enfranchised women upon achieving partial independence from the Russian Empire) was "perhaps more comparable with the American territories and the English colonies [New Zealand and Australia] than with truly European states."[23]

In other words, suffrage was not a standard of behavior for the old civilized world. There was simply no reason why these states should imitate the experiments of new, second-rate countries. As the Swedish report explains:

In these New countries, the "state" is in reality not an independent being, since, on the one hand, a large portion of public office is filled by elected officials and the remaining offices lack the independent and traditional power that is enjoyed by the public organs of Old civilized states, and, since on the other, the government itself is hardly anything other than an executive organ of the electing citizenry. It should be clear that what in these New countries is a necessity in order to avoid the oppression of women and which may lead to the development of a true *state* could be the very thing that undermines the independence of state authority in the Old states ... There is a significant difference between the application of the principle in a state-in-the-making and a fully grown state, even though women's suffrage cannot be rejected on principle in the latter case.[24]

The report spells it out quite clearly: the principle of women's suffrage, while applicable to states-in-the-making, was not valid for fully grown states. These new states' experiments with women's suffrage simply had "neither applicability nor importance for fully sovereign states of old European civilization with developed political institutions and traditions."[25]

Women's suffrage may never have materialized in the "old culture-states" of Europe had it not been for the crisis generated by the World Wars. World War I signified a breakdown of enormous magnitude in the relations between civilized states, demonstrating that international law and diplomacy could not guarantee the non-violent settling of interstate conflicts. With 8.5 million people dead from battle and dis-ease, the aptness of men to run the affairs of state could be questioned

---

[22] Reuterskiöld 1911: 63, my translation.
[23] Reuterskiöld 1911: 23, my translation.
[24] Reuterskiöld 1911: 76, my translation.
[25] Reuterskiöld 1911: 110, my translation.

with more force. The peaceful nature of women appeared more necessary and useful than ever before. Women had also proven their public
worth on the home front during the war, points underscored by the
suffrage proponents, who regrouped as the war ended.

A wave of states of European civilization enfranchised women in the
years immediately preceding or following the war: Denmark and
Iceland[26] in 1915, Canada in 1917, Germany, Austria, Hungary,[27]
the UK and Ireland in 1918, Belgium and Luxembourg,[28] the
Netherlands and Sweden in 1919, Czechoslovakia and the USA in
1920. As we shall see below, a host of states that were emerging as
independent from the Russian Empire and governed by socialist councils also granted women the vote during this time.

In 1918, Catt, like numerous others, stated that "the question of votes
for women is one which is commanding the attention of the whole
civilized world."[29] And indeed, once these additional "civilized" states,
including those of "old culture," had extended the vote to women, the
norm changed. Women's suffrage now became approached as a standard of civilization, a reversal of the prior expectation that civilized
states keep women out of formal politics. It is interesting to note that in
the 1930s, both Thailand and Turkey enfranchised women without the
presence of domestic suffrage mobilization, apparently in an attempt to
situate themselves well within civilized international society.[30] In the
words of Kemal Atatürk, Turkish women were enfranchised in 1934 in
an effort to bring Turkey to the "level it deserved in the civilized
world."[31]

But far from all societies were classified as "civilized" in the early
twentieth century. Nor did all care to be part of civilized society and
adhere to its standards of behavior. What did the close link between
suffrage and civilization imply for women in these other societies? What
were the implications of tying the female vote so intimately to

---

[26] Iceland was still not fully independent from Denmark in 1915.
[27] Austria, Hungary and Czechoslovakia came into existence from the Austro-
Hungarian Empire in 1918.
[28] Neither Belgium nor Luxembourg had any suffrage mobilization to speak of.
[29] Catt 1918.   [30] Arat 2000; Loos 2004.
[31] Atatürk, quoted in Arat 2000: 108. Even so, *women's suffrage was not
represented as an invention of European civilization.* Suffrage was defended as a
Turkish tradition reaching back to the pre-Islamic Turkish culture that had been
interrupted by the Islamic-Ottoman period. On this point, see Arat 2000;
Kandiyoti 1989.

civilization? Subsequent suffrage movements all had to grapple with the claim that suffrage was a trait of European civilization. As we shall see below, they handled the claim in very different ways.

Suffragism and socialist transnationalism

In the first years of the twentieth century, as the suffragists' agitation on behalf of "civilization" developed into a mass movement, the importance of women's suffrage as an explicit goal also won ground among socialist organizations. A second and distinctive wave of suffragism developed within socialist transnationalism between then and the early 1920s. This wave was distinctive in two regards. First, socialist women organized separately from the suffragists, and the core of their organization was located more towards the east of Europe. Second and not surprisingly, these women had a different diagnosis of the problem that suffrage was meant to rectify. What others termed Western civilization was to them "bourgeois capitalism" and the source of female subordination. The claim that women's suffrage was a standard of civilization, an indicator of civilized progress, thus posed a challenge for socialist women.

Since the 1860s, there had been failed attempts to organize women as a separate collective within the socialist transnational infrastructure. These attempts were rejuvenated in the late 1890s. Among others, Clara Zetkin of the German Social Democratic Party (SPD) worked relentlessly for a formalized Women's International. This work came to fruition at the 1907 Congress of the Second Socialist International in Stuttgart. A permanent International Women's Bureau was created, with an adjacent journal, *Gleichheit* (*Equality*), which reached an impressive circulation of 125,000 by 1914. A key resolution was passed requiring all socialist parties to fight for universal male and female suffrage.[32] Although a few parties had already incorporated female suffrage as part of their demands for universal enfranchisement, the others were now required to fight for women's vote as well.[33]

---

[32] For partial accounts that can be pieced together as a history of the Socialist Women's International, see Clements 1979; DuBois 1994; Zetkin 1984; Honeycutt 1975; Riddell 1987; Stites 1978; Waters 1989; Wood 1997.

[33] For instance, the German SPD (1891), the Argentine Socialist Party (1900) and the Russian Social Democrats (1903) had endorsed female suffrage, whereas the Swedish, Belgian and Austrian parties had not.

Commanding all socialist parties across Europe and beyond to place universal suffrage on their platform was no small accomplishment.

As was the case with the IWSA, the geographical scope of this circle of women was to remain limited until the 1920s. During its first decade of existence, the Women's International was almost entirely made up of nationals of Europe and North America.[34] The working language was one – German – rather than the two (English and French) of the IWSA. The choice of working language tells us much about the core of the organization. In the Women's International, German and Russian women were most active, in contrast to the Anglo-Europeans of the IWSA.

The socialist activists understood themselves to be distinctive from the civilized suffragists and worked for a different and superior world. Any cooperation with "bourgeois" transnational suffragism was thus expressly prohibited. As Alexsandra Kollontai of the Russian Bolsheviks explained: "Different aims and understandings of how political rights are to be used create an unbridgeable gulf between bourgeois and proletarian women."[35] This gulf included distinctive understandings not only about the ideal society but also about the nature of womanhood and women's relation to the state. Although the civilized and socialist activists endorsed the same standard – political rights for women – the rationales and goals of this standard diverged dramatically.

Socialist approaches to the woman question did share a view of history as a set of progressive stages. In 1879, August Bebel of the German Social Democratic Party had published the first of over fifty editions of his groundbreaking *Woman and Socialism*. His book gave suffrage a lengthy and favorable treatment and became central in the strife for women's political rights. Influenced by Lewis Morgan's work on the progress from savagery to barbarism, he attempted to lay bare "the entirely different relation of the sexes at an early period of human development from their present relation."[36]

Bebel's assessment of this early period differed considerably from most European ideas about women in savage society. Rather than

---

[34] I have been unable to find comprehensive information on the nationality of the parties represented besides Germany, Italy, Austria, England, Russia, and Belgium. However, it would be surprising if the participation in the Women's International was broader than that of the International itself, whose scope Riddell (1987: 11) documents as limited to Europe.

[35] Kollontai 1909: 72. See also Zetkin 1920.   [36] Bebel 1910: 17.

being belittled, the primitive stage became appreciated as a form of primitive communism governed by matriarchy. And contemporary Europe was identified as the low point in the relation of the sexes:

In present day bourgeois society woman holds the second place. Man leads; she follows. The present relation is diametrically opposed to that which prevailed during the matriarchal period. The evolution from primitive communism to the rule of private property has primarily brought about this transformation.[37]

The social relations and general emancipation embedded in a mode of production were theorized as productive of the condition of women. In other words, the status of women was understood as an effect of general emancipation.

The situation of women could thus be viewed as a clear indicator of the miseries of "civilized society." Capitalism and Christianity, seen as the key components of Western civilization, were presented as the two prime causes of the contemporary oppression of women. Capitalism produced a number of institutions necessary for its maintenance that subjugated women to a greater extent than men. Most important of these were the creation of women as property, sex beings, prostitutes, housewives, and particularly exploited workers. These social institutions were embedded in the bourgeois state. Capitalism used "the backward character of old-style housekeeping ... to keep women intellectually and politically backward by blocking them from participating in society," proclaimed Communist International instructions to communist parties around the world in 1920.[38] Christian morality and the reactionary influence of the clergy on women did not help matters. Women, as being most heavily under the influence of the Catholic Church and enduring the most difficult effects of capitalism, became a symbol and the very embodiment of the backwardness of the civilized world.

With a change in mode of production and advancement away from bourgeois capitalism, the situation of women would allegedly improve. The political emancipation of women in socialist society thus became a site for demonstrating its distinctiveness from and superiority to the capitalist, civilized world. Paraphrasing Fourier at length, Marx and Engels had stated in *The Holy Family* that

[37] Bebel 1910: 96.   [38] Zetkin 1920: 911–12.

the transformation of a historical era can always be determined by the condition of progress of women toward liberty, because it is here, in the relation of women to men, of the weak to the strong, that the victory of human nature over brutality appears most evident. *The degree of female emancipation is the natural measure of general emancipation.*[39]

The status of women was thus seen as indicative of prior developments, a gauge of the degree of emancipation of a society. While drawing on Fourier, Marx and Engels had reversed his argument about female emancipation being causal of general progress. This in turn meant that the status of women could be used to gauge the level of general emancipatory progress of different kinds of societies.[40]

The conceptualization of women as particularly backward and retrograde posed a difficult dilemma. On the one hand, women were victims of bourgeois capitalism and in dire need of liberation. However, their backwardness was also a concrete impediment to the victory of socialism. To many, women's alleged reactionary disposition made them unsuitable political actors, since it was expected that they would advance clerical and reactionary political forces. The contention by the IWSA and others that suffrage was a sign of civilization did not precisely help matters.

The influence of bourgeois suffragism on proletarian women became further evidence of their unreliability and political backwardness, since the suffragists suggested that the category "women" had certain unified interests distinguishable from class. Even "a few *leading* women comrades who had fallen head over ears into the bourgeois Woman Suffrage movement forgot all the same, in their support of the right of the female purse, their elementary duty as Socialists," lamented Zetkin.[41]

Until the turn of the century, this was reason to exclude women from participating in political life. Zetkin herself had initially been ambivalent about the separate organizing of women, because in such organizations "the woman and not the proletarian acts and speaks."[42] Shifting her views in response to the growth of civilized suffragism, Zetkin came to argue that women should have "Universal Suffrage, not as a reward

---

[39] Marx and Engels 1956: 259, my emphasis.

[40] An interesting twist on the woman question had thus developed. Marx and Engels had reversed the causal order of Fourier's argument – no longer did the "progress of women toward liberty" *cause* general progress, but general progress caused the emancipation of women. (See Fourier, *Oeuvres Complètes* I, 145–50.)

[41] Zetkin 1906.   [42] Zetkin 1896.

for the political maturity, but as an effective means of educating and organizing the masses ... it is our duty through intensive work of enlightenment and organization so to raise the standard of political intelligence and maturity in our proletarian women that it will soon be impossible for the reaction to count on the women's vote."[43]

Socialists thus came to see the suffrage norm in relative terms: advances made by "bourgeois" suffragists were at the expense of workers and threatened to undermine socialism. An intensely competitive attitude thus developed among socialist suffrage advocates, situating women's political mobilization in the struggle between socialism and capitalism. And just as the IWSA had transformed previous claims about women's civilizing mission to argue in favor of suffrage, the socialist women were thereby able to transform the idea of women's backwardness into a reason for their political emancipation. It was precisely *because* women were so backward that special agitation for women's suffrage became a necessity.

Whereas "civilized" women had celebrated and drawn strength from women's difference, socialist suffrage activists approached suffrage as a key institution for educating women out of the backwardness they suffered by means of active political participation. Women had to be turned into proletarian fighters that would aid and strengthen the coming socialist society. It was important that their womanhood not taint the struggle, however. "We must not conduct special women's propaganda, but Socialist agitation among women. The petty, momentary interests of the female world must not be allowed to take up the stage. Our task must be to incorporate the modern proletarian woman in our class battle," Zetkin had roared in a speech at an 1896 SPD Congress. Special efforts among women were necessary to change the "unpolitical, unsocial, backward psychology of women, their isolated sphere of activity and the entire manner of their life," Lenin proclaimed in 1918 before 1,000 delegates at the first Congress of Peasant and Working Women in Moscow.[44]

To be sure, women had a fair amount of agency as socialists and the Bolshevik ranks counted on a substantial mass of women. However, it was only as *socialists* that women had agency – the category "women" as such retained no ability to raise itself out of its misery and had to be "drawn" into socialist liberation, presumably with considerable

[43] Zetkin 1906: 18.   [44] Lenin 1918.

resistance. "You cannot draw the masses into politics without drawing in the women as well," Lenin proclaimed.[45] "The 'woman question' for male and female workers is a question of how to draw the backward masses of women workers into organization, how best to explain to them their interests, how best to make them into comrades in the general struggle," Bolshevik activist Nadia Krupskaia argued.[46] To be liberated as political actors, women thus had to be helped out of their woman-hood, and transformed from a "woman" into a "comrade" and "citi-zen" via political enfranchisement.

Unlike the civilized suffrage activists who had gathered force as *women*, a distinctive sex, the large numbers of Bolshevik women under-stood themselves to act primarily as socialists and comrades in efforts to overcome their femininity. Women's suffrage thus drew on and assigned dissimilar meanings to women. In the "civilized world," it entailed making use of woman's difference, her particular feminine qualities, to civilize the state polity. In this framework, the state enfran-chised women as beings different from men. Within socialism, in con-trast, woman and her feminine traits had to be remolded and overcome in the creation of the new political subject. As Kollontai put it, with the establishment of socialist society, "the self-centered, narrow-minded and politically backward 'female' becomes an equal, a fighter, and a comrade."[47]

Although the Stuttgart resolution had directed that universal suffrage be placed on all socialist party platforms in 1907, it would be a decade until these parties would actually govern any states. The socialist suf-frage efforts came to fruition only after World War I as a host of new states emerged under socialist rule. Communist workers' and peasants' governments enfranchised women in the newly created states of Belarus (1919), Latvia (1918) and Lithuania (1918). Suffrage in Ukraine came about with the establishment of a second embattled socialist council government in 1919. In 1918 the Bolsheviks adopted a new Russian constitution that endorsed suffrage rights, closely following the 1903 party guidelines.[48] With that change, suffrage was simultaneously extended to the women of what is today Kyrgyzstan. In a number of other new states, women's suffrage came with their formal incorpora-tion in Soviet Russia: Armenia and Azerbaijan in 1921, and Kazakhstan

---

[45] Lenin 1921: 7.   [46] As cited in Wood 1997: 33.
[47] As cited in Wood 1997: 1.   [48] Wood 1997: 49–50.

and Tajikistan in 1924.[49] The Mongolian constitution of 1924, closely modeled on the Soviet Union, also recognized universal suffrage. For reasons still unknown to me, Uzbekistan did not enfranchise women until 1938, although it was incorporated into the USSR as the Uzbek Soviet Socialist Republic in 1924.

The Women's International had succumbed with the outbreak of World War I and the nationalist fervor that preceded the war. A few years later, Bolshevik Russia became a state champion of women's political rights. The Third International, also known as the Communist International or Comintern, was founded in 1919. Although formally run by an International Women's Secretariat (IWS), the new Women's International was in effect under the command of one national communist party – the Russian. Via a series of International Communist Women's Conferences, appeals, speeches, organizing and other efforts, Russia and the IWS were to continue the work to politically enfranchise women.

After socialism had become a form of state and Soviet Russia took charge of socialist internationalism, an even more competitive dynamic around woman and suffrage took hold as the suffrage norm was understood in thoroughly relative terms. The political emancipation of women became a means for the Bolsheviks to challenge the society of civilized states and the very language of civilization. The political advancement of women under socialism would help tear "the benevolent mask off the *real* barbarian – the capitalist regimes of the most 'advanced' and most 'civilized' countries," in the words of Bukharin.[50]

The "barbarous" and "savage" treatment of women was henceforth routinely used to demean the bourgeois West and demonstrate the superiority of socialist states. In a typical speech on "Soviet Power and the Status of Women," Lenin proclaimed that

In the course of two years of Soviet power in one of the most backward countries of Europe, more has been done to emancipate woman, to make her the equal of the "strong" sex, than has been done during the past 130 years by all the advanced, enlightened, "democratic" republics of the world taken together. Education, culture, civilization, freedom – all these high-sounding words are accompanied in all the capitalist, bourgeois republics of the world

---

[49] Azerbaijan appears to already have granted women suffrage in 1921, but I have been unable to find out when and how.

[50] Bukharin 1919.

with incredibly foul, disgustingly vile, bestially crude laws that ... give privileges to the male and humiliate and degrade womankind.[51]

Russia had of course long had a vexed relationship with the civilized West as well as with the East.[52] Improving the lot of women via political enfranchisement helped the new Soviet society not only to challenge the civilized status of Europe but also to distance Russia as more advanced and more liberated from the backward East. Claims were time and again made about the barbarity of the colonial powers, which not only degraded European women but had also retarded the social development of Oriental peoples. Evidence of this was consistently found in the alleged oppression of women in the East, whose situation was seen as even more dire than that of European women.

The plight of Eastern women took on exceptional importance in demonstrating the progress of socialism. The 1920 Comintern Appeal "To the working women of the world" stated that

[the Communist International] knows that more than any others the peoples of the East have suffered the harshest forms of colonial exploitation at the hands of the imperialists of the West, robbers of the whole world, as well as Japan, the imperial power of the East. The overthrow of capitalist rule is the only way to liberate the toiling masses of the East. If the nations of the East are more backward, that is precisely because of this merciless exploitation that has held back their natural free development, and their economic, social, political and intellectual emancipation. The Communist International calls on the peoples of the East to struggle both against landlords and capitalists of their own countries and against the imperialist yoke. If you, working women, want to see yourselves and your children free, if you want to end the enslavement of the colonies and the enslavement of the East, your place is in the ranks of our union, the Communist International. For it is only side by side with your more liberated brothers and sisters in the other countries of Europe and America that you will liberate yourselves.[53]

The indictment of Europe as barbaric and backward thus failed to release the colonies, and particularly the East, from being understood as backward as well. The message was clear – the "more liberated sisters" of "Europe and America" were key agents for the liberation of "Eastern"

---

[51] Lenin 1919: 5. See also Lenin 1921.
[52] On the Russian Empire and its relation with Europe and the East, see Geraci 2001; Neumann 1999.
[53] First International Working Women's Conference, 1920: 975–6.

women.[54] "In agitational and organizational work among women in countries with a precapitalist level of development, special use should be made of the experiences acquired by the Russian comrades since the Russian revolution in their work among women of the Eastern peoples," the IWS instructed communist women in 1920.[55] The sense was that Russian women, as formerly backward themselves, were particularly well suited to this work with the backward East. As Trotsky proclaimed before the Second World Conference of Communist Women in 1921:

Generally speaking, in the world labor movement the woman worker stands closest precisely to ... that section of labor which is the most backward, the most oppressed, the lowliest of the lowly. And just because of this, in the years of the colossal world revolution, this section of the proletariat can and must become the most active, the most revolutionary, and the most initiative section of the working class.[56]

The geographical scope of the Women's International was expanded in the 1920s, moving beyond the European and North American membership of the Second International to incorporate some parties of colonial and pre-capitalist areas. However, just as the Women's International was beginning to reach outward from Europe and the USA, it dwindled. The last international conference was held in 1926, a conference which was attended by the newly founded Chinese Communist Party (CCP). The institutional means of the socialist women's movement to promote the enfranchisement of women was dismantled at the same time as the IWSA moved away from suffrage work. From the mid-1920s on, European women were no longer important as a force in the extension of suffrage. However, by then the baton had been passed on.

Pan-American suffragism

It is rarely recognized that the suffrage laws passed in Latin America between the 1930s and 1940s were preceded by a transnational struggle to demand the vote. This is possibly the case because the transnational mobilization was carried out in the pan-American context, far away from Europe. But a third and distinctive suffrage wave did develop in the Americas between the 1920s and 1940s, bringing together not only

---

[54] First International Working Women's Conference 1920: 976.
[55] Zetkin 1920: 992–3.   [56] Trotsky 1945: 156.

the transnational mobilization but also the timing of the grand suffrage debates and the adoption of suffrage. Most importantly, the rationales for suffrage as an appropriate behavior identified Latin American states as distinctive from others, as a "new" part of Western civilization that was still not as advanced as the old world of Europe. Suffrage was initially not interpreted as a standard that separated categorically different kinds of states but was rather seen as a measure indicative of whereabouts on a continuous scale of civilization a state was located. However, as we shall see below, these ideas were then to merge into the competitive ideological battles between socialism and market liberalism that erupted in the hemisphere in the 1930s.

By the turn of the twentieth century, voices were already raised in favor of enfranchising women in the Americas. For instance, the Argentine socialist party had endorsed universal suffrage for both sexes in 1900, much earlier than most European counterparts.[57] In 1910, the first transnational discussion of suffrage in Latin America took place, at the First International Feminine Congress in Argentina. The take-off in mobilization for suffrage across the continent came in the early 1920s, not due to any activities of the IWSA or Socialist Women's Internationals. Although some efforts were made by newly enfranchised US women to bring suffrage to the rest of the Americas, the essence of the transnational activism consisted of the traveling, networking, active borrowing and selective importing of ideas and strategies by Latin American women. Although IWSA president Carrie Chapman Catt proposed in 1920 that the organization "really ought to go hot and fast after those Spanish countries and wake the women up to demand their rights,"[58] the Alliance never acted on her call. Instead, Latin American women – apparently already awake – launched suffrage organizations in the 1920s and 1930s, often after traveling or studying in Europe or the USA.[59]

---

[57] Lavrin 1995: 259–60.   [58] Pernet 2000.

[59] Paulina Luisi, the first main suffragist of Uruguay, had done extensive travels in Europe (Lavrin 1995: 328), and her compatriot Sara Rey Alvarez of the 1932 Comité Pro-Derechos de la Mujer had studied in Brussels and London in the mid-1920s, where she had met Emmeline Pankhurst, Louise Van Den Plas and a number of other suffragists (Lavrin 1995: 343). Aurora Cáceres was a Sorbonne student and resident of France from 1924 to 1930, when she returned to Peru to form its main suffrage organization, Feminismo Peruano ZAC. Bertha Lutz (Brazil), also a Sorbonne student for seven years, had followed the English

Ideas about the unity of the Americas served as an enabling and delimiting transnational framework for these suffrage struggles. The suffragists organized as "American" women, and as such they could meet across national borders. Seeing themselves as American, they made no attempts to bring suffrage to women outside the continent. A momentous 1922 Pan-American Conference of Women brought together almost 2,000 women from all but two American countries to discuss suffrage, making the conclave the largest gathering of women in the Americas to that date.[60] At the meeting, the Pan American Association for the Advancement of Women (PAAW) was created, whose platform included the aim "to educate public opinion in favor of granting the vote of women, to secure political rights."[61] As PAAW's honorary chairperson, Catt toured South America in 1923 to spur suffrage work. However, by 1925, Catt had turned to peace work and suggested dissolving PAAW.

The formal pan-American institutional infrastructure was made into the primary arena to advocate for women's suffrage.[62] The suffragists secured the unanimous adoption of a motion to study the status of women at the pan-American conference in Santiago in 1923.[63] Suffrage activists could soon turn to the Inter-American Commission of Women (IACW), which was created "to take up the consideration of the civil and political equality of women in the continent" at the meeting in Havana in 1928.[64] The IACW had an official mandate, making suffrage part of the formal diplomacy of interstate relations of the Americas and indeed the world for the very first time. At the seventh meeting, in Montevideo in 1933, the world's first international resolution to recommend suffrage – Resolution XIX, Civil and Political Rights of Women – was adopted unanimously.

In most cases, the great onslaught of suffrage campaigning and the grand parliamentary debates came in the early 1930s, showing a clear

suffrage campaign and had fruitful meetings with Catt in the USA (Hahner 1990: 138), as did Chilean Amanda Labarca in 1918 (Pernet 2000) and Argentine Alicia Moreau in 1919 (Lavrin 1995: 266). Chilean suffragist Aida Parada had studied at Columbia University, and her fellow member of the Unión Femenina de Chile, Delia Ducoing, had visited Alice Paul and her pro-suffrage National Women's Party in the late 1920s (Pernet 2000).
[60] Miller 1986: 178.   [61] Miller 1986.
[62] On the pan-American work by and for women, see Cáceres 1946; Miller 1986, and 1991; Pernet 2000.
[63] Cáceres 1946: 1–3; IACW 1965: 3.   [64] J. Scott 1931: 408.

hemispheric trend. In 1929, Ecuador had become the first state of the hemisphere to grant women suffrage. Soon thereafter, many governments collapsed or were overthrown during the turbulence of the Great Depression, creating windows of opportunity for suffrage organizations across the continent as new electoral codes were debated in constituent congresses. The great suffrage debates took place in Brazil in 1931, Argentina in 1932, Peru in 1932, Uruguay in 1932, Colombia in 1933 and Chile in 1934. Though not for lack of mobilization, these debates resulted in the approval of national female suffrage in only three cases: Uruguay in 1932, Brazil in 1932 and Cuba in 1934.

If the geographical scope and timing suggest a pan-American wave of suffrage advocacy and debate, the understandings of what suffrage was and did also points to "the Americas" as a distinctive region situated in a hierarchical international society. By 1930, veteran Brazilian politician José Francisco Assis Brasil, previously an opponent of women's suffrage, proclaimed that suffrage was a "victorious idea of the civilization to which we belong."[65] This was a position that the suffragists of the Americas had advocated for well over a decade. They located the historical origins of the advancement of women, including suffrage, almost exclusively in the "civilized" world and primarily Europe, in stark contrast with later representations that were to emphasize precolonial traditions and unity with non-European "developing" countries. With the exception of Japan, the suffrage struggles that had now developed in Asia did not seem to register among Latin American suffragists. Instead, it was proclaimed that "in the whole civilized world, in secular Europe as well as in young America and the transformed Japan, the feminist movement is developing with an incomparable force."[66] Enfranchising women had indeed become the expected behavior for civilized states.

However, young America was prevalently characterized as "less advanced" on the scale of social evolution. And suffrage became seen as characteristic of more advanced societies that had already experienced changes that had not yet reached the Americas. Many of those who agitated on behalf of women from the 1910s to the 1930s embraced suffrage in principle. However, like suffrage opponents,

---

[65] Hahner 1990: 159.
[66] María Jesús Alvarado at the First International Feminine Congress in Argentina, 1910.

even women's rights activists expressed deep skepticism about the propriety of granting women the vote in a "less advanced" cultural and social environment. The particular cultural circumstances of the Americas became interpreted to mean that these countries were "not ready" for women's vote, something considered appropriate only for fully civilized states. Just as the experience of the new states of Australia, New Zealand, Norway and Finland did not give rise to automatic mimicry among those who considered themselves the core of old civilization, the political condition of women of the advanced states was not interpreted as entirely relevant for Latin America (other than as an indication of what was to come, in a more or less distant future). The fact that suffrage was seen as a standard of civilization, a stage desired for the Americas, did not help to move suffrage advocacy forward.

Even if Europe was upheld as the pinnacle of civilization, it was furthermore the *Anglo* tradition that was widely signified as empowering for women. *Latin* American women suffered from a cultural deficiency that was partially blamed on the region's "cultural tradition, with all the impediments of colonial Spain that place the woman in a socially inferior level, devoid of impulse and initiative of her own."[67] The Spanish heritage, including Catholicism and legal systems based on the Napoleonic Code, was thought to give rise to a "Latin tendency" that inhibited the "rapid granting of justice to women" that had taken place in areas with English common law.[68]

Lack of education and literacy was central: with lower levels of formal schooling than men, it was argued, women of the Americas had less culture and consciousness. They were also excessively influenced by the clergy and the Catholic Church, thus incapable of voting independently and rationally. Conceptualized as lacking in culture, it was only proper that Latin women be kept out of politics. It was only proper that less advanced Latin states, with their less advanced women, waited to adopt suffrage. "Woman's absolute and unconditional civil and political equality signifies an exceedingly radical change for the Latin American society, since its women are perhaps not properly prepared," the National Women's Council of Peru proclaimed in a statement against suffrage in 1938.[69] With the vote, women would

---

[67] Portal 1933: 10, my translation.   [68] IACW 1965: iii.   [69] *El Comercio*, 1938.

allegedly threaten the advancement of their societies and thus, by exten-sion, they posed a threat to their own wellbeing.

In Ecuador (1929) and Spain (1931), the conservative political estab-lishments saw women as loyal Catholics, congenitally conservative, whose votes could be mobilized accordingly. These examples were not lost on the suffrage debaters in the rest of the Americas. The Mexican Institutional Revolutionary Party saw support for women's suffrage as a sure electoral defeat and held out against such reform until 1953. Being of incipient culture, women were allegedly prone to traditional ideas and prejudice; thus for those on the left in states such as Chile, Mexico and Peru they were still inept for politics, while to a limited few on the right they were seen as attractive candidates.

Comparable to the links made between woman and the savage in Europe, as we saw in Chapter 4, the lack of culture pulled woman into the same fold as the so-called "Indian" in the Americas. Although the Orient figured in the American imaginary, there were much more pressing concerns erupting in the relations with the internal "uncivi-lized." Like woman, the indigenous were thought to suffer from a lack of culture and to retard the advancement of the American states. Illiteracy and inability to speak Spanish – emblematic of this alleged lack of culture – were strong markers of ethnic belonging, so much so that in states with large indigenous populations, illiterates were virtually synonymous with Indians. Learning Spanish as well as reading and writing, conversely, "culturalized" a person, providing the foundation for voting rights. Explicit comparisons, parallels and contrasts between woman and the Indian as two culturally lacking groups were further-more commonplace in suffrage debates. Even though "[woman's] cul-tural level has been very neglected in our country," Sayan Álvarez contended in the 1931 Peruvian congressional suffrage debate, "I don't want to establish a close comparison between the indigenous and the fair sex, which has reached a much superior level. But I am afraid that [like the Indian], the woman with the vote in her hands will only hurt herself."[70]

Contributing to "national advancement" remained a robust premise for being worthy to vote for all those involved in the suffrage debates. The task thus fell on the suffragists to demonstrate woman's worth. Indeed, as the well-read women's rights activist Magda Portal argued,

[70] Peruvian Constituent Congress 1931: 493, my translation.

"Culture opens all doors."[71] There was an opening in the fact that women figured simultaneously as effect *and* cause of cultural advancement. If the less advanced status of the Americas was reason to deny women the vote, the backward condition of American women could also be held forth as a cause of this unfortunate status. It would thus have been possible to follow the women of the Socialist International and argue that suffrage was needed as a form of political education, to help women out of their backwardness and turn them into a positive force for national progress.

Developments in the Americas would proceed more cautiously, however. Sustained efforts were allegedly needed to prepare women culturally before they could vote, rather than by means of the vote, so as to avert catastrophic consequences. The 1923 Inter-American Resolution on Women's Rights, arguing that legislation must "correspond to the present cultural condition of American women," simply called on the American governments to "promote the moral, intellectual and physical education of women" so that "political rights for women" could be eventually granted.[72] Resolution XIX, Civil and Political Rights of Women, similarly called for granting political rights to women "to the extent allowed by cultural circumstances."

In this context, the suffragists came to argue that granting *some* women the vote would help the states of the Americas to progress within civilization – the votes of women *of culture* would advance the states of the Americas, whereas granting suffrage to the uncivilized segments in society would inhibit progress. To attain the vote, suffragists in countries with substantial indigenous populations such as Bolivia, Colombia, Guatemala and Peru struggled to distinguish themselves from the Indian, alleging that woman was not this illiterate, this problematic Indian without culture.[73] They argued that certain women were already cultured enough to shoulder voting responsibilities: "It is not only unacceptable but deeply embarrassing that [the proposal for the

---

[71] Portal 1933: 43, my translation.   [72] J. Scott 1931: 244–5.
[73] In states with less indigenous presence, variations on the view that "culture" as literacy was a necessity for the vote were commonplace as well. The participants at the 1910 Congress in Argentina, many of the National Women's Councils, the Chilean Partido Femenino Progresista and Partido Cívico Femenino of the 1920s (Pernet 2000), the Argentine National Council of Women and the 1930 Argentine Comité Pro-Voto de la Mujer (Lavrin 1995: 277–9) and doubtlessly many other women's groups all expressed such views.

new electoral law] suggests granting the vote to an 18-year-old child
and to the illiterate while denying it to the woman," the organization
Feminismo Peruano reiterated in article after article.[74] Bolivian suffragists similarly advocated suffrage for woman, while not for the illiterate
Indian. Expressing herself in the grandiloquent language so typical of
the time, the director of *Mujeres de América*, in the Bolivian national
report to the 1933 Seventh International Conference of American
States, made this appeal:

[Bolivia's] legislation still does not treat women's rights as in other States or
nations of more advanced civilization ... [Although cultured women should
be granted suffrage], there are not sufficient reasons why the semi-literate and
wretched masses, under the unconditional servitude of the sordid *caudillismo*
and with unspeakable passions, should suppress the cultured elements of
either sex, in a country that – sincerely or sarcastically – calls itself democratic.
Therefore, in the legitimate and prudent interest of the citizenry and as
members of the Bolivian community for whose institutional progress we
honorably struggle, we strongly desire that the results of the elections not be
allowed to degenerate – perhaps accruing corruption and major shortcomings – by being carried out without the necessary elementary political and
cultural education.[75]

"Culturalization is of great importance," Peruvian suffrage leader
Aurora Cáceres agreed in a discussion of political rights in an *America
Today* radio interview in Washington DC in 1944:

In the aboriginal Aymara and Quechua regions, there is an experimental
school and they teach Spanish as well as literacy. This culturalization crusade
that is extended to the indigenous will strengthen the ties and unite the
citizenry, destined to uphold democratic rights, and the aborigine will cease
to be a national problem.[76]

As the franchise was extended to women, literacy remained a commonplace requirement for voting rights in many parts of the Americas,
excluding large segments of the populations from suffrage. Such restric-
tions tended to exclude female voters to a much larger extent than male,
as women's literacy rates were far lower. Furthermore, since illiteracy
was one of the criteria that determined one's status as "Indian,"

---

[74] E.g. "El voto femenino" *La Prensa*, June 15, 1931.
[75] Merino Carvallo 1936: 111, my translation.
[76] Cáceres 1946: 36, my translation.

women's lower literacy rates led to the perhaps surprising existence of a larger number of female than male Indians.[77] In cases such as El Salvador (1939), Panama (1941) and Guatemala (1945), literacy requirements were furthermore placed solely on women, while not on the male electorate. As the least cultured of the less civilized, women had to be especially prepared via education and literacy to be entrusted with the responsibility of citizenship.

In sum, women's suffrage was understood as indicative of advanced civilization, a condition Latin American states were striving to attain. What was not clear was the relation between suffrage and advancement in a context in which national progress was understood to depend on a competitive struggle between civilizing and savage elements of society. Was women's suffrage a measure that would help bring about progress, or was cultural progress a prior process that would subsequently bring women the vote? The view that often came to prevail was that Latin American women were culturally backward, and that as voters they would thus pose a risk to national advancement as well as to themselves.

By the mid-1930s, the understanding of what suffrage was, the reason it was appropriate and legitimate for certain kinds of states, began to change. The issue now also became embedded in the emerging contentions between Western democracy and the growing tide of communism (and, to a lesser extent, fascism). The Russian Revolution and the emergence of socialist states had lent support to claims about an impending socialist stage of history, which helped to unsettle the previously predominant unilinear views of evolutionary progress. At least two and possibly three paths were now imagined in the move away from savagery: towards Western democracy rooted in capitalism, towards socialism or towards fascism.[78] The world became seen as divided into unique areas, areas that were not necessarily related as stages but that were nonetheless engaged in a competitive struggle for survival. This competitive struggle was to engulf the Americas for the decades to come.

Women's suffrage was increasingly advocated as a behavior appropriate for Western, democratic states. The conceptualization of suffrage as a "democratic" behavior was more effective than the link between Western civilization and suffrage on its own, particularly since various US administrations began seeing the value of women voters in Latin

---

[77] E.g. De la Cadena 1995.   [78] Leacock 1972: 15–16.

America. It was primarily in the conflict with communism that the US state came to support the establishment of suffrage in the Americas. Understood as clerical and conservative, women seemed to offer a valuable base of political support in the fight against communism. At the 1938 VIII Inter-American Conference in Lima, the "Lima Declaration on Women's Rights" was proposed by the Mexican delegation and adopted, calling on the American republics to urgently grant women political rights equal to those of men. At this meeting, the autonomy of the IACW was withdrawn and the commission was reshaped as a subsidiary of the Pan-American Union. As such, the IACW was charged with organizing the women of the Americas "in defense of democracy," and to this end it encouraged the formation of *Acción Femenina* (Women's Action) groups, which were subsequently formed in a number of countries.[79] Western democracies, it was now argued, grant women the vote.

Since women were widely conceptualized to be uncultured, clerical, and conservative, their enfranchisement largely came to depend on how each state was situated in the antagonistic and competitive relations between "Western democracy," "socialism" and "fascism" in international society. For much of the socialist left in the Americas, women were looked upon with suspicion, and the socialist parties did not take a united position on women as voters.[80] In the PRI-governed Mexico of the late 1930s, apprehension once again grew about letting women vote. News of the female support for Franco in Spain and the bloody destruction of the Spanish Republic of 1937–9 with the help of Hitler and Mussolini was spread by newspapers as well as the growing

---

[79] Cannon 1943; Miller 1991: 115.

[80] Socialist parties were an important force for women's suffrage in Uruguay and Argentina in the early part of the century, and a number of other socialist parties advocated women's suffrage (e.g. Peru) but were violently purged from the political arena. Though socialism was an important force in parts of the Americas from the turn of the century, I have found no evidence of separate *transnational* socialist women's organizing for suffrage. In cases such as Mexico and Chile, the socialists opposed women's vote. There was thus no united stance on suffrage among the socialist parties of the Americas. Suffragism furthermore often united women across the liberal–socialist divide. Alicia de Moreau de Justo (a leading member of the Argentine socialist party) and Paulina Luisi (co-founder of the Uruguayan socialist party) were both in contact with Catt and subsequently founded the suffrage organizations Comité Pro-Sufragio Femenino and Alianza Uruguaya por el Sufragio Femenino in 1919. These women were also important in the pan-American organizing for suffrage.

numbers of Spanish refugees who fled to Latin America. "In Mexico, without preparation, [suffrage] must be considered carefully, as must that which has just happened not long ago in Spain," argued Luna Arroyo of the PRI. "Taking the most advanced attitude," the PRI could therefore allow women full suffrage rights only upon their developing a "revolutionary conscience."[81] Despite the enfranchisement of women in the socialist states of Europe and Central Asia, allowing women to vote was not necessarily considered appropriate behavior by leftist governments of the Americas.

In other cases, woman's suffrage helped to demonstrate allegiance to Western democracy. During World War II, the USA temporarily abandoned its policy of direct military involvement in Central America, and its previously strong political ties to the dictatorships of Trujillo in the Dominican Republic, Hernández in El Salvador, Somoza in Nicaragua and Ubico in Guatemala grew more tenuous. With the USA publicly dedicated to democracy, its previously strong ties with these dictatorships became an embarrassment. Granting presumably conservative women voting rights thus became a seemingly inconsequential way for dictators such as Trujillo to show dedication to "democratic" reform and loyalty to the North American patron.[82] In fascist-friendly Argentina, in contrast, the alignment of suffrage with Western democracy repelled the military rulers of 1942–6 and furthered their resistance to the measure.[83]

By the end of the war, a series of regimes across the Americas were toppled by mass upheavals, once again generating the prospect of electoral reform.[84] A new resolution XXVIII on the Rights of Women in America was furthermore adopted in 1945, and the work of the IACW was intensifying.[85] National suffrage coalitions such as the Federación Chilena de Instituciones Femeninas and the Peruvian Comité Nacional Pro-Derechos Civiles y Políticos de la Mujer were created, campaigning vigorously for the introduction and passage of suffrage bills in the constituent congresses. At the Ninth International Conference of American States at Bogotá in 1948, the world's first treaty on women's political rights was approved – the Inter-American

---

[81] Luna 1936: 7.   [82] Miller 1991: 114; NACLA 1974.   [83] Lavrin 1995: 285.
[84] Dictatorial regimes fell in Guatemala (1944, Ubico), Cuba (1944, Batista), Venezuela (1945, Betancourt), Peru (1945, Prado), Brazil (1946, Vargas), Argentina (1946) and Costa Rica (1948).
[85] Inter-American Commission on Women 1965: 9.

Convention on the Granting of Political Rights of Women – and it was signed by fourteen states.[86] A number of the ensuing new constitutions granted (some) women suffrage: Guatemala (1945), Panama (1941), Argentina (1947), Venezuela (1947), Chile (1949) and Costa Rica (1949). The ruling left establishments of Mexico (Alemán of the PRI) and Peru (Bustamante of the Frente Democrático Nacional) still would not risk granting the vote to presumably conservative women. In Peru and Paraguay, it was the right-wing dictatorships of Odría and Stroessner that would finally find women beneficial as voters.[87]

The 1945 Resolution XXVIII on the Rights of Women in America called on governments to grant suffrage and abolish any sex discrimination that "retard[s] the prosperity and the intellectual, social and political development of the nations of this Continent."[88] The importance of the status of woman for the advancement of the states of the Americas was the predominant, indeed, *the* meta-narrative of the suffrage debates well into the 1950s. The desire to leave "backwardness" behind was furthermore a shared ongoing premise of the suffrage debates. The initial hierarchy was unilinear and concerned advancement further away from savagery and towards civilization. By the 1930s, a multilinear conceptualization of the world emerged in which states could develop in three directions: towards liberal Western democracy, socialism or fascism. All of these were seen as modern forms of statehood and, in that sense, advancements from backwardness. The shared ideas about women as conservatives made them a factor in such advancement. And although the ranking of Western democratic, socialist and fascist states was highly contested, they were always seen as superior and inferior in relation to one another. Various interpretations of social hierarchies were indeed an integral aspect to the struggles about suffrage as an appropriate behavior in the Americas.

---

[86] The 1948 signatories: Argentina, Brazil, Chile, Colombia, Costa Rica, Cuba, Dominican Republic, Ecuador, Guatemala, Panama, Peru, USA, Uruguay and Venezuela. Nicaragua signed and ratified the treaty in 1956, the year after suffrage was granted. Peru and Colombia signed the treaty in 1948, but waited until 1955 and 1957 to grant suffrage, and ratified the convention thereafter. Paraguay signed in 1951 but did not ratify it or grant suffrage until 1961.

[87] Odría explicitly situated women's suffrage in the fight against communism and as a response to the social revolution in Bolivia.

[88] Pan American Union 1945: 61–2.

Suffragism, liberation struggles and Afro-Asian solidarity

In the colonized areas of Asia and Africa, women's suffrage first emerged as a concern within the vast dominions of the colonial empires of France and Great Britain and the less extensive colonies of Portugal, Belgium, the Netherlands and the USA. In many cases, female suffrage was granted in the context of limited self-government within the auspices of the imperial state. The British Empire seems to have been more reticent about supporting female suffrage within its colonies and protectorates than the French, particularly in regard to the African colonies. Whereas France quickly enfranchised women in five African colonies upon granting French women suffrage in 1944, the British allowed women to vote in the West Indies and Singapore in the 1940s and 1950, but waited until the mid-1950s before extending the vote to women of the first African state (Ghana).

In many other cases, women achieved suffrage only with liberation from colonialism. For instance, in Gabon (1956), Mauritania (1961), Algeria (1961) and the Congo (1963), women gained the right to vote with independence from France. Likewise, in Jamaica (1944), Malaysia (1957), Uganda (1962) and Bahrain (1971/3), suffrage came with liberation from British rule. Portugal is notable for not extending the franchise to women within the colonies, all of whom were enfranchised upon independence in 1975 (Angola, Cape Verde, Mozambique, São Tomé and Principe, and Guinea-Bissau). In a number of cases, such as Cambodia, Morocco, the Central African Republic, Egypt, Sudan, Jordan, Yemen and Iraq, suffrage was not extended to women until several years after independence.

Although the research on women's suffrage struggles in post-colonial states is still limited, that which exists makes clear that the granting of suffrage rarely took on an automatic logic. Despite the large number of states that had accepted women's suffrage by the mid-1940s, it was not a given for these states to do so. Women's suffrage had not become a standard held out for all states, irrespective of rank. The extension of the vote to women within colonial rule was preceded by widespread suffrage activism from the 1930s to 1960s – among women of the Bahamas, Nigeria and India, to name three examples – prompting general concern about suffrage in the colonies among the British.[89]

---

[89] Burton 1994; Grewal 1996; Johnson-Odim and Mba 1997. Excellent new collections of documents on "Empire and Suffrage" from the British Public

Similar mobilization for suffrage within colonial rule took place in the Dutch East Indies.[90] Among the states that enfranchised women upon their creation, furthermore, the women of the national liberation movements had often organized for and demanded political equality before liberation.[91] In Sudan and Egypt, where suffrage was not extended to women until eight or nine years after independence, suffrage mobilization was similarly a crucial antecedent to the vote.[92]

There were also important organized transnational dimensions to these suffrage demands, generated within the emergent Asian-African liberation from colonialism. The first Asian-African Conference on Women was held in Colombo in 1958, and the first Afro-Asian Women's Conference in Cairo in 1961, both direct offspring of the Non-Aligned and Afro-Asian Solidarity movements. Their stated aim was to coordinate and formalize the interaction among women of former colonies, with women's suffrage on the agenda.[93]

The national liberation struggles and the Non-Aligned Movement furthermore developed ties with the new Soviet-led Women's International Democratic Federation (WIDF) as well.[94] In WIDF, a new form of state-sponsored women's transnationalism emerged that linked up with and sometimes helped to form pro-independence, pro-suffrage nationalist women's organizations all over the world. For instance, in Nigeria, the Federation of Nigerian Women's Societies became affiliated to the WIDF in 1953. The Federation was successful in organizing women in the south, and pressured the British colonial government to extend the vote to women in the (Muslim) north.[95]

Women of Africa and Asia forged a common Afro-Asian speaking position as victims of "civilized" colonial oppression. At the 1935 International Alliance for Suffrage and Equal Citizenship congress in

---

Record Office were released in 2003. See www.adam-matthew-publications.co.uk/collect/p633.htm.

[90] Blackburn 1999.

[91] E.g. Blackburn 1999; Johnson-Odim and Mba 1997; Tripp 2000.

[92] Ahmed al Amin and Abdel Magied 2001; Botman 1999.

[93] See Proceedings of the First Asian-African Conference of Women, Colombo, Ceylon, February 15–24, 1958; and Proceedings of the First Afro-Asian Women's Conference, Cairo, January 14–23, 1961.

[94] Founded in 1945 in Paris, and relocating to East Berlin in 1951, the WIDF was present in 106 countries by the 1980s.

[95] Johnson-Odim and Mba 1997. The Federation of Nigerian Women's Societies was previously the Nigerian Women's Union and before that the Abeokuta Women's Union.

Istanbul, Indian delegate Shareefeh Hamid Ali had warned "you of the west that any arrogant assumption of superiority or of patronage on the part of Europe or America ... will alienate Asia and Africa and with it the womanhood of Asia and Africa ... The Ethiopians might as well some day pretend to go and civilize Italy, or China to civilize Japan." Indians, she made clear, did not "admire European civilization."[96] The distinction and release of the Afro-Asian world from Europe informed suffrage mobilization and arguments, serving as an organizing principle akin to "civilization," "socialism" or the "Americas." And the post-colonial Afro-Asians were not interested in simply mimicking the behavior of their European colonizers.

The insistence by European women and statesmen that suffrage and the advancement of women were *European* inventions, intrinsic to "civilization," did not facilitate the efforts of Asian and African suffragists. In a context of enmity with the colonial West, such an insistence instead prodded forward arguments for the rejection of political equality. Opposing suffrage as a European invention became a manner of rejecting the West and guarding non-Western "tradition."[97] Afro-Asian suffragists responded not only by referring to examples of women's political emancipation in Turkey, India, China and the Philippines, but also by crafting arguments about the political power of women in pre-colonial societies.[98] They drew on intellectuals such as Turkish Kemalist ideologue Ziya Gökalp, who had proclaimed that "Old Turks were both democratic and feminist."[99] Likewise, when introducing the suffrage bill to parliament, Turkish prime minister Inönü claimed that "the Turkish nation prospered and pervaded the whole world with its power and civilization only when its women had occupied their just and prestigious place along with men and worked together with men in the complicated and difficult tasks of their country."[100] Despite what the Europeans may claim, female political agency was not a European invention, they insisted. Far from it.

It is important to note that the liberation from Europe, the insistence on *not* being European, was crucial in these suffrage struggles. And while the extension of the vote to women may have brought these states into the fold of "international society," the interpretations of suffrage

---

[96] As cited in Rupp 1997: 79–80.   [97] See e.g. Blackburn 1999: 214.
[98] E.g. Blackburn 1999: 214.   [99] Arat 2000: 109.   [100] Arat 2000: 111.

simultaneously helped to render these states as distinct, with traditions of their own.

Conclusion

In a now classic statement, Tilly claims of the extension of political rights that "nothing could be more detrimental to an understanding of this whole process than the old liberal conception of European history as the gradual creation and extension of political rights."[101] This chapter seconds that statement in its analysis of the worldwide emergence of women's suffrage. Although suffragism first emerged in Europe, the subsequent development of suffrage laws around the world is not testimony to the progressive expansion of a liberal, European international society of more similar states. Indeed, this chapter challenges several central claims made in prior attempts to address this development.[102]

Prior analyses of the worldwide emergence of women's suffrage all share the assumption that this is a case of homogenization; the puzzle to be explained is why so many states have engaged in presumably the same behavior. The accounts also share the view that once a critical mass of European countries and Anglo-European settler states had instituted suffrage as a result of activism, an imitative logic took hold among remaining states, those of Latin America, Asia and Africa. In these later cases, the causal power is thought to rest with a new international suffrage norm. The states of the Americas, Asia and Africa mimicked a standard that the Europeans had set up, creating an outcome of similarity among states worldwide.

This account takes us some of the way in understanding the global emergence of women's suffrage. Transnational suffrage mobilization did start among European nationals and women of Anglo-European settler countries. A number of these states were the first to grant women political rights. And suffrage did become an international standard of appropriate behavior for states. The rationales for why women should be allowed to vote furthermore became part of the shared language of

---

[101] Tilly 1975: 37.
[102] More specifically the analyses by Berkovitch 1999b; Finnemore and Sikkink 1999, Keck and Sikkink 1998, Ramirez *et al.* 1997, Ramirez and McEneaney 1997.

international society. Notions of suffrage as progress, linking the political status of women to the advancement of the state, circulated across the world. In these ways, suffrage is a story of state similarity emerging out of the European core of international society.

International social hierarchies were built into the new norm from the get-go, however. The initial transnational activism developed in the society of civilized states and not in the world at large. This fact is not well explained simply by reference to the strength of liberal ideals about political equality in Europe as opposed to elsewhere. Not only can liberalism accommodate the exclusion of women from politics, as we saw in Chapter 4, but many non-European societies had recognized female political authority and could have been included in the struggle. The scope and content of the first wave of transnational suffragism are better accounted for as a response to a prior international norm, the standard that civilized states (in contrast with allegedly inferior societies) keep women out of politics. By reinterpreting this prior norm, "civilized" suffragists helped to change the standard governing their states. Civilized states were now to grant women suffrage.

The ensuing process that made suffrage a worldwide phenomenon provides further testimony to the link between international norms and social hierarchies. Since suffrage was presumably indicative of having reached an advanced stage of European civilization, it was far from clear whether this was an expectation for other societies as well. If they were to enfranchise women, on what grounds? It would take imaginative reinterpretations of this norm to make the case that other states, states whose representatives indeed may have loathed such "civilization," should adopt suffrage legislation.

Large-scale activism also developed to legitimate women's suffrage in societies not part of "advanced European civilization." In this chapter, we saw the mass nature of the mobilizations for female political empowerment in the socialist East, the Americas and the newly emerging states of Africa and Asia. Prior accounts have overlooked these waves of transnational suffragism. Had they not, they would likely have agreed that this level of mobilization outside of the core of civilized society is not well captured as a process of "mimicry."

Nor did activists outside the core simply mimic the rationales for women's suffrage provided for civilized states. They did argue that the political status of women was a means for general national advancement in a hierarchical world. And the suffrage proponents all had to come to grips with and transform the challenging European proclamations of suffrage as exclusively a sign of "civilization." However, they did so in different ways.

The suffrage advocates of Latin America largely accepted the division of the world into progressive levels of civilization, topped by the states of Western Europe and followed by Latin America as "less advanced" among the civilized. They challenged the idea that a state needed to reach a certain level of civilization before women could attain the vote, arguing instead that allowing "cultured" women to vote would in fact advance a society. It was thus made appropriate also for less advanced societies to adopt suffrage legislation.

Socialist and Afro-Asian suffragists vehemently rejected the idea that the political emancipation of women was the creation of European civilization. Pointing to socialism or pre-colonial traditions as a basis for female emancipation – and to developments in Western Europe as a source of patriarchy – they made suffrage a mechanism for distancing their societies from and superseding the West. While they could not dispense with the European West altogether, they provided distinct interpretations of the nature of the category "women," of international hierarchy, and of how the political emancipation of women related to the progress of their country in that hierarchy. The shared practice of relating the status of women to the state as progress thus gave rise not only to differentiation and rank among states but also to the challenging of an emergent Eurocentric international order. Rather than the spread of Western norms and institutions, these developments suggest an international society whose Eurocentric hierarchy was contested.

6 | *National women's policy bureaus and the standards of development*

When it comes to institutionalizing women's interests in policy processes, no country in the world can be considered "developed."

Anne Marie Goetz[1]

Introduction

Partially because of the continuous addition of new states, it took almost a century before women's suffrage would become a worldwide phenomenon. The development of national women's policy bureaus, so-called "national women's machinery" (NWM), was much more rapid, becoming a global fact within a couple of decades. National women's machinery consists of formalized institutions officially part of either the administrative or governmental state structure. Although their specific directives vary, they all address the situation of women in some manner and thus bring women's issues into the formalized public policy planning and implementation processes of the state. Their organization can take several forms, ranging from a more permanent ministry of women's affairs that employs civil service staff to a council or commission populated by partisan government officials.

Between 1976 and 1985, during the United Nations Decade for Women, over two thirds of UN member states created some form of bureaucracy to formally oversee and direct public policy related to the status of women.[2] During this period, there was furthermore a general shift away from what had initially been advisory commissions to the establishment of more permanent government units. It is important to

---

[1] Goetz 2003: 69.

[2] In most cases, the creation of a bureaucracy for the advancement of women was only the beginning of the power-laden battles over public policy and other forms of state involvement in the status of women. To learn more about the particularities of national machinery through case studies, see e.g. INSTRAW 2000; Goetz 2003; Lovenduski 2005; Sawer 1996a; Stetson and Mazur 1995.

remember that a century earlier, legislation to bar women from entering state office had spread among states. Now, not only were women allowed to hold public employment, but they apparently merited a bureaucracy of their own. The stunning worldwide creation of these bureaucracies between 1961 and 1986 is the focus of this chapter.[3]

The promotion of NWMs took place within the United Nations context, with the result that all member states became faced with the question of creating a NWM simultaneously. Addressing the situation of women was furthermore set out as an expectation for all states from the beginning, in contrast with women's suffrage. NWMs nevertheless developed in and became a constituent part of a highly stratified international society in which some states were upheld as more advanced with regard to the status of women than others. Importantly, it was not "developed" states of the West that were set up as the model to be emulated by others. Quite to the contrary. As this chapter will show, First World states were understood to have serious problems with inequality between men and women. They were furthermore charged with having exported doctrines of male superiority to the developing world and for creating an unjust international economic order highly harmful to "Third World women."

Not all states were considered substandard, however. The UN discussions of NWMs set socialist states apart and held these up as an ideal for others in terms of providing a more just environment for women. Women in socialist countries had reached higher levels of education, were more involved in public life and the labor market, enjoyed better legal protection and benefited from healthcare systems that significantly improved their physical wellbeing, UN reports argued. Being most advanced in terms of meeting the expectations regarding the status of women, socialist states became exempt from creating NWMs. Why adopt a problem-solving measure if there was no, or at least only a negligible, problem?

---

[3] Other organs may of course also influence the governmental position on policies and issues affecting women, serving as a *de facto* national women's machinery in a sense – such as mass organizations of women with institutionalized ties to the government. The Vietnamese Women's Union is an example of such an organization. The focus of this chapter is on the establishment of formal state policy bureaucracies specially commissioned to advance women rather than the myriad organizations that may also carry on work with relevance for women in public policy.

First World and Third World states alike were considered to be in need of NWMs. For the Third World, this allegedly involved reversing and overcoming the negative impact of colonialism as well as modernization based on First World models. Core states of what had previously been called "civilized society" and whose liberal principles had been championed as vital for the advancement of women thus hardly set the standard for others to emulate. Instead, the formal documents of international society pointed to socialist states as well as some "traditional" societies as the most progressive and just polities for women.

The story about the international spread of policy bureaus for women is a story of norms and social hierarchies. Two primary dimensions of distinction and rank were present in the deliberations around NWMs – between states of the capitalist West and of the communist East, on the one hand, and between the "developed" and the "developing" world on the other. Importantly, the policy bureaus were created among states ranked as lesser in terms of the advancement of women and thus emerged from below. And they did not spread to the states considered far ahead with regard to sexual equality. It would take the fall of communism before these states would create national bureaus to oversee the advancement of women.

National women's policy bureaus have largely been seen as a technical response to the problematic of the status of women. As such, the establishment of these bureaucracies has generated very little mobilization among activists. In contrast with suffrage and legislature quotas, there were no transnational activist movements advocating the creation of NWMs, even though a few domestic women's organizations have backed their creation. The promotion of NWM instead was largely in the hands of political officials and what Sawer (1996a) calls *femocrats*: civil servants and international organization bureaucrats advocating for the advancement of women within official state and interstate organs. The United Nations was the primary associational arena within which the idea of a national policy bureau for women was discussed and promoted. UN debates and deliberations thus serve as the empirical entry point to study the emergence and proliferation of NWM.

The rest of this chapter is organized in four sections. It begins by exploring the origin and trajectory of NWMs, asking the "what, where and when" questions that provide the first indications of the norms and identities at stake. The subsequent section continues with a textual analysis of the many UN documents surrounding the discussions of

NWMs, bringing into the analysis the webs of meaning of the state representatives and of UN bureaucrats who deliberated the change. The section is organized to discuss social hierarchies along two broad dimensions, namely the communist East as superior to the capitalist West, and the differentiation and rank between the First and the Third Worlds. The third section briefly analyzes NWMs as creatures of ongoing constitution and asks questions about international rank subsequent to their initial creation. The chapter ends by drawing out the implications of the worldwide proliferation of NWMs for the study of norms and stratification in international society.

The global trajectory of national machinery on the status of women

The trajectory of the creation of national policy bureaus on the status of women provides the first clues as to the norms and hierarchies entailed in the commissions' proliferation. Before we turn to look at the worldwide path of state agencies for the general advancement of women, there are precursors that merit some attention. Specialized bureaucracies dealing with women as laborers developed in the wake of the post-World War I resurgence of mobilization around the woman question. Unlike the contemporary women's machineries, these bureaus were not concerned with a general advancement of women but rather with women specifically in their role as workers. These agencies oversaw the working conditions of women laborers in attempts to ensure compliance with labor regulations (e.g. legislation regulating overtime, night work, safety conditions, and special protection of mothers and pregnant women).

From a brief examination of the trajectory of their proliferation, it is clear that the creation of a formal organ for women workers on a national level cannot be traced authoritatively to a single founding state. In this sense, the emergence of women's machineries is similar to that of suffrage and quotas. However, whereas suffrage was first adopted in states that were largely peripheral to what was then known as "civilized international society," the first women's bureaus were created in two states emerging as central to international society. In August of 1919, after two years of pressure and maneuvering within the party by the Bolsheviks most committed to the woman question, possibly the world's first formal state bureau for women was created in

Russia.[4] Known as the Zhenotdel (Women's Department), the bureau
had a central directing staff of forty employees.[5] A similar federal
agency to create "standards and policies which shall promote the welfare of wage-earning women" was established by the US Congress in
1920, called the Women's Bureau of the Department of Labor. Between
then and the mid-1960s, at least thirty additional state labor divisions
for women were set up around the world.[6] It is noteworthy for our
purposes that the vast majority of these bureaus were located in Latin
America, and were often created before women of the Americas were
granted voting rights, with European states establishing such agencies
relatively late. The Inter-American Commission for Women appears to
have been an important catalyst for their establishment.

A change away from labor bureaus to the institutionalization of a
general or unified concern with the "status of women" in all spheres of
life emerged with the December 1961 creation of a President's
Commission on the Status of Women by the Kennedy administration.[7]
Unlike suffrage mobilization and legislation, which developed in discursively, geographically and temporally distinct waves, subsequent
divisions for the advancement of women came into being quite quickly,
almost explosively, in various parts of the world. If we look at
Table 6.1, a seemingly wide range of states is among the first twenty
to create advisory commissions. At first sight, no clear overall pattern
emerges akin to that of suffrage. What we can say is that even though
the first such commission was established in the USA, the subsequent
trajectory of creation does not indicate a uniquely European or Western
nature of the change, nor does it suggest that Western state identities are
necessarily the ones centrally at stake.

[4] Hayden 1976: 157; Stites 1976.   [5] Hayden 1976: 165.
[6] Although there is mention of the existence of women's labor departments in
socialist states, I have been unable to find data on the exact years of creation with
the exception of Russia (1919), Bulgaria (1945) and Cuba (1960). In non-socialist
states, between 1919 and 1965, the following women's labor bureaus were
created: USA (1920), Mexico (1936), Argentina (1944), Peru (1945), Netherlands
(1946), Japan (1947), Haiti (1950), Panama (1950), Papua New Guinea (1950),
West Germany (1950), El Salvador (1951), Colombia (1952), Canada (1954),
Dominican Republic (1954), Bolivia (1955), Guatemala (1957), Norway (1959),
Central Africa (1960), Philippines (1960), Italy (1962), United Kingdom (1962),
Australia (1963), Brazil (1964), and France (1965).
[7] Duerst-Lahti 1989: 255; Harrison 1980: 634.

Table 6.1 *Divisions for the advancement of women, 1961–1986*

Year of creation	Advisory commissions or committees	Permanent units or divisions	Ministries
1961	United States		
1963	Australia		
1964	Argentina		
	Malaysia		
	West Germany		
1965	Denmark		
	Nepal		
	Sweden		
1966	Finland		
	Japan		
	Philippines		
1967	Canada		
	Taiwan		
1968	Chile		
	Indonesia		
1969	United Kingdom		
1970	Belgium		
	India		
	Ireland		
	Madagascar		
	Netherlands		
1971	Costa Rica		
	New Zealand		
	Portugal		
1972	Egypt		
1973	Colombia	Australia	
	Guyana		
1974	Ethiopia	Gabon	
	France	Sudan	
	Pakistan		
	Somalia		
	Sudan		
	Venezuela		
	Zambia		
1975	Peru	Ghana	
	Sierra Leone	Japan	

Table 6.1 (*cont.*)

Year of creation	Advisory commissions or committees	Permanent units or divisions	Ministries
	Sri Lanka	Kenya	
	Surinam		
	Swaziland		
	Uganda		
1976	Barbados	Bangladesh	Ivory Coast
	Grenada	Canada	
	Kuwait	Madagascar	
	Lesotho	Malaysia	
	Malaysia		
	Rwanda		
1977	Thailand	Egypt	Jamaica
		Iran	
1978		Burkina Faso	Bangladesh
		Kenya	Dominica
		Senegal	Togo
		Spain	
		Sri Lanka	
1979	Cyprus	Chile	
	Maldives	Grenada	
		Lesotho	
		Nicaragua	
		Pakistan	
		Uruguay	
1980	Iceland	Bahamas	Antigua
		Colombia	Venezuela
		Costa Rica	Zimbabwe
		Dominica	
		Ecuador	Mauritania
		Equatorial Guinea	Mauritius
		Guyana	
		Nepal	
		Rwanda (Dept. for the integration of women in development)	Paraguay
		Zaire	

Table 6.1 (*cont.*)

Year of creation	Advisory commissions or committees	Permanent units or divisions	Ministries
1982	Belize	Chad	Grenada
		Greece	Rwanda
		Guinea-Bissau	
		Sweden	
1983	Bolivia	Barbados	Burundi
	South Korea	Malaysia	Cameroon
		Peru	Indonesia
			Sri Lanka
1984	Malawi	Dominican Republic	
1985	Brazil		Chile
	Mexico		New Zealand
			Zaire
1986		Belize	

Table assembled from data provided in Gruberg 1973; Åseskog 1998; Asian Development Bank 1998; Berkovitch 1994; INSTRAW 2000; Sawer 1996a; Sveriges Riksdag 2000. Judicial equality ombudsman offices are *not* included in this listing.

The seemingly random trajectory of these changes appears less puzzling when we consider that NWMs developed within the United Nations context after the Economic and Social Council (ECOSOC) quickly swept the issue away from the USA. Instead of several generative frameworks as was the case with women's suffrage, all member states were thus in immediate conversation about NWMs within the UN.

At the urging of the UN Commission on the Status of Women, in 1963 ECOSOC passed a resolution making its first recommendation on the creation of national commissions on the status of women only two years after the US commission was created, the first of four such resolutions between 1963 and 1972.[8] Between 1963 and 1970, a series of

---

[8] Resolution 961F (XXXVI, as recommended by Social Committee, E/3810, adopted unanimously by Council on July 12, 1963, meeting 1280) called on member states to appoint "national commissions on the status of women,

primarily UN-initiated meetings subsequently discussed and recommended the establishment of national women's commissions in all regions of the world, a sign of the measure receiving virtually immediate worldwide consideration.[9] Whereas the advocacy for suffrage developed in waves across the globe over a sixty-year period, the UN promotion of these advisory commissions made possible the simultaneous worldwide attention to the matter by all member states.

The UN calls for women's full integration into national life did not develop in the total absence of social movement demands, and there was in many cases some sort of domestic trigger for the creation of national machinery. The President's Commission was indeed established without any such demands, responding instead to internal bureaucratic pressures from the US Women's Bureau. It is noteworthy that the commission preceded the appearance of a new and forceful US women's movement by several years.[10] A brief investigation suggests that at least some of the subsequent commissions were prompted by domestic demand by women's organizations that had picked up the model from the USA. Not long after its 1960 creation, the Malaysian National Council of Women's Organizations advocated for the establishment of the 1964 commission, which "would seek to improve women's status in terms of equality of opportunities to education and access to legal

---

composed of leading men and women with experience in government service, education, employment, community development and other aspects of public life, to develop plans and make recommendations for improving the status of women in their respective countries" (United Nations 1963: 351). ECOSOC resolutions 1068 D(XXXIX) of July 1965; 1209 (XLII) of May 1967; and 1682 (LII) of June 1972 also called for the establishment of national commissions.

[9] The following meetings passed resolutions or otherwise urged states to establish national commissions to study and make recommendations on problems affecting the status of women: 1963, Seminar on the Status of Women in Family Law (Bogotá, Colombia); 1964, African Seminar on the Status of Women in Family Law (Lomé, Togo); 1966, Seminar on Measures Required for the Advancement of Women, with Special Reference to the Establishment of a Long-Term Programme (Manila, the Philippines); 1968, International Conference on Human Rights (Teheran, Iran); 1968, Seminar on the Civic and Political Education of Women (Accra, Ghana); 1971, working group on national women's machinery (Rabat, Morocco); 1972, Seminar on the Status of Women and Family Planning (Istanbul, Turkey). United Nations Branch for the Advancement of Women 1987: 3–4.

[10] On the importance of US government initiatives for prompting the US women's movement of the 1960s, see Duerst-Lahti 1989; Harrison 1980.

aid."[11] Organized Philippine women likewise promoted the creation of their 1966 commission. In Canada, similarly, the first aim of the 1966 Committee for Equality of Women (representing 2 million Canadian women of thirty-three groups) was to advocate for a Canadian version of the US commission, established in early 1967 with the Federal Royal Commission on the Status of Women.[12] Many commissions, such as the Swedish and Danish ones, were not preceded by women's movement demands. In yet other cases, intervention by political parties or parliamentary women's caucuses prompted the creation of the commission. In Australia, for instance, it was the involvement by the parliamentary organization Women's Electoral Lobby (WEL) in the 1972 federal election that served as the trigger for the creation of a prime minister's advisory body in 1973 as well as the Office for the Status of Women.

If the first advisory commission appeared out of bureaucratic pressures within the US state, a premier representative of the liberal West, it was the Soviet-supported transnational women's organization Women's International Democratic Federation (WIDF) that in 1972 proposed the declaration of a UN Women's Year for 1975.[13] The decision to convene a related world conference on women was made only in 1974, however, leaving a mere year – unusually little time – for preparation. The early 1970s nonetheless saw the convening of regional and preparatory world meetings by the UN, several of them specifically on the question of more permanent institutional structures for the advancement of the status of women, to replace the advisory commissions. There was a subsequent shift to advocacy for and establishment of enduring institutional structures during this period and thereafter.

The first document to elaborate specific guidelines on the type and form of permanent machinery was published by the UN Economic Commission for Africa (ECA) in 1973.[14] The 1974 Interregional

---

[11] Asian Development Bank 1998: 37.   [12] Gruberg 1973: 23.

[13] Pietilä and Vickers 1994: 76. The proposal was presented by the Romanian representative on the UN Commission on the Status of Women. In 1972, the Commission subsequently recommended to the General Assembly the declaration of 1975 as International Women's Year.

[14] The publication was titled "National Commissions on women and development and women's bureaux." United Nations Branch for the Advancement of Women 1987: 4.

Seminar on National Machinery to Accelerate the Integration of
Women in Development and to Eliminate Discrimination on
Grounds of Sex (Ottawa, Canada) was particularly important in
developing the concept of national machinery as an umbrella term,
denoting any of a broad range of institutional forms.[15] Like each
of the following UN world conferences on women, the 1975 World
Plan of Action recommended the establishment of an "inter-
disciplinary and multisectoral machinery within the Government for
accelerating the achievement of equal opportunities for women and
their full integration into national life."[16] The surge in commissions
established in the 1974–6 period points to the importance of UN
activities. Well over half of the NWMs were set up during the
Decade for Women.[17]

Between the first and the second World Congress (1975 and 1980), a
series of national, regional and international meetings discussed NWM
as a mechanism for such integration, as a primary question or as a
complementary one.[18] During this period, according to the UN Branch
for the Advancement of Women, "national machinery was not seen, by
any means, as a way of solving all the problems of women."[19] Another
UN report explained that "it was important to base national machinery
on some well thought-out philosophy relating to the society as a
whole."[20] The question we will turn to next is what these national
goals and needs were for which national machinery appeared a feasible
solution. What were the overall philosophies that were to undergird

[15] United Nations Branch for the Advancement of Women, Background Paper 1,
1987: 7.
[16] United Nations 1975c: para. 46.
[17] United Nations Branch for the Advancement of Women 1987: 7.
[18] E.g. the 1976 Latin American Seminar on the Participation of Women in
Economic, Social and Political Development: Obstacles that Hinder Their
Integration (Buenos Aires, Argentina); the 1977 Regional Seminar on the
Participation of Women in Political, Economic and Social Development, with
Special Emphasis on Machinery to Accelerate the Integration of Women in
Development (Kathmandu, Nepal) and the 1979 first meeting of the African
Regional Coordinating Committee (Rabat – the African Research and Training
Centre for Women [ARTCW] produced a report and directory on national
machinery for women in development). United Nations Branch for the
Advancement of Women 1987: 5–6.
[19] United Nations Branch for the Advancement of Women 1987: 6.
[20] United Nations 1975a: 15.

these measures? Does the apparently random emergence of NWMs indeed suggest an undifferentiated society of states concerned with the problems of generic, modern statehood?

National machineries and international stratification

By 1985, the vast majority of UN member states had formally accepted the "integration of women into national life" as a state planning objective.[21] As part of this objective, most states had furthermore created some sort of specialized bureaucracy to work for the advancement of women. It was argued that "although the problems of the full integration of women in the development effort varied greatly from country to country both in nature and scope, there were factors common to all countries, whether developing or developed."[22] The commonality identified by those deliberating the notion of a national machinery was "the many and varied problems facing women in *modern society*," "modern society" denoting all societies or sectors touched by industrial development.[23] In contrast with the European suffragists and the quota debaters of the late 1990s, the identification of "culture" as an important causal force had receded into the background in the deliberations of NWMs. Structures and relations of the *economy* – including national "level of industrialization" and the "sexual division of labor" – sometimes coupled with doctrines of *male superiority* were the forces most widely identified as the primary causes of what was now signified as relations of inequality between men and women.

As world polity scholars would argue, establishing NWMs to address the status of women had indeed become "a necessary task of the modern state."[24] In the most abstract sense, the norm articulated by representatives of the world's states in UN discussions could be summed up as "Modern states [should] create a women's machinery." Of the three worldwide institutions under scrutiny in this book, NWMs seem to be the best candidates for one, generic categorical state identity, as all states are identified as modern polities in some sense.

And yet NWMs were championed in a complex and highly contentious global environment. Differentiation and hierarchies were manifest

[21] United Nations 1980a: 3.   [22] United Nations 1977: 3.
[23] United Nations 1977: 3.   [24] Finnemore 1996b: 36.

in all the debates around these bureaucracies as well as in the form the machineries were to take. On the one hand, as we shall see, the norm of modernity entailed stratification of rank, where some states were signified as more advanced than others. On the other, there were also differences in kind among modern states, most conspicuously between socialist, Western capitalist, and Third World states. Multiple interpretations of how the ideal modern state polity should be organized in the continuous adjustments of modernization differentiated among several varieties of modern statehood. Whereas NWMs were advocated as a means for sexual equality as a component of modern statehood, the intensity and dynamism around their creation derived from the differentiation and hierarchal ordering among groupings of modern states rather than from some quest for generic statehood.

Modernization was approached primarily as economic processes of industrialization in the deliberations around NWM. The NWM discussions thus distinguished among states along two broad dimensions: (1) degree of modernization or development and (2) type of economic system. In the sections that follow, I first tend to the contention and differentiation between the communist East and capitalist West. We then turn our attention to the strife and stratification between the First and the Third World.

NWMs and competitive hierarchies between the communist East and capitalist West

The contention between communist and capitalist states had been central to the creation of the very first national machinery, the 1961 US President's Commission on the Status of Women. Like some other Americans, commission chair Eleanor Roosevelt had long been concerned about the Soviet world leadership and advancement on the status of women.[25] The Soviets were relentless in upholding the progress of Soviet women as an indication of the superiority of socialism to capitalist democracy, approaching the advancement of women in relative terms. Demonstrating that women were *more* liberated under socialism than under Western capitalist systems was an important component in the struggle against the West. In response, the President's Commission was charged with "recounting the story of

---

[25] See Roosevelt 1995.

women's progress in a free, democratic society."[26] The justification for the commission was rather utilitarian, making little if any mention of justice for women and emphasizing instead the importance of women for the progress of the American nation as the leader of the free world. "It is in the national interest to promote the economy, security and national defense through the most efficient and effective utilization of the skills of all persons," the Executive Order that established the commission read, emphasizing that "prejudices and outmoded customs act as barriers to the full realization of women's basic rights which should be respected and fostered as part of our Nation's commitment to human dignity, freedom, and democracy." Strengthening the free world in its struggle with communism involved ceasing to treat women as a "marginal group whose skills have been inadequately utilized." The advancement of women was thus approached both as an important symbolic marker of the freedom women enjoyed in the USA and as an important source to strengthen its economic and security interests.

The report of the commission, *American Women*, was subsequently published in 200,000 copies and widely distributed, helping to repoliticize and make more widely respectable to the US public the discussion of a broad range of issues as women's "status" and "role."[27] The creation of this commission almost immediately became part of foreign policy, if only peripherally, as the US government sought to spread information about the commission via the publication of a booklet on the commission for international consumption among other activities.[28] *American Women* was translated into a host of languages, including German, Italian, Japanese and Swedish, and helped to prompt the creation at least of the Canadian commission, as we saw above.

Within a short period, the United Nations became the main arena for debating the status of women and the creation of national machineries. In UN documents, the status of women was discussed in absolute rather than relative terms, with equality set out as something any state should aspire to and could attain, regardless of the sexual equality situation in other states. The discussions were nevertheless comparative and upheld socialist states – not those of Western capitalism – as having come closest to meeting the expectations of advancing the status of women.

---

[26] US President's Commission on the Status of Women 1963: iv.
[27] Duerst-Lahti 1989: 257.   [28] Gruberg 1973: 1.

Despite the US initiative with the President's Commission, a major UN review of national machinery explained that:

As stated above in the review of national machinery, the approach of the socialist countries differs from that of the market economies. Significant progress has been achieved in the socialist countries in increasing the participation of women in all aspects of national life and the protection of their rights. Specifically, the involvement of women in social production through the advancement of their educational standards and occupational skills has become a distinctive feature of the socialist economies, where women constitute 42–51 per cent of the factory and office workers of the Council for Mutual Economic Assistance (CMEA) member countries. Women's political awareness has increased, enabling them to participate more fully in public life and the administration of government, while a comprehensive system of protection of female labor and mother and child care has significantly improved the health status of women. The experiences of the non-socialist countries have been different and merit a more detailed approach.[29]

Many of these market economies whose neglect of women warranted larger scrutiny by the UN – e.g. Great Britain, the United States, France – had of course been core states of the prior civilized society whose liberal principles these states had championed as vital for the advancement of women in the world at large. Now, the formal documents of international society celebrated not the states of Western civilization but rather their socialist rivals as the most progressive and just polities for women. Indeed, as Tinker and Jaquette sum up the decade, "the UN consensus moved ahead of that in the United States."[30]

If we take a second look at Table 6.1, there is a noticeable absence of socialist states among those listed as having created NWMs. Having already officially resolved the woman question, there was allegedly little if any need for a state bureaucracy to integrate women into national life. Preparing a 1973 paper for the American Political Science Association, its author received a letter from the head of the Czech International Relations Division of the Ministry of Labor and Social Affairs, stating that a commission on the status of women was not under consideration because

[29] UN 1980b: 10. *Review and Evaluation of Progress Achieved in the Implementation of the World Plan of Action: National Machinery and Legislation.*
[30] Tinker and Jaquette 1987: 423.

women enjoy in Czechoslovakia the same status and the same rights and opportunities as men in every field. The contribution of women to society is fully recognized and their integration in the total development process in all sectors is in accordance with the Constitution as well as the Government's policy.[31]

In their stead, socialist state representatives pointed to a long tradition of women's wings of the socialist party.[32] Rather than being civil servant units, these women's wings were expressly political units of the state, created to mobilize women peasants, workers and housewives and to draw them into political organization in the manner discussed in the previous chapter. As a result of these differing forms of state organization, a 1980 UN report explained that "the nature of the machinery varies according to the specific socio-economic and political system of each State."[33]

Rather than leading to a world of isomorphism in which undifferentiated states respond to general calls to be modern, the creation of NWMs so far demonstrates systematic differentiation among socialist states and market democracies. These states were not simply differentiated, however, as the distinctions involved moral evaluations and hierarchical ordering. The particular order may be startling to those who presume that states identified as liberal, Western democracies would be the ones validated as most advanced in their treatment of female nationals. The expectation, as expressed in the UN deliberations on national machinery, may be better summed up as: "Due to their inadequacies, non-socialist states should create a bureaucracy for the advancement of women." Socialist states apparently had no need to do so.

NWM and hierarchies among the First and Third Worlds

The supposedly advanced nature of the developed, Western states as measured by the progress of women was perhaps even more vehemently

[31] As quoted in Gruberg 1973: 32.
[32] An incomplete list of such women's wings of ruling socialist parties (and year of creation) include Vietnam (1930), North Korea (1945), East Germany (1947), China (1949), Bulgaria (1950), Romania (1952), Laos (1955), Cuba (1960), Tanzania (1962), Poland (1966), Syria (1967), Yemen (1967), Iraq (1969), Kampuchea (1971), Somalia (1971), Sudan (1971), Angola (1980), Cape Verde (1981) and Laos (1984).
[33] United Nations 1980b: 4.

challenged by delegates from Africa, Latin America and Asia. The prevalent understandings of the relation between the status of women and the modern–traditional hierarchy were consistently questioned by state representatives of the developing world, as well as certain European government representatives, Western WID scholars, and activists. To understand the significance of this challenge, we shall step back momentarily to discuss prior representations of women and development.

The intensified concern with the status of women within the UN system and its specialized agencies had emerged out of the UN decades for development, and more specifically the UN's Second Development Decade. Development as a discourse entailed an impending sense of crisis in what became known as the developing world, where mounting collections of data demonstrated the enormous gaps between the First and Third Worlds in what were taken to be indicators of the basic necessities for a dignified human life: life expectancy, literacy, access to potable water, medical care and so on. Beginning in the late 1960s and escalating in the early 1970s, so-called women's issues came to the fore in several of the UN-convened world conferences to address challenges to world development, particularly on the issue of population and poverty.

Until this time, the sparse treatments of women and Third World industrialization by West European and US scholars had presumed that modern economic development would automatically raise the status of women, reminiscent of the views of the liberating effects of Western civilization. Modernization had been thought to be a linear process away from traditional life, similar for all societies, with positive effects for women. The liberating effects of industrialization and technology had been taken for granted rather than investigated, however, and they rested on the assumption that these developments would necessarily reduce the social impact of presumed sexual asymmetries in physical strength between women and men. Moving away from the brute facts of nature, it was thought, men would no longer be able to dominate women through sheer strength. As an excerpt from an influential advocate of Third World industrialization may illustrate, these assumptions appear to be mere reiterations of the postulations of "civilization" that were discussed in Chapter 4:

Women benefit from [growth] even more than men ... Woman gains freedom from drudgery, is emancipated from the seclusion of the household, and gains at last the chance to be a full human being, exercising her mind and her talents in the same way as men. It is open to men to debate whether economic progress is good for men or not, but for women to debate the desirability of economic growth is to debate whether women should have the chance to cease to be beasts of burden, and to join the human race.[34]

Such understandings obviously rested on a division between the traditional and the modern world and the reproduction as an unquestioned given that tradition needed to give way to state-led modernization to assure human progress. Modernized states were presumed to produce egalitarian sexual relations, at least as a long-term end result, whereas traditional societies were taken to be oppressive to women. The identification of tradition as tyrannical was indeed analogous to the representations of women in "savage society" that had circulated a mere half century earlier. However, there seems to have been almost complete, collective amnesia within the development establishment about savage society having been chastised by the Europeans for retaining a political role for women and for their failures to establish appropriate, separate sexual spheres. Indeed, if we recall from Chapter 4, Europeans used to hold that it was their unique consciousness of sexual difference that distinguished them from savages.[35]

In Europe and the USA, feminist critiques of sex-role theory emerged in the 1960s. These critiques responded to predominant views that sexual divisions of labor functioned as a form of specialization that would bring about economic growth and other forms of progress through the principle of comparative advantage. A wide range of scholars and politicians, including prominent sociologist Emile Durkheim, contended that sexual differentiation was part of an efficient and thereby necessary division of labor.[36] Differentiation, it was widely held, was indeed necessary for sexual attraction and thereby ensured the reproduction of the species.

Arguing that sex roles were neither complementary nor a rational adaptation to modernization, feminist interpretations contended that many sexual differences – even those most intimately part of sexual life – should be understood as an expression of a power-laden subordination of women to men. The most vibrant arena of European feminist debate in the 1970s was socialist feminism in its grappling with the integration

---

[34] Lewis 1955: 422. I was initially made aware of the work of Lewis and of this quotation through Kabeer 1994: 19.
[35] See also J. W. Scott 1996: 9.   [36] E.g. J. W. Scott 1996.

of historical materialism and patriarchy. Even the scholars that shied away from the core tenets of socialism drew on and developed earlier socialist work on the woman question, most notably that of Engels. In the United States, in turn, liberal feminism was most animated, developing the concepts of equal opportunity and discrimination to challenge sex roles.

The notion that the technological and structural economic changes brought about by industrialization had harmed rather than benefited European and North American women became widespread among liberal and socialist feminists alike and permeated the international fora where NWMs were discussed. As an example, the Swedish report to the 1975 UN Women's Conference states that

In the 1850s Sweden was a poor agricultural country on Europe's fringe ... Peasant women and middle-class townswomen played an important role as producers of food, clothing and other necessities of life for a large family ... The process of industrialization during the second half of the nineteenth century wrought great changes in the social and economic situation of the Swedish people ... Industrialization brought with it a ruthless exploitation of women and children, not because labor was scarce but because they were cheap labor.[37]

Delegates from Africa, Asia and Latin America (together with some European and North American WID scholars, activists, and government representatives) also intervened in the discussions about modernization and the status of women. Like their northern counterparts, they largely accepted the division of the world into modern and traditional spheres and First and Third World states. However, they re-signified the presumed relation of state categorization and rank to the status of women by charging that it was *modernization* and the modern world that had harmed women in developing states. Development was thereby importantly identified as a cause of the subordination of women rather than its automatic solution. Indeed,

there was a consensus that over-all economic and social progress did not automatically benefit women and place them in the mainstream of development as full partners with men. At the highest level women rarely had a voice in the formulation of policies on broad issues affecting the development of society. At the lowest level, women frequently did not benefit from the

---

[37] Sandberg 1975: 11–12. Swedish report to the UN World Conference on Women.

modernization process ... The participants therefore welcomed the convening of the seminar which would permit them to pool among themselves the knowledge and experience gained in the establishment of bodies to review and evaluate women's positions, as well as recommend and implement measures and priorities to ensure the full participation of women in all sectors of national life on an equal footing with men.[38]

The problem for women was not necessarily "tradition" in this view, but rather the inequality that modernization created between men and women.[39] Men may have advanced with modernization, whereas "insufficient attention to women has meant retardation of their advancement," a development that in turn created a gap in power and resources between men and women.[40] A regional UN seminar in Africa concluded that "a division of activities between the sexes was understandable, but, as advancements were made in the modernization process, the traditional ways often became handicaps and discriminatory against females."[41]

It was to counter the male marginalization of women's productive and reproductive capacity and potential, the arguments went, that NWMs must be established. "The predominant economic analyses of labor and capital insufficiently trace the linkages between production systems in world economics and women's work as producers and reproducers; nor is the subjection, exploitation, oppression and domination of women by men sufficiently explained in history," the introduction to the 1980 UN report of the World Conference on Women stated. NWMs were therefore charged with generating statistics and economic analyses that traced such linkages and identified the main areas of oppression of women in all non-socialist states alike.

At this juncture, it may be helpful to pause and reconsider the suggestion that "obviously ... the poor and weak and peripheral copy the rich and strong and central ... [these states] would undoubtedly turn first to American, Japanese, or European models for much of their social restructuring."[42] It was not Western capitalist states but socialist ones that were upheld as models in advancing the status of women in the

---

[38] United Nations 1975a: 3–5. *Interregional Seminar on National Machinery to Accelerate the Integration of Women in Development.*
[39] For two prominent examples, see Boserup 1970; Rogers 1980.
[40] United Nations 1975b: 7.   [41] United Nations 1975c: 8.
[42] Meyer *et al.* 1997: 164.

1970s and 1980s UN context. Rather than being beneficial for women, and more in line with earlier socialist interpretations of the effects of capitalism on women, modernization was furthermore now charged with having lowered the status of women relative to men. Non-European tradition was thereby also endorsed as empowering for women, defying the common claims that Western-led modernization would bring liberation and dignity to women. As we shall see, rather than merely copying the "rich and strong and central," Asian, Latin American and African NWMs were created in complex attempts to challenge, subvert and come to terms with the developed world. The norms of national machinery thereby not only prompted the creation of similar state institutions; they drew upon and spawned social hierarchies among states as well.

The discussions surrounding the establishment of NWMs often held that the integration of women into economic life had not been a problem for "traditional" society. As one scholar noted, "Women are in a qualitatively different position in [modern] societies than they are in societies where what has been called the 'household economy' is the *entire* economy."[43] In defense of the status of women in traditional life, the report of an African regional seminar on women in development similarly argued that "women are fully engaged in the economic and social tasks in the traditional sectors of African life." However, "the traditional role of African women in economic life is neither evident nor acknowledged in the modern sectors of agriculture, industry, commerce and government."[44] As Nigerian representative Bolanle Awe argued at a 1975 UN seminar, "it was known that [prior to industrialization and colonialism], women had been village chiefs in many parts of Africa."[45]

The presumed causal relationship between modernization and the status of women was thereby turned on its head. Proponents for the advancement of the status of women once again operated within existing international hierarchies but reversed and re-signified the implications for women. This reversal is quite remarkable, if we consider the prevalence of the notion that "general progress" would bring advancement for women. What is more, Western industrialized states and the modernization they had allegedly set in motion in the developing world

---

[43] Leacock 1978: 250.   [44] United Nations 1975c: 1, "Plan of Action."
[45] Tinker and Bramsen 1976: 143. From the "Proceedings of the Seminar on Women in Development, Mexico City, June 15–18, 1975."

were charged with hindering the advancement of the independent and alternative, if modern, national polities of the Third World.

The focus on economic processes did generate momentary expressions of a shared experience among women of North and South, East and West, as oppressed subjects of similarly modernizing states. Shared notions of a common female experience of subjection, with women as subjects of modernizing states differentiated only by rank, proved brief and elusive, however. Many Asian, African and Latin American women argued that their lack of advancement was not simply the effect of similar but laggard structural modernization processes. Developed states, modern international institutions and First World feminist scholars were indicted for having advanced at the expense of the Third World, for having actively created and sustained an unjust international order. In other words, there was a difference in *kind* between the experiences of First World and Third World women, as nationals of categorically different states. First World feminists were chastised for having misinterpreted and mischaracterized the nature of sexual differentiation in "traditional" society. It was argued that contrary to the accounts provided by First World academics and policy-makers, separate sexual spheres in traditional society were often complementary rather than hierarchical in function and power.[46] The inequalities between men and women in "traditional" society, many contended, were simply not as stark as suggested in First World accounts.

Rather than "traditional" patriarchy, the international economic system was put forward as a more important determining force for the unequal status of women. Retorting to the claims that general progress in developing states would bring about an advancement of women, it was widely argued that "the inequality of women in most countries stems to a very large extent from mass poverty and general backwardness of the majority of the world's population caused by underdevelopment which is a product of imperialism, colonialism, neo-colonialism and also of unjust international economic relations."[47] The vice-president of the Peruvian women's commission charged that the participation of women, "particularly those from developing countries, is central in the vindication of workers, peasants and Third World

[46] E.g. Rogers 1975; Rosaldo and Lamphere 1974.
[47] "Roots of Inequality of Women," UN World Conference of the United Nations Decade of Women 1980a: 7.

women through the revolutionary processes and the struggles of
national liberation against colonialism and neo-colonialism."[48]

First World international development institutions were also taken to
task for the oppression of women in developing countries. A body of
feminist WID scholarship emerged, from nationals of developing and
developed states alike, which charged development organs with the
marginalization of women. This literature plainly challenged the prevailing wisdom within development discourse that "traditional societies
are male-dominated and authoritarian, and modern societies are democratic and egalitarian."[49] Influenced by First World doctrines of male
supremacy and populated by men, the UN Development Programme
was indicted for the omission of women from its programs.[50] It was
emphasized that "in several countries [national development] planners
resort to program evaluation manuals which are issued by international
organizations and agencies. None of these manuals, however, contained
any references to the evaluation of programs with regard to women."[51]

Some significant aspects of development planning that were harmful to
women were singled out as follows: failure to take into account women's
economic contribution and traditional economic activities in the informal
sector and in land use; inadequate knowledge of and concern with economic
resources at the household level; insufficient consideration of the likely impact
of innovation schemes on existing patterns of food production and proces-
sing; and weak inadequate provisions for consultation with people, especially
women, whose future is affected by development plans; strong male
predominance in planning and tokenism of women.[52]

The worldwide creation of NWMs cannot be characterized as a simple
imposition of Western institutions or a clear set-up of the industrialized
North as superior to the developing South. Inverting contentions that
placed the West as most advanced, many argued that in "pre-
industrialized societies, women had a positive role from which they
derived power, but that the West is 'exporting' a middle-class definition
of women's work to these countries which undermines this traditional

---

[48] Oviedo de Sarmiento at the first UN World Conference on Women in Mexico
City. Comisión Nacional de la Mujer Peruana 1975b: 2.

[49] Jaquette 1982: 269. Other influential critical WID works include the classic by
Boserup 1970 as well as Staudt 1978 and 1982, Tinker 1976 and many others.

[50] E.g. United Nations 1975a: 10.   [51] United Nations 1977: 3.

[52] United Nations 1977: 4.

role."[53] The advocated NWM solution was not an emulation of those very states that had allegedly exported doctrines of male superiority to the developing world, but rather an attempt to find modern alternatives to the European West. Indeed, as the proceedings from a major 1975 UN seminar preceding the first World Conference concluded, "there was a clear consensus that the Western model of development is not a panacea for improving the condition of women."[54] Rather than fostering institutions to replicate developed states, it was stated over and over again that national machinery must be created and understood "in the context of the historical, cultural and social background of each country ... types of machinery could not be transferred *in toto* from one country to another. They had to be adapted to national goals and needs."[55]

Conclusion

In the last chapter, we saw that the adoption of suffrage legislation first moved from the periphery to the core of the European society of civilized states, spreading from there with considerable effort and in clustered waves over almost a century. National women's policy agencies became a simultaneous concern of virtually all states of international society. Their trajectory of creation appears random, though with a slight over-representation of Western capitalist states, and they were not the target of any transnational or domestic activism to speak of. How are we to best account for the worldwide emergence of these state bureaus for the advancement of women? And what, if anything, does their creation have in common with the spread of suffrage?

True and Mintrom (2001) explain the creation of national machinery with reference to transnational networks of women's advocates, including formal efforts by governmental officials and informal struggles by NGOs. They carefully show that the more inclusive and prestigious the official delegation attending UN conferences on women (containing not only public officials but also NGO representatives, and including a minister rather than lower-level representatives), and the higher the

---

[53] Tinker and Bramsen 1976: 142. From the "Proceedings of the Seminar on Women in Development, Mexico City, June 15–18, 1975."

[54] Tinker and Bramsen 1976: 142. From the "Proceedings of the Seminar on Women in Development, Mexico City, June 15–18, 1975."

[55] United Nations 1975a: 13.

number of women's international non-governmental organizations (INGOs) with affiliate organizations in the country, the higher the likelihood of adopting a national machinery. While there is no reason to doubt these correlations as such, the subsequent conclusions about the causal dynamic – that the absence of NGO/INGO activism would explain the absence of a national machinery, for instance – are fundamentally flawed. First, no evidence is presented that domestic or transnational women's activists advocated for the creation of NWMs *per se*, although they are clearly responsible for raising the issues of gender inequality that these agencies address. Second and more importantly, the presence of NGO representatives and the number of women's INGOs is not a good indicator of advocacy for gender equality in socialist societies, since these do not distinguish between public and private life and do not support the existence of NGOs. It is hardly surprising that socialist countries would have a low score on any NGO measures. The third problem is the assumption that the non-creation of a national machinery equals a lack of interest in women's issues and in the norms of international society. For instance, what are we to make of the fact that it was the Soviet-led WIDF that suggested the declaration of a UN Women's Year for 1975, and that the proposal was presented by the Romanian representative on the UN Commission on the Status of Women? Had the authors looked at the meaning attributed to the creation of women's policy agencies, they would have recognized that the absence of these agencies among socialist countries was an indication of their alleged compliance with the expectations about sexual equality expressed in the United Nations. In the absence of a problem, presumably, there is no need for problem-solving measures such as a women's policy agency.

World polity scholars have paid considerable attention to state ministries and bureaucracies, although a 1994 dissertation chapter by Berkovitch remains the only treatment of national women's agencies from this perspective. Berkovitch argues that NWMs were created "by states' response to world models, not by internal pressures"; UN bodies picked up the notion from the US Presidential Commission and popularized the idea among remaining states.[56] Relations among states do not figure in the explanation, and social hierarchies are certainly not theorized as significant, presumptions shared by True and Mintrom. What took

---

[56] Berkovitch 1994: 147.

place is allegedly a change in the generic, categorical scripts of modern statehood, a change that is not presumed to be power-laden. Creating NWMs was simply the appropriate thing to do for modern states.

This chapter lends support to the world polity claim about national women's agencies becoming part of the requirements of modern statehood. It is important to note that the understanding of what "modern" statehood entailed was broad and included a number of distinctive models of advancement. The deliberations on NWMs consistently made reference to the diversity in aims and forms of modern states and the legitimacy of such diversity. Even if we agree with the world polity scholars that all states were engaged in a shared endeavor of demonstrating rationalized progress, the more specific objectives were not common to all. Instead, the ongoing constitution of these states took place in relational and often contentious terms, with some states seeking to be what others were not. What we have seen in this chapter is that the creation of NWMs, while indicative of isomorphism in one sense, also entailed systematic differentiation and rank among developed and developing states, on the one hand, and in the capitalist West and communist East, on the other.

The claim that core, Western states initiate new state institutions and then supply scripts of statehood to the remaining majority of states does not capture the dynamic by which NWMs spread around the world. Although some Western states were among the first to adopt a national women's agency, the trajectory does not unequivocally point to these states. More importantly, the developed West was not upheld as a model for the advancement of women. Socialist states were set apart as having largely solved the woman question. And their compliance with the norm largely exempted socialist states from creating a NWM at all, given their alleged solution to the woman problem. The First World was, in contrast, confronted with having problems with sexual inequality, and it was because of their inadequacies that they were called on to establish NWMs to address the subordination of women.

The First World was not simply charged with injustice at home. These states were also held responsible for the negative effects of modernization for women and were charged with bringing Western doctrines of male supremacy to the developing world through the intrusion of colonialism. The solution for developing states was not to create NWMs that simply mimicked the very states that had produced many of the miseries of "Third World women," but rather to find alternatives that advanced their status and ensured national progress. Isomorphism and more similar state identities were hardly the source or outcome of these contestations.

Instead of a simple quest for isomorphism, we need to turn to the social hierarchies of international society to account for the worldwide transformation in state institutions for the advancement of women. And in comparison with the suffrage debates and particularly with the quota deliberations that are the subject of the next chapter, it is quite remarkable that modernization and the modern world, rather than "tradition," were identified as the source of women's misery. The portrayal of modernization as damaging for women was quite novel and its predominance was indeed to prove temporary. However, it is extraordinary that for a brief moment of time, the discussions of NWMs centered on the damaging effects of modernization (the prized accomplishment of allegedly male-driven advancements) and on the injustices suffered by women.

7 | Legislature sex quotas and cultural rank

What I am against is quotas. I am against hard quotas, quotas they basically delineate based upon whatever. However they delineate, quotas, I think, vulcanize [*sic*] society. So I don't know how this fits into what everybody else is saying, their relative positions, but that's my position.

George W. Bush[1]

Introduction

A quick look at the emergence of sex quota laws to bring women into national legislatures in the past decade suggests that we may be witnessing the global development of a new measure to bring women into state institutions. The increasing use of national quota provisions suggests that the position articulated by George W. Bush above does not fit "what everybody else is saying." In fact, outside of the United States, there is growing agreement that national legislatures need to raise their levels of female delegates via quotas. This chapter focuses on the adoption of constitutional or electoral quota laws to increase the level of women in the national legislature, in other words sex quota laws regulating the national legislature.[2] Nearly fifty states, ranging from Nepal to Uganda, Ecuador and Djibouti, have adopted affirmative measures to boost their number of female legislators since 1990, and mobilization for quotas is present in over fifty other states across the world.[3]

The swift emergence of quotas has been paralleled by an equally impressive growth in quota scholarship within the subfield of women

---

[1] Spoken by Bush when he was US Republican presidential candidate, as quoted by Molly Ivins in the *San Francisco Chronicle*, January 21, 2000.

[2] Individual political parties may of course also adopt internal sex quota measures. Since political parties are not formal state institutions, their internal practices fall outside the focus of this book.

[3] IDEA 2008.

149

and politics, almost all of which centers on the relative importance of various domestic factors.[4] And yet as Krook (2006 and 2009) effectively points out, there are also crucial international dimensions to the rapid emergence of quota laws in different parts of the world, dimensions that are largely overlooked and certainly under-studied in the quota literature. The existing research, including Krook's examination of international factors, asks many important questions of quotas: How did such measures come about? Are quotas effective in bringing higher numbers of women into legislatures? What accounts for the variation in quota types and effectiveness among states?

In this chapter, I begin by asking a different and more elemental question of the worldwide emergence of quotas: *What* are quotas *about*? In other words, what are quotas a case of? Generally pointing to the importance of women's movement demands for the materialization of quotas, feminist and other scholars of women and politics claim or presume that quotas are a case of an increased democratization of states and gender justice for women as a collective.[5] In fact, such presumptions often give rise to the questions raised around quotas mentioned above.

Scholars within the constructivist international relations spectrum would most likely agree with characterizations of quotas as enhancing states' democratic nature and would concur that they provide justice and rights for women. However, in addressing what quotas are about – what makes them significant and worthy of analysis – they would shift the emphasis and claim that quotas constitute yet another instance of increasing similarity among states as well as among men and women in their ever-increasing capacity as desexed individual citizens of those states. Such outcomes would likely be traced to the existence of a new norm for state behavior.

To make this claim about isomorphism, world polity and norms scholars treat states as formally equal, individuated and unrelated to one another, subjected to a norm whose meaning is constant.

---

[4] This literature is too large to reference here. For one crucial example, see Dahlerup 2006.

[5] Scholarship making theoretical arguments about women in political decision-making, democracy and justice include Diamond and Hartsock 1998; Phillips 1991; Sapiro 1998; Squires 2000; Young 1990. Virtually all scholars who empirically study the causes and effects of quotas start with the premise that their essential meaning and implication are democracy and justice.

The given identity entailed in the proliferation of quotas is presumed by world polity scholars to be generic modern statehood, a simple "modern state" writ large. Norms scholars, in turn, would emphasize the increasingly liberal democratic identity of states and international society. In either approach, states are approached as individuated beings with no specific relations to other states or actors. Both approaches furthermore expect worldwide changes in state institutions to first take place in the "core" Western states of international society.

As this chapter will show, the global trajectory of legislature quota laws does not suggest a measure initiated in the states of the liberal West. The quota trajectory could furthermore hardly diverge more from that of women's suffrage and national machinery for the advancement of women. The present quota wave emerged primarily among Latin American states in the late 1980s and early 1990s and is now increasingly adopted in Africa and Asia.[6] The use of quotas in Europe and North America is still rare, and the question remains whether these parts of the world are capable of learning about quotas or being socialized into using quotas by the Latin Americans, Asians and Africans.

Like suffrage, quotas are presently advocated by transnational advocacy networks. The contexts of the campaigns have changed quite dramatically from that of suffrage, so that present quota debates and practices have become embedded in a more singular post-Cold War global order. Rather than developing in waves within distinct transnational contexts that generated fundamental and antagonistic fault lines among states, the contemporary quota campaigns emerged almost simultaneously in various parts of the world, being promoted as an objective for *all* states. As world polity scholars would contend, quotas are a new development in the ever-changing transformations of modern polities. However, providing one sole measure for evaluation and success, predominant representations of the world are heavily imbued with ideas of social evolution and progress away from "tradition" towards "modern" state-formation. Social hierarchies are thereby of the utmost importance in the proliferation of quotas.

[6] National legislature quotas first developed widely among socialist states in the 1950s and in intermittent and rare cases in Asia and Africa. As a "socialist" measure, these quotas never spread to other kinds of states and were abandoned with the fall of socialism as a state form. These quotas are not discussed in this chapter for space reasons. Instead, see Towns 2004.

Two variants of modern statehood emerge in these debates, coexisting uneasily. On the one hand, quotas are promoted as a modern measure to yield more *democratic* states, such states treating women at large *justly* by bringing some of them into the national assemblies. This interpretation predominated in the Latin American quota debates, among others, and is prevalent in the transnational NGO advocacy campaigns. Higher levels of women legislators are furthermore supported as a means of ensuring the success of *market-led economic reconstruction* and growth. This interpretation is spearheaded by the UNDP and the World Bank, the powerhouse global governance organs that have recently discovered the benefits of female rule. Democracy and markets are both upheld as integral to modern statehood, and both components have been present in quota discussions since they emerged in the late 1980s. The political status of woman – in this case the percentage of women legislators a state can exhibit – is once again held to be emblematic of progress. A state's moving up in the hierarchy between the "modern" and the "traditional" provides much of the urgency for passing quota legislation and thus gives leverage to quota proponents.

The analysis will be presented in four sections. The first begins by examining the global adoption trajectory, and the second section then examines the overall problematic that quotas are thought to address – modern democratic market statehood. Third, the analysis moves to the hierarchical ordering that is involved in the construction of these modern states, the hierarchy between the "advanced" and the "traditional" world. This third section includes an examination of how exactly women as a category help to move states from "tradition" to "modernity." I end with a discussion of the tactics and strategies of quota proponents that are thereby enabled, tactics that help to prompt the promulgation of quotas.

The global trajectory of quotas, 1990–2003

Legislature sex quota laws have now become an almost worldwide object of debate. The landscape of organizations, networks, states and campaigns involved in increasing the ratios of what is known as "women in decision-making" is dizzyingly enormous, spanning the globe from Latin America to Asia. Certain organs stand out as crucial nodes in this network of activities, however, including the intergovernmental organizations UNDP, the UN women's agencies, the Inter-Parliamentary Union (IPU),[7] the International Institute on Democracy and Electoral Assistance (IDEA) and the World Bank; the foreign ministries of the Netherlands, Norway and Sweden, and the transnational NGO the Women's Environment and Development Organization (WEDO). Connected to all of these organs are regional initiatives and networks of domestic and transnational NGOs, development banks, intergovernmental organizations and other actors.

Whereas the transnational concern for women's suffrage was raised and sustained by women's movements that primarily operated outside of formal institutions, the attention worldwide on women in decision-making was fairly quickly embraced by established international organizations in collaboration with NGOs and scholars after initial promotion by women activists. The UN Decade on Women (1976–85) heightened the interest in the status of women, though the recommendations and treatment of women in political decision-making were vague and general.[8] During that period, efforts to increase the numbers of women in political parties and legislatures developed in a number of states across the world, initially with most success in the Scandinavian countries and the Netherlands.

Transnational mobilization advocating affirmative action quickly emerged in Latin American states in the second half of the 1980s, at the outset stimulated by social democratic debates on internal party quotas in Europe. The party quota debates of the Partido Socialista Obrero Español in 1987 and 1990 were closely followed by the parties of the left in Latin America.[9] Two Socialist International conferences were crucial for establishing the notion that quotas are the most effective way to bring women into decision-making. In June 1986, at the

---

[7] Examples of regional or national organizations of parliamentarians advocating larger ratios of women in national legislatures include the Association of West European Parliamentarians for Africa (AWEPA) (Netherlands), Center for Asia-Pacific Women in Politics (CAPWIP) (Philippines), Organization of Women Parliamentarians from Muslim Countries (Pakistan), and Parliamentarians for Global Action (PGA) (US).

[8] The 1952 Convention on the Political Rights of Women simply spells out the legality of women holding public office. The Convention on the Elimination of All Forms of Discrimination Against Women, in turn, does not directly advocate increasing female levels of representation but rather establishes the legality of affirmative action.

[9] Lubertino Beltrán 1992: 28.

XIII Congress of Socialist International Women held in Lima, Peru, the participants rejected the idea of gradual reform in favor of affirmative action: "Only the Scandinavians, who had modified this [gradual] strategy with that of quotas (40%) had finally had a relative success: the election in Norway of a female prime minister and seven ministers."[10] The Socialist International itself endorsed affirmative action as a principle for gender equality at its XVIII Congress in Stockholm in 1989, an endorsement that was crucial for the initiation of the quota debate in Argentina that same year.[11] In 1989, bills demanding that a certain percentage of all party candidacies be reserved for women had been proposed in Costa Rica, Argentina and Paraguay. This demand amounted to a legislature quota law, a qualitative difference from the internal quotas that individual parties may adopt. In 1990, the V Encuentro Feminista Latinoamericano y del Caribe declared itself in favor of such quotas and La Red Latinoamericana de Feministas Políticas was formed to promote their promulgation across Latin America.[12]

In 1990, the year of the Encuentro and the formation of the Latin American feminist network, sustained and focused international action to enhance the levels of women in parliaments took off among global governance organs. That year, the Commission on the Status of Women named equality in political participation and decision-making a priority theme, and recommended that quotas be used as an interim measure to increase the levels of women in elected office.[13] Two states in very different parts of the world – Nepal and Argentina – passed quota legislation in 1990 and 1991 respectively. In the next few years, various international organizations began urging *political parties* to put forth

---

[10] *Mujer y Sociedad* (1986: 11), my translation.   [11] Lubertino Beltrán 1992: 30.
[12] Lubertino Beltrán 1992: 39.
[13] In preparation, the Commission requested that the Division for the Advancement of Women hold an Expert Group Meeting, which was held in Vienna in September 1989. The Expert Group recommended that "as an interim measure, substantial targets, such as quotas or similar forms of positive action to ensure women's candidacy for office and participation in political party posts, should be adopted" (United Nations Division for the Advancement of Women 1990, annex, para. 22) (UN Office at Vienna 1992). The Commission similarly recommended that governments and other representative organs take measures to increase women's representation to 30 percent by 1995 (1990:21). See also ECOSOC Resolution 1990/4: "Equality in Political Participation and Decision-Making."

female candidates, demonstrating a heightened concern with women in political decision-making but falling short of advocating legislature quota laws.[14] The work intensified in 1995 on the occasion of the UN Fourth World Conference on Women in Beijing. The Conference as well as the processes leading up to it generated discussions and recommendations on how to increase the levels of women in public office.[15] Crucially, the *Human Development Report 1995*, prepared by the UNDP for Beijing, argued for targeted measures such as quotas to attain a short-term threshold of 30 percent women in national assemblies, a goal the UNDP subsequently increased by calling for 50 percent women in national assemblies by 2005.[16] The Beijing Platform for Action, while not binding, saw 189 governments commit to taking measures to increase the levels of women in political decision-making, if necessary through positive action.[17]

Since Beijing, we have seen a virtual explosion of activity to increase the levels of women in parliament. A series of large international and regional conferences have been convened[18] and development projects

---

[14] E.g. the IPU work in 1992–3, the 1992 UN Commission on the Status of Women resolution "Women in Decision-Making Bodies." In March 1994, the Council of the IPU adopted a Plan of Action to Correct Present Imbalances in the Participation of Men and Women in Political Life, which was subsequently presented at the Beijing Conference.

[15] The 1992 resolution "Women in Decision-Making Bodies," put forth by the UN Commission on the Status of Women, asked that the regional group meetings pay attention to women in decision-making, and all of the 1994 Regional Platforms prepared in anticipation of the Beijing Conference subsequently named insufficient participation of women in public decision-making as one of the critical areas of concern. The regional group meetings were organized in Europe, Latin America and the Caribbean, Asia and the Pacific, Africa and the Arab region. At Beijing, a Parliamentary Declaration was made, urging states to establish legislative measures for equal participation of women and men in the political decision-making process.

[16] UNDP 1997.

[17] Strategic objective G.I. 190 of the Platform of Action calls on governments to "(b) take measures, including, where appropriate, in electoral systems that encourage political parties to integrate women in elective and non-elective public positions in the same proportion and at the same levels as men."

[18] E.g. IPU 1997c; UNDP, "Governance and Sustainable Equity," New York, USA, July 28–30, 1997; Netherlands Ministry of Foreign Affairs, "Women and Good Governance," Harare, Zimbabwe, May, 1998; UN Economic Commission for Africa (1998); UNDP 1999b; SADC Gender Unit, "Beyond 30 percent in 2005: Women in Politics and Decision Making in SADC," Botswana, May, 1999.

initiated,[19] by the IPU, UN agencies, IDEA, development banks, foundations, certain donor states or, most commonly, a combination of these. These international organs came to argue more forcefully that *affirmative action* was the preferable manner of achieving "gender balance" in decision-making.[20] The embracing of quotas as an appropriate state measure by *regional* intergovernmental institutions and networks of mostly elite feminist organizations has also developed remarkably since 1995.[21]

The most impressive effects to date have been in Latin America,[22] where the great majority of states have adopted quota measures

[19] E.g. the Belgian government approved a $6 million Program for Strengthening Parliaments in 1998 for UNDP implementation in twelve pilot countries, a program that gives preference to activities targeted to redressing gender imbalances in parliamentary representation (UNDP 2000: 96). The UNDP funded a $4 million governance program in Bangladesh, entitled Strengthening Parliamentary Democracy, which allegedly resulted in the extension to thirty reserved seats for women in 1997 from the prior seven, and a promise to increase to 30 percent the seats that are directly elected (rather than the present indirect election) (UNDP 2000: 97). The organ also co-financed a similar project in Vietnam together with the Dutch government.

[20] For instance, the Commission on the Status of Women called for "positive action, including such mechanisms as establishing a minimum percentage of representation for both sexes," for the first time in 1997. Essentially all of these efforts to establish quotas build on and refer back to the Platform of Action.

[21] *Africa*: in 1997, Heads of Government of the Southern African Development Community (SADC) adopted a "Declaration on Gender and Development" that pledged to reach a target of 30 percent women in all spheres of decision-making by 2005. *Asia*: South Asian Network for Political Empowerment of Women (SANPEW – India); the Advocacy Network for Gender Balance in Political Representation (Philippines). *Arab region*: the UNDP Programme on Governance in the Arab Region.

[22] After the 1990 embrace of quotas by the V Encuentro Feminista and the Red Latinoamericana de Feministas Políticas, other regional fora (e.g. the annual meetings of the "Foro Cono Sur de Mujeres Políticas," the Women's Leadership Conference of the Americas (WLCA) of the Inter-American Dialogue, and feminists of the Andean Community) came to promote quotas. The Inter-American Commission of Women has advocated the use of national legislature quota laws since 1994. The Inter-American Development Bank has funded these meetings and other projects on women in national decision-making, and it convened the conference "Women's Leadership and Representation" in September 1996. The Summit of the Americas has made proclamations in favor of increasing the ratios of women in decision-making, although without explicitly supporting quota measures. Article 18 of the first 1994 Summit of the Americas Plan of Action. See also Summit of the Americas 1998, section IV, and 2001, section 15.

Table 7.1 *Adoption of quota measures for national assemblies, 1990–2003*

Year	State	Mandated seats or candidacies for women
1990	Nepal	5%
1991	Argentina	30%
1994	Eritrea	30%
	Belgium	33%
1995	Philippines	20% women *and others*
	Uganda	56 of 304
1996	Costa Rica	40%
	Mexico	30%
	Paraguay	20%
1997	Bolivia	30% and 20%
	Brazil	25%
	Dominican Republic	25%
	Ecuador	20–50%
	Kenya	6 appointed seats
	Panama	30%
	Peru	25–30%
1998	Venezuela	30%
1999	Guyana	33.3%
	Armenia	5%
2000	France	50%
2001	Bosnia and Herzegovina	30%
2002	Djibouti	10%
	Morocco	30 of 325
	Macedonia	30%
	Serbia	30%
2003	Indonesia	30%

Table assembled from data provided by IDEA 2003.

(see Table 7.1). Of the three measures under consideration in this book, quotas are the ones least clearly linked to European and North American states. Indeed, in addition to all those of Latin America, more African and Asian – including Islamic – states than European ones have passed quota legislation. Quota bills have been introduced in numerous other parliaments, and debates are underway that will surely result in the passage of quota measures in the not so distant future.

There are good grounds for anticipating that quota legislation will be accepted in more states around the world. In 2000, the efforts to promote quotas intensified yet again. The UN five-year Review and Appraisal of the Platform for Action – Beijing + 5 – concluded that it was states such as those of Latin America, that used quotas, that had seen a significant increase in women in public office. For the occasion, the UNDP launched its landmark report *Women's Political Participation and Good Governance: 21st Century Challenges*, widely cited and subsequently translated into a number of languages. In the UN General Assembly Special Session for the five-year Review, "governments agreed to set time-bound targets, including quotas, to promote gender balance." That same year, the international advocacy network WEDO launched its program on Gender and Governance, central to which is the "50/50 Campaign: Get the Balance Right!" The campaign has since been adopted by 154 organizations in 45 countries worldwide.[23] In a milestone move, the World Bank threw its weight behind women in decision-making in two momentous publications: *Engendering Development* (2001)[24] and the follow-up *Strategy for Action* (2002). As the surest and quickest way to achieve an increased numbers of women in national legislatures, quotas seem to have become the darling of the global governance system.

Modern democracy and the business case for women in political decision-making

Given the increasing predominance and expansion of market economies, quotas are unmistakably being championed in a global economic context of neoliberal restructurings of states. However, there are many ways in which higher levels of women in decision-making could be interpreted and promoted even within our contemporary environment of free-market orthodoxy: as a matter of democratic representation, human rights, a step in eradicating men's domination of women, or, as we shall see below, specifically a matter of market-led growth. Higher levels of women legislators are overwhelmingly understood as a

[23] See www.wedo.org.
[24] Funded by the governments of Norway and the Netherlands.

question of promoting democratic institutions, on the one hand, and the presumably complementary markets enabled by such institutions on the other. As a matter of democracy and markets, quotas are advocated as not only beneficial for women but as productive of general welfare. The NWMs of the 1970s were often conceived to counter male privilege relative to women. Quotas, in contrast, are not understood to draw on any sort of conflict of interest between men and women, having instead become a win-win measure, a good for women *and* "general" society. "The attainment of power by women results in greater well-being for humanity," the Inter-American Commission stated in its 1999 *Plan of Action on Women's Participation in Power and Decision-Making Structures.* The IPU calls this the "Partnership between Men and Women in Politics," a partnership "from which society as a whole will benefit."[25] The Union explains that "what has to be developed, in modern democratic societies, is nothing less than a new social contract in which men and women work in equality and complementarity, enriching each other mutually from their differences."[26]

As a question of fair representation for women, increasing the levels of female legislators is represented as a question of justice that consti-tutes a cornerstone of "modern democracy." This was indeed the pre-dominant understanding of quotas in the Latin American quota debates and mobilizations of the 1990s. As Mexican senator Carvajal Moreno Gustavo explained at a 1997 IPU conference: "What is at stake is not just the inclusion of women in Parliaments but democracy as such: our countries want to grow, our countries want more justice. Women are key actors for the renewal of democracy."[27] Latin America of the 1990s had of course just emerged out of a traumatic period of authoritarian rule, characterized by the military administration of state bureaucracies and political units and widespread persecution of the organized political left. Latin American quota proponents, themselves of the left, capital-ized on the general elation surrounding the end of formal authoritarian rule and the prospects for democracy. As a matter of democratic justice, the very essence of the meaning of modern forms of representation was debated, centering on whether allegedly disembodied interests or

---

[25] IPU 1997a. In fact, as a tribute to this notion of complementarity, the Indian government as conference host of the 1997 IPU conference on women in decision-making released coins as well as special stamps, embodying the concept of "partnership" in the symbol of a man and a woman.
[26] IPU 1997b.   [27] As cited in IPU 1997e: 9.

embodied identities were the proper object of representation and the implications for the composition of national legislatures. Modern democracies, all sides in these debates publicly agreed, do not mistreat women. Modern democracies, the quota proponents argued, in fact take affirmative measures, if need be, to provide just representation for women by bringing some of them into the legislature. In the words of Argentine senator Margarita Malharro de Torres, those who oppose higher levels of women legislators "hold women back in the name of old, traditional prejudices more worthy of a feudal era than of modern times, than of an *aggiornado* and firm democracy that is founded on the representation of all." In passing the quota bill, on the other hand, "the Senate [is] taking the advanced, modern, *aggiornado* step of transitory quotas to incorporate women into the legislative powers as they deserve."[28]

When legislature quotas were embraced by the major global governance organs in the mid- to late 1990s, the democratic justice arguments receded into the background in favor of arguments that emphasize the advantages of women legislators for the market economy. A second understanding of the importance of women legislators for modern states has thereby come into play, namely that gender-balanced institutions are conducive to market economies and particularly to market-led growth. In a global market economy, it is often charged, states simply cannot afford not to bring more women into national assemblies:

Today, all our countries face global, political and economic challenges that are partly beyond our control, and many are undergoing radical institutional and structural changes whose long-term social, political and economic effects are extremely hard to manage in view of an unsatisfactory international order and insufficient economic co-operation. In such a context, no country can any longer afford to overlook any portion of its human resources. This means redirecting our perspectives and policies. Our domestic policies must henceforth, at all levels, be shaped and applied not just by men but with the full and equal participation of women.[29]

A larger percentage of women legislators is thus a "critical dimension of the UNDP's efforts to help meet the overarching goal of halving world poverty by 2015," as the *very first* introductory sentence of the landmark *Women's Political Participation and Good Governance: 21st Century*

[28] Lubertino Beltrán 1992: 73.   [29] IPU, 1995, *Beijing Parliamentary Declaration*.

Challenges reads. The significant *Road Map towards the Implementation of the United Nations Millennium Declaration* tellingly lists "supporting the inclusion of women in government and other decision-making bodies at a high level" as a strategy for the goal of development and poverty eradication.[30] It is worth pausing to reflect on this focus on poverty eradication (presumably achieved through economic growth), since higher levels of women in parliament could also be considered an end in itself or as a strategy for human rights and democracy. Instead, "disparities between males and females in power," as the subsequent *Strategy for Action* claims, "act to undermine economic growth."[31] In a surprisingly sharp tone, in an introduction to "The Business Case for Mainstreaming Gender,"[32] the World Bank similarly emphasizes that "Gender Equality is an issue of development effectiveness, not just a matter of political correctness or kindness to women." Senior World Bank economist Andrew Mason (co-author of the groundbreaking 2001 World Bank report *Engendering Development Through Gender Equality*) states that "societies that discriminate on the basis of gender pay a significant price in greater poverty, slower economic growth, weaker governance, and a lower quality of life."[33]

"Democracy," to the extent that it is mentioned at all in the UNDP and World Bank elaborations, takes on a particular meaning in the discussions of bringing more women into legislatures, namely the creation of public institutions that are conducive to so-called good governance. A "gender-balanced representation," one is told time and again, is a matter of "good governance."[34] For those unfamiliar with the concept, the UNDP defines governance as "the exercise of economic, political and administrative authority to manage a country's affairs at all levels,"[35] and it centrally involves "providing an enabling environment for private sector activity."[36] After a period of skepticism about the importance of state institutions for the market economy, democratic political institutions have come to take center stage in the production of such an enabling environment.

---

[30] Section III, §125, p. 25. [31] World Bank 2002: 4.
[32] "The Business Case for Mainstreaming Gender" is a chapter in the World Bank's 2002 *Strategy for Action.*
[33] As cited in Mutume 2001. [34] E.g. Karam 1998: 15; UNDP 2000: 24.
[35] UNDP 2000: iii. The UNDP launched its Global Programme for Governance in 1997.
[36] UNDP 2000: 29.

Summing up the significance of good governance, the then UN
Secretary General Kofi Annan declared that "a new consensus is emerging on the nature, role and function of official institutions," concluding
that "we are moving from old ideologies to a new pragmatism."[37] With
alternatives to the market economy apparently not only defeated but
also relegated to the world of "old" ideologies, a higher number of
women legislators are becoming part and parcel of the new and "modern" pragmatism of good governance. Precisely *what* women are made
out to be in order to bring about democracy and economic growth as
office-holders will be more carefully analyzed below, after an examination of the hierarchy between "modernity" and "tradition" in the
discussions around quotas.

Social hierarchies and quotas: overcoming "tradition" in the development of "modern," market democracy

In the brief section above, I introduced the notion that quotas are
promoted as a component in the construction of "modern" statehood
that brings into tenuous union markets and democracy. Having become
embedded in the production of modern, neoliberal democracy, much of
the drive of the quota debates across the world derives from efforts to
move away from tradition and its associated practices. "Modern"
statehood is articulated together with "less advanced" or "traditional"
polities or groups of humans on a single scale of development and
success. The quota struggles thus draw upon and are constitutive of
two broad categories of states and the hierarchical relations between
them: those that have already attained the modern status (generally so-
called developed states) and those that are understood to be still developing away from tradition and in the direction of meeting the demands
of the global economy.

"Cultural tradition" is widely identified as the primary causal force
behind low levels of female representation. In sharp contrast with the
NWM debates and the earlier communist theorizing of women's political participation, which located the source of women's subordination
in the effects of economic industrialization and/or imperialism, the
structures of the economy and even economic scarcity have now been
forcefully dismissed as determinants of under-representation of women

[37] Annan 1997.

legislators. Poor and wealthy states alike have managed to increase the numbers of women legislators, it is argued, demonstrating that the wealthy part of the world does not have a monopoly on the political empowerment of women. The *UNDP Human Development Report 1995* showed that women's political empowerment does not depend on "national income or wealth," or the "level of economic development," a claim that has since been widely reproduced and presumably accepted.[38] The primary cause of the problem is thought to preside in *culture*, a concept carefully separated out from the economy and politics. It is through cultural development, the move away from "traditional" society towards "modern" state institutions, that women are empowered in decision-making.

In an interesting reversal of the representations of culture in the suffrage debates of the first few decades of the twentieth century (in which culture was equivalent to civilization and progress, something which non-Europeans allegedly lacked), culture is now approached as "tradition" and antithetical to progress as a remnant of an economically inefficient and undemocratic past not yet overcome. Contrasted against modernity, culture is understood as a set of national beliefs, values and customs that have been passed down from pre-modern eras and that hinder economic and democratic advancement. As states modernize, we are expected to see a "weakening of traditional values" and therefore "changes in perceptions regarding the appropriate role for women – all factors that increase women's political resources and decrease existing barriers to political activity,"[39] according to IDEA's quota website. "Traditional understandings of space as private and public, women generally being relegated to the former," we are told by the UNDP, "lie at the very heart of most of the difficulties women face entering politics."[40] The Southern African Development Community (SADC) and others agree that "at the heart of the under representation of women in politics are age old attitudes and stereotypes that assign women to the private, and men to the public domain."[41] This, of course, is a total reversal from the representations of the early twentieth century, when much of the non-European world was

---

[38] E.g. Karam 1998: 2; Lowe Morna 2000: 4; UNDP 1995; UNDP 2000: 2, 23, 72. See also Nelson and Chowdhury 1994.

[39] Matland 1998, on the IDEA website.

[40] UNDP 2000: 23.   [41] Lowe Morna 2000: 12.

chastised as "primitive" for *not* maintaining separate spheres and for *not* keeping women out of political power. The Inter-American Commission on Women similarly argues that it is "socio-cultural patterns" that inhibit women from taking part in "modern society." "Prejudices and customs" – as low levels of women legislators are now interpreted – "limit [women's] participation in public life."[42] These "customs" have been institutionalized as "traditional practice in many political parties and government structures."[43]

Despite the scathing critiques of modernization theory that emerged in the 1960s and 1970s, state officials across the world now share the view that traditional culture is to blame for the lack of progress in bringing more women into national legislatures. Operating in this framework, the Latin American quota debates centered on cultural deficiencies as one primary source of women's under-representation. "[The low level of female deputies] demonstrates clearly that a patriarchal and *machista* political culture is responsible for the fact that of a total of 2031 parliamentarians, only 84 have been women," Peruvian deputy quota legislation author Luz Salgado argued in 1997, like many of her colleagues.[44] "The nature of the discrimination that we are debating is cultural and it permeates Argentine society profoundly," the Argentine minister of the interior likewise claimed during the 1991 quota debates.[45] His fellow legislators agreed:

The law that we are debating today arises from the problematic of a society which has suffered a strong cultural retrocession, because if this had been a democratic people which had long ago overcome authoritarianism and discrimination, we would not need to discuss the 30 percent female representation for electoral lists. The fact that we are debating how to protect women through affirmative action shows that we in some way accept that there is a problem in Argentine society.[46]

Such an understanding of the problem leads to certain preferred solutions: quotas are understood as transitory electoral reforms that serve as one step in "achieving a transformation in the political culture of

---

[42] Inter-American Commission of Women 1994: n.p., section on "Participation of Women in the Structures of Power and Decision-Making."

[43] Inter-American Commission on Women 1999: section 2:4.

[44] Congress of Peru 1997: 2520.   [45] Lubertino Beltrán 1992: 107, my translation.

[46] Deputy Carlos A. Álvarez, Argentine debate in the Chamber of Deputies, November 6, 1991, from Lubertino Beltrán 1992: 87, my translation.

society,"[47] in "overcoming the sociocultural obstacles that impede or limit [women's] participation."[48] Once such cultural change has taken place, quotas will no longer be needed. States that are truly "modern," that have progressed towards a modern national culture, would have no need for such measures, as half of the legislature would automatically be female. Swedish statesmen often point out with pride that the Swedish legislature and cabinet attained their high levels of women without "coercive" quotas. Furthermore, whereas the transfer of *economic* resources from rich to poor states is not seen as a solution within this schema, the transfer of modern *values* and the eradication of traditional culture *are*. Women, as we are about to see, are an important component in this cultural transformation.

How women legislators advance the state from a traditional to a modern polity

In the 1991 quota debates, Argentine delegate Cecilia Lipszyc cited nineteenth-century French Utopian Socialist Charles Fourier's famous thesis: "*Social progress and historic changes occur by virtue of the progress of women toward liberty, and decadence of the social order occurs as the result of a decrease in the liberty of women.*"[49] Even though general progress from traditional to modern statehood is now widely held to be the fundamental force behind the political empowerment of women, an increase in women legislators, as this quotation suggests, is concurrently thought to bring about general progress. State officials and quota debaters are thus faced with an apparent tautology, a chicken-and-egg situation for which quotas appear as a good intervention. General modernization is understood to be beneficial for women, while at the same time the changing status of women allegedly brings about general progress. To be sure, women are sometimes validated as a category of inherent worth in the quota debates, a category that deserves a relation to the state polity that is equal to that of men. Women are simultaneously approached as a resource for general society, a category whose inclusion in public institutions will help to

---

[47] Inter-American Commission for Women 1999: section 3.I "Cultural Change."
[48] Inter-American Commission for Women 1994: section 1.B.1.
[49] Lubertino Beltrán 1992: 60, emphasis original.

advance the country in becoming a modern democracy conducive for market growth.

For quotas to be promoted as a matter of modern democratic justice across the globe, *women* must obviously be understood to form an at least partially homogeneous group that will be represented in some sense by the few women that end up in parliament. Similarly, for women legislators to stabilize and enhance market economies, they must be conceptualized as a group united by common traits amenable to markets. Reflecting on the issue of *how* women legislators advance the state thus involves the logically prior question: *What* is it that allegedly unifies women? How have women been constructed as a category so that quotas (asking for *anyone* sharing the female label) appear as a feasible measure? We shall momentarily turn to address this question before proceeding with the analysis of how women bring about general welfare.

Most fundamentally, the discussions of quotas rest on a base conceptualization of women and men as two mutually exclusive sexes whose difference is rooted in allegedly natural biology. This biology is in turn understood to provide the base for gender as socially constructed identities and behaviors. Such a differentiation has been quite effective, and indeed appears necessary, for the successful advocacy for quotas. As half of humanity, quota proponents argue, women are entitled to half the legislative seats, making "a gender-balanced representation" and "getting the balance right" goals for the composition of legislatures. In many cases, to be sure, a portion smaller than half may be advocated as more politically feasible in the short run. In others, such as that of France, anything less than half would have been impossible. As Kramer explains, "While 25% is a quota, 50% is merely the female half of the 'universal,' or of 'the people' or of 'neutral citizens.'"[50]

Gender is in turn approached as the cultural interpretation of biological sexual difference, and is as such notably not represented as an effect of politics or of the economy.[51] As a cultural construct, gender-based separation of the two sexes – in fact, *gender itself* as anything other than natural and biological difference – potentially becomes understood as something "traditional," a remnant of a superstitious and prejudiced past that modern democracies and modern economies

---

[50] Kramer 2000: 115.
[51] E.g. Lambsdorff 1999: 13; Swamy *et al.* 2001: 53; World Bank 2002: 2.

leave behind.[52] To take a quotation from the World Bank that is representative of the approach, gender

refers to *culturally* based expectations of the roles and behaviors of males and females. The term distinguishes the socially constructed from the biologically determined aspects of being male and female. Unlike the biology of sex, gender roles and behaviors can change historically, sometimes relatively quickly, even if aspects of these roles originated in the biological differences between the sexes. Because the *religious or cultural traditions* that define and justify the distinct roles and expected behaviors of males and females are strongly cherished and socially enforced, change in gender systems often is contested.[53]

Gender, as any distinction between males and females that cannot be attributed to allegedly natural differences stemming from sex, is thus itself rendered suspect and understood as a potential source of inequality between men and women. Such cultural difference between men and women often becomes understood as a limiting and perverting stereotype or prejudice that locks men and women into presumably unnatural roles. In fact, were it not for gender, the female sex would allegedly not have been under-represented in national assemblies to begin with! However, as we shall see below, the fault line between gender and sex is markedly ambivalent, and many of the participants in the quota debates express uncertainty about whether to attribute observed differences between men and women to gender or to sex. What is more, gender is sometimes seen as comprising beneficial, if temporary, traits for democracy and growth.

Most norms and world polity scholars implicitly share the assumption that women are unified by a shared, naturally given fact of biological sexual distinction. With this as a basis, quota measures may appear to generate a diminution of gender, as women and men alike hold legislative positions rather than the "gendered" public/private distinction that kept legislatures an almost exclusively male domain. With quotas, difference seems to be giving way to as much sameness as nature may allow. It may be helpful to remember that sexual difference itself remains a social construct, as so many feminist scholars have demonstrated and as Chapter 4 laid out. The allegedly natural and immutable

[52] E.g. Lambsdorff 1999; Swamy *et al.* 2001; World Bank 2002.
[53] World Bank 2002: 2, my emphasis.

sexual distinctions are certainly not understood to be disappearing but are rather reproduced in the quota debates. The recognition of women's difference is thereby once again made necessary for their equality.

What is more, few of the actual quota proponents approach the issue of increasing the number of women in parliament as a mere head-count, as simply ensuring that half of the legislators are of female sex. If women were thought to share nothing more than genitalia, making the case that bringing a few such reproductive organs into a legislature is a source of justice for *all* women in a state would be difficult. Skeptics such as Peruvian feminist Maruja Barrig have asked: "Can [some] women, by the simple fact of being women, represent all women? Personally, I believe that whatever sisters me with Margaret Thatcher is nothing but a biological accident."[54]

Such skepticism about the politically relevant unity of the sexual category "women" is rare among quota proponents, however. Quotas are advocated as a manner of looking after women's interests via "the difference that is made, as a result of having women in politics."[55] According to the Beijing Platform for Action, "Women's equal participation in decision-making is not only a demand for simple justice or democracy but can also be seen as a necessary condition for women's interests to be taken into account."[56] A UNDP policy paper explains the rationale: "The basic idea behind why women can contribute differently is that women share men's lives anywhere in the world, yet they have their own experiences, specificity's [sic], attitudes, and life-styles, which are reflected in different approaches, needs, insights, and goals from politics and decision-making. As the other half which shares life and planetary interests, women are also a different half with different life-experiences."[57]

While cognizant of the possible disruption of this sex/gender unity by differences stemming from class, nationality, ethnicity, age, sexual orientation, religion or any other line of differentiation of social relevance, quota advocates carefully bring together women as a coherent category with certain shared interests. "There are many commonalities between what is seen as crucial concerns by women, regardless of geopolitical location and aspects. The examples quoted here were violence

---

[54] Barrig 1990: 44, my translation.   [55] Karam 1998: iv.
[56] Under section "Women in Power and Decision-Making."   [57] Karam 1998: 16.

against women and economic participation."[58] WEDO agrees that "when women enter decision-making bodies in significant numbers, such issues as child care, violence against women and unpaid labor are more likely to become priorities for policy-makers."[59] A 2000 opinion piece in *The Hindu* likewise argued that "given the composition of the legislatures all these years, it is not surprising that none of the basic problems affecting women – landlessness, domestic violence, lack of control over decisions and, above all, female infanticide – has been addressed seriously by our majestic law-making bodies."[60]

Academic research from across the world lends support to the existence of differing legislative behavior and priorities of male and female delegates.[61] Given such different practices and the understanding of what women do as legislators, it is problematic to simply equate equality with sameness as is the tendency in world polity and norms scholarship. Clearly, the empowerment of women as legislators rests on their construction as simultaneously equal to *and* different from men, as one of two different halves of a common humanity. The promulgation of quotas has resulted not in the dismantlement of sex/gender systems but rather in their reinterpretation.

Having analyzed the unification of women as a category, we can now turn to the primary question of how such women legislators presumably advance and modernize the state. While furthering women's interests is a goal of quota proponents, bringing more women into legislatures is expressly *not* about furthering women's interests at the expense of men. As we saw above, more women legislators are said to be good for everyone, men and women alike, in a world of no inherent conflicts of interest. How, then, are women in national legislatures supposed to bring about general welfare? First, by enhancing general economic growth, a feature central for modernity and the quest away from tradition. Interestingly, if the level of a state's economic development is not an important determinant of women in decision-making, the reverse is certainly said to hold true: the number of women in decision-making has been positively related to a state's level of economic development. The landmark 1997 UNDP conference on Governance for Sustainable Growth and Equity – the first global UN conference on governance, which officials from more than 153 member states

---

[58] Karam 1998: 2.   [59] WEDO 2003a.   [60] Chandhoke 2000.
[61] See e.g. Towns 2003 and the scholarship listed therein.

attended – highlighted a close relationship between the low number of women parliamentarians and the high number of women in poverty.[62] A close relationship between low numbers of women parliamentarians and a high level of general poverty has been established and underscored time and again.[63]

Empowered as a distinctive category with unique experiences and interests, women legislators are valued for contributing towards poverty eradication by bringing their difference into the policy process. "Women's interests," such as equal opportunity for education and employment, reproductive health, nutrition and childcare, are understood to benefit the economy as a whole. The "failure to include women in the political running of societies is regarded by the IPU as a major impediment to development," the Secretary General of the IPU proclaims in unison with other quota proponents.[64]

If the pursuit of women's interests is said to be an important strategy for the welfare of all, women are even more predominantly celebrated in a second manner, as the honest sex. Allegedly less corrupt and less selfish, women have become ideal for the construction of transparent states. The honest sex has come to play a crucial part in the struggle to lessen corruption, the reduction of which is thought to advance markets and, by extension, purportedly to reduce poverty, all according to relatively recent discoveries by global governance organs. A series of studies shows strong positive correlations between women and good governance, arguing as a rule that "the greater the representation of women in parliament, the lower the level of corruption."[65] (As an interesting aside, new all-female traffic police forces were created in Mexico City and Lima in the late 1990s with the hope of reducing corruption, an initiative that has allegedly had the expected effects.[66]) The World Bank explains that "good governance is critical for sustainable development. A growing body of evidence suggests that gender equality in rights and resources is associated with less corruption and better governance."[67] In a widely cited study commissioned by the

---

[62] The Conference also called upon countries that have attained 30 percent women in parliament to share their experiences and strategies with others.

[63] E.g. UNDP 1999b; Asplund 2003.   [64] IPU 1997e: 4.

[65] Dollar *et al.* 2001: 1. See also Frey Nakonz 1999; Stückelberger 2003; Swamy *et al.* (2001); UN Development Fund for Women 2000; UNDP 2000; World Bank 2001 and 2002.

[66] Moore 1999; McDermott 1999.   [67] World Bank 2002: 9.

World Bank, we learn that "numerous behavioral studies have found women to be more trust-worthy and public-spirited than men. These results suggest that women should be particularly effective in promoting honest government."[68] The authors of the study elaborate:

Men are more individually oriented (selfish) than women ... women will be less likely to sacrifice the common good for personal (material) gain. This may be particularly relevant for the role of women in government since, almost by definition, one of the most significant difficulties faced by public bureaucracies is designing institutions that discourage their agents from acting opportunistically, at the expense of the public.[69]

Such research findings about the selflessness of women – analogous to claims of nineteenth-century scholars Louis-Aimé Martin and Sarah Lewis, but with reversed implications for women in politics – are echoed time and again across the world. "Women have stabilized politics in a way because they tend not to be so opportunistic. They tend to go after the interests of stability. They're not so reckless as men," Uganda's President Museveni stated in 2000.[70] "Women generally refuse corrupt behavior and are less inclined to adopt corrupt behavior than men," the Swiss Protestant aid organization Bread for All declared in 2003.[71] Peruvian delegate Luz Salgado, co-author of the quota bill that won approval in 1997, explained in the brief parliamentary debates that

being a woman gives us a special condition that doesn't simply consist of having a different color, stature or texture. We women have different life experiences from men. The quota system will put things in order, like they should have been from the beginning ... politics will be clean when there are clean characters, when there are transparent characters, when there is a decision to work, when there is solidarity.[72]

Some quota debaters are still unsure whether such honesty is inherent in women's sex or a malleable matter of gender: "The reasons are unclear, various hypothesis [sic] could be established, such as socialization, less access to the networks of corruption, less access to the 'corruption currencies,' less know-how of corrupt practices." Whatever the verdict, women are presently understood, at a minimum, as important for the fight against corruption in the short run: "Efforts to promote the

---

[68] Dollar *et al.* 1999: cover page.   [69] Dollar *et al.* 1999: 1.
[70] As cited in Simmons and Wright 2000.
[71] Stückelberger 2003: 47.   [72] Congress of Peru 1997: 2521, my translation.

involvement of women in public life could at least in a short term represent an effective strategy to fight corruption."[73]

As Luz Salgado's statement above suggests, women legislators and politicians have been active proponents of the understanding of women as more honest in politics. The surge in interest in the honest sex as well as in women's issues may, in turn, have importantly helped to create an opening for women to enter political office. Even if the transnational campaigns and global governance organs emphasize non-confrontation between the sexes, female political candidates indict the rule of men as tending to corruption. Mexican Senator Maria Elena Chapa argued in 1997 that "because citizens in Latin America are increasingly demanding a more virtuous political system, new opportunities may open for women in the political arena."[74] A number of women legislators or candidates have indeed stepped into this speaking position, campaigning on platforms of greater honesty and promoting anti-corruption measures once elected. For instance, Peruvian presidential candidate Lourdes Flores Nano used her status as a woman to launch herself as an anti-corruption candidate in 2000. Margaret Dongo in Zimbabwe, Wangari Maathai and Charity Ngilu in Kenya, and Winnie Byanyima in Uganda have come forward as among the most ardent opponents of corruption in their respective countries.[75] In arguing in favor of quotas, Argentine deputy Lubertino, while skeptical of the natural origins of women's honesty, claimed that "having been left on the sidelines of power ... each one of us women, from our distinct ideologies, would like to move ahead without frivolities, corruption, in-fighting."[76] The Women's Caucus of the Ugandan Parliament furthermore initiated "transparency measures" by pushing for making government disbursement information available to the public.[77] Women are understood to literally bring about state-led general progress by carrying their different life experiences into the policy-making process and by reducing corruption, both aspects that are seen as key in the development of modern, market-led economies that have moved away from tradition.

If women quite literally help to advance the state and general welfare through making use of their different characteristics, they also do so symbolically by serving as a crucial marker of modernity. Since neither the economy nor politics is approached as important in generating

---

[73] Stückelberger 2003: 47–8.   [74] As cited in UNDP 1997: 86.
[75] Tripp 2001: 151.   [76] Lubertino Beltrán 1992: 57.   [77] UNDP 2000: 4.

higher levels of women in national legislatures, only "traditional" states governed by culture rather than by modernity would exhibit low levels of female representation. As was stated above, the causal relation between the status of women and cultural advancement is circular. Quotas, as a quick fix for bringing more women into national assemblies, help to mark states as modern, a point that has clearly not been lost on state officials. So when Ugandan parliamentarian Beatrice Kiraso claims of the quota legislation that "women are now the main instruments of modernization in Uganda. We're also leading the way for women in Africa – It's hard to believe we've come so far,"[78] she suggests that Uganda has inched closer to the vanguard of modernity simply by passing the quota law, before the women legislators have had time to have their expected effects. Senior World Bank economist Andrew Mason explains that a higher level of female political representation "signifies a country that is more open in general, with more transparent government and a more democratic approach."[79] In other words, having produced more women legislators, the country must be more transparent and democratic. In a world where being ranked as corrupt has serious effects for a country's total capital inflows,[80] such symbolic representation can potentially have financial consequences.

Advocacy, hierarchy and the adoption of quotas

World polity and international norms scholars have argued that the initial stages of making a state practice a norm involves intense domestic or transnational mobilization to prompt change. This indeed is the case with sex quotas, even though the mobilization began in Latin America and then emerged in Africa and Asia rather than in the European-led trajectory predicted by these scholars. A decade after quotas were first promoted, we can take stock of some of the initial developments to ask how the adoption of quotas came about.

First, it should be clear from the discussion above that mobilization and organized activism have been directed towards most of the state legislatures that have embraced quotas. However, rather than networks

---

[78] As quoted in Simmons and Wright 2000.   [79] As cited in Moline 2002.
[80] For instance, Lambsdorff (1999) shows in a cross-section of 65 states that being labeled "corrupt" decreases capital inflows at a 99 percent confidence level.

made up primarily of non-governmental activism[81] seeking support
from governments and intergovernmental organizations to effect state
change, the quota transnationalism is heavily predominated by "partnerships" and "alliances" between various global governance organs
representing modernity. The UNDP proclaimed that establishing
mechanisms that bring women into decision-making "means taking
advantage of the unprecedented opportunities for national, regional
and global networking and alliance-building."[82] These opportunities
have so far entailed international financial institutions such as the
World Bank and the regional development banks in "partnership"
with UN agencies (primarily UNDP, DAW, UNIFEM and the regional
UN organs), "modern" states in terms of women legislators (the
Netherlands, Norway, Sweden and others) and transnational NGOs
such as WEDO.[83] In 1999, Mr. G. Shabbir Cheema, Director of the
Management Development and Governance Division of the Bureau for
Development Policy (UNDP) announced that the "UNDP was explor-
ing the possibility of supporting a global network on gender and gov-
ernance, which would take forward the processes initiated at [the 1999
UNDP meeting in Delhi]."[84]

Domestic legislators and women's organizations of the culturally
modern and economically elite variant are often crucial components
in these alliances. Domestic mobilization does not seem entirely necessary, however. The Peruvian legislature passed a quota law in 1997
without prior pressure from domestic women's organizations and with
minimal debate, presumably because the then president, Alberto
Fujimori, had sensed the advantages of such a measure and thus supported the initiative. There is furthermore a marked elation and opti-
mism among global governance organs about the prospects for change
as a result of these partnerships and alliances. The *Millennium
Declaration* and its 2001 *Road Map* are said to "have paved the way

---

[81] Such as the advocacy organizations, social movements, foundations, media
organs and churches that made up the bulwark of the transnational advocacy
networks analyzed by Keck and Sikkink (1998).

[82] UNDP 2000: i.

[83] As one example, the World Bank and the UN Economic Commission for Africa
collaborated with the Association for Progressive Communications' "Women's
Africa Program" in orchestrating a 1998 conference that called for the use of
affirmative action to increase the numbers of women in African parliaments.

[84] UNDP 1999a.

for the type of collaboration amongst UN system agencies that is unprecedented."[85] UN assistant secretary-general (Special Adviser on Gender Issues and Advancement of Women) Angela King affirmed that "I am heartened by the growing solidarity and common view shared with our Bretton Woods colleagues on many of these [gender equality] issues," rejoicing that the World Bank "is increasingly participating with the whole United Nations system."[86] The UNDP similarly refers to quotas as an effect of the "building of alliances between different stakeholders in the political process."[87] The stakeholders in the sexual composition of a state's legislature are clearly not simply the national citizenry of that state.

So how, then, do these modern partnerships operate? If the transnational advocacy networks analyzed by Keck and Sikkink were said *not* to be powerful in a conventional sense, the participants in these quota partnerships suffer no shortage of financial resources.[88] An impressive wealth of reports, conferences, press releases and studies has thus been produced and disseminated across the world, and development projects on women in politics funded. The sheer volume and scope of such publications and initiatives are bound to have effect, at least in bringing the attention of policy-makers to the issue of women legislators.

For those not immediately convinced by the utter mass of arguments favoring quotas, various other tactics are in place. A number of partners have developed ranking systems to grade states' performance on bringing women into decision-making, thus clearly identifying the traditional states that are lagging behind their modern models. Most notable among these is the Gender Empowerment Measure of the UNDP, but the IPU also puts out a ranking report annually, as does the Women's Leadership Conference of the Americas with its wide distribution of a country-by-country "report card" on women's leadership in politics and government (first presented at the 2001 Summit of the Americas in Canada) and others. These reports often sound a bit like the commentary on a sporting event, a typical summary reading as follows:

The top of the chart has traditionally been occupied by the Nordic countries which show the highest regional level, averaging 39.9% of women in parliament. In this group, Sweden, the leader, has managed to improve its score by a 2.6 percentage point increase: women now account for 45.3% of

---

[85] King 2002.   [86] Ibid.   [87] UNDP 1999a.   [88] Keck and Sikkink 1998: 16.

parliamentarians in the Swedish Riksdagen whereas they represented 42.7%
of parliamentarians in the previous legislature. Despite showing the lowest
regional average, the Arab countries have consolidated their move towards
gender equality in politics. In Morocco, women now account for 10.8% of the
lower House, a 10 percentage point leap. In Algeria, women MPs have
doubled from 12 to 24, a 3.3 percentage point increase.[89]

What Keck and Sikkink call "moral leverage,"[90] or the mobilization of
shame, is clearly at work in the publication of these reports. Keck and
Sikkink contend that "countries that are most susceptible to network
pressures are those that aspire to belong to a normative community of
nations ... thus moral leverage may be especially relevant where states
are actively trying to raise their status in the international system."[91]
Swedish and Ugandan state representatives have widely expressed their
pride in the high levels of women legislators that have brought them to
the apex of the modern world, whereas the French conveyed a deep
sense of embarrassment over their Republic – the cradle of democracy –
showing such low numbers of female delegates before the passage of the
parity law. The norms literature overlooks or fails to develop the fact
that the social hierarchies of international society enable such moral
leverage. In conveying the norm that modern market democracies dis-
play at least 30 percent female legislators, presumably "traditional"
practices are obviously stigmatized and devalued as keeping women
from political empowerment. The shame involved is that of being
branded traditional, backward, lagging behind.

Shame and embarrassment alone are not the only or perhaps even the
principal elements of importance in the adoption of quota measures.
Whereas developed and developing state officials alike may express
shame about being stuck in age-old "tradition," they are differently
situated in international society and thus under different kinds of pressure to increase the levels of women legislators.

Although European states are more securely positioned as modern
democracies, the failure to raise the levels of female legislators via
quotas apparently does not appear as a full-fledged contradiction in
Europe. Liberal, Western states can apparently still reconcile low
levels of female elected representatives with being modern market
democracies. As we have learned, it is not necessarily the wealthiest or

[89] IPU 2003.   [90] Keck and Sikkink 1998: 23.
[91] Keck and Sikkink 1998: 29.

"developed" states that rise to the top of these women-in-decision-making modernity rankings. The United States and Britain, to name two noteworthy examples, show dismal results and negligible if any prospects for passing quota measures. In the USA, what appears as a contradiction elsewhere (e.g. the status as advanced democracy along with low levels of women legislators) has not given rise to quota debates.

As a cultural construction, quotas open one possibility for states other than the economically developed to reach a modern benchmark and outperform developed states. So far, however, there is little evidence that such challenges register on the radar screen of developed state representatives, or that they can even *see* the activities of states in Asia, Africa and Latin America as worthy of serious consideration, possible emulation or as a source of shame. For the developed world, the horizon of "modern democracies" is clearly limited, reducing the universe of possible cases to draw lessons from and be embarrassed by to those of the liberal West. "Do people seriously believe British women less capable of running their country than their European sisters?" a recent *Guardian* opinion piece asked, with no mention of any state other than European ones. Instead, the piece simply contends that "modern democracies with between 30% and 44% female representation in parliament include Sweden, Finland, Norway, Denmark, Iceland, the Netherlands and Germany."[92] What is more – and this is noteworthy – Belgium, France and Spain are the only states in the developed world to have adopted quota measures, although the French case has given renewed fuel to such efforts in Italy.

Using the French quota debates as an example,[93] it is clear that the low levels of women's representation cast France as "backward" in the context of the liberal West rather than in the world at large.[94] Kramer argues that the Socialist Party strategists behind the quota bill were "embarrassed *in Europe*" and that one crucial function of the Parity Law was to help France "look modern and 'not like Greece' – the only

[92] Abdela 2001.

[93] After enormous debates, France adopted a constitutional amendment on June 28, 1999, assuring "equal access" to elected office. The amendment was followed on May 3, 2000, by a new law obliging political parties to allot 50 percent of candidacies to women or else lose a share of public campaign funding (Lenoir 2001: 244, note 93).

[94] E.g. Lenoir 2001: 235.

country in Western Europe with a lower percentage of women in its parliament."[95] Arguing that "the aim of this parity is to place France at the cutting edge of the promotion of access of women to political responsibility," French Constitutional Court member Lenoir similarly comments that "the fact is that in terms of women's representation in politics, France still shares with Greece the bottom place in the European Union."[96]

French levels of female parliamentarians were also closely compared to another state of the West, for whose institutional structures the French have much more contempt – the United States. Interestingly, even though the USA has not seen a semblance of a debate on sex quotas for Congress, French sociologist Éric Fassin claims that the entire parity debate was an attempt not to turn the French Republic into an American communitarian democracy.[97] To pass the parity laws, these therefore had to be interpreted *à la française*. Rather than "the prelude to a society on the American or Canadian model," Lenoir underscores that the parity laws do not mean that France is moving towards becoming "a State which acknowledges that it is made of a variety of ethnic, linguistic or religious minorities. Nor is it to say that, by admitting a more active form of citizenship made up of diversified forms of cultural expression, the French Republic is ready to give up its belief in the universality of rights, *a major central feature of civilization*."[98] The prior implementation of comparable measures in the states of Latin

---

[95] Kramer 2000: 112, my emphasis.   [96] Lenoir 2001: 217.

[97] See discussion of Fassin's work in Kramer 2000: 115. This issue of how not to be American was thornier than one might expect and is absolutely fascinating. On the one hand, the French level of female representation "is comparable to that observed in the United States Congress," as Lenoir lamented (2001: 239). On the other hand, the idea of *quotas* to rectify this situation would "get tossed into the trash can of American ideas that the French reject – ideas having to do with affirmative action and multiculturalism and communitarianism and all the other isms of an invasion that spells the beginning of the end of France" (Kramer 2000: 115). The concept was discussed as "parity" rather than "quotas" in terms of its impact on the very heart of the meaning of the Republic. To critics, "the universalist republican tradition is said to be giving way to the Anglo-Saxon tradition, which is differentialist and 'communitarian'" (Lenoir 2001: 243). For instance, leading anti-parity campaigner and French philosopher Elisabeth Badinter argued that "the defenders of gender parity suggest nothing less than *a modification of the political system*; they try to impose a communitarian democracy based on quotas, imported from the United States" (as cited in Sgier 2001: 11).

[98] Lenoir 2001: 246–7, my emphasis. See also Sgier 2001.

America as well as in Taiwan, Nepal, Eritrea, Uganda and Kenya did
not enter the French discussions. Clearly, certain modern democracies –
those sharing the central features of "civilization" if we are to believe
Lenoir – understand themselves to have little to learn from others.

If this analysis appears unfairly harsh, consider the following – typical if colorful – interpretation of "traditional" states using quotas to
modernize in a 2000 *Los Angeles Times* article entitled "Gender quotas
puts Uganda in role of rights pioneer."[99] The readers learn that

The customs still practiced in this lush East African nation are strikingly
archaic: Women expected to kneel when serving food to their husbands.
Mothers forbidden permanent custody of children after a divorce. Men
"inheriting" widows of their deceased brothers. Legal polygamy. Yet
Uganda has become a key testing ground for a radical political experiment.
All elected bodies, from village councils to the national parliament, must have
a minimum number of women.
In a word, quotas.
The requirement has helped transform a country ranked as one of the world's
most wayward states during the brutal rule of President Idi Amin in the 1970s
into a pioneer for women's rights in the 2000s. Almost 20% of Uganda's
parliament is female – nearly 1½ the percentage in the U.S. Congress. Seven
Cabinet members are women.
A third of local council seats must, by law, go to women.
The difference involves more than just a proliferation of female names and
faces. With gutsy energy, Uganda's female politicos are tackling centuries-old
traditions – and recasting their futures.

Lest the reader be deceived by the degree of modernizing transformation,
the article uses deterring examples from *other* African states – presumably related to the case of Uganda through their shared "traditional"
culture – to demonstrate the severe threat that lingering tradition still
poses for women's equality, despite the use of quotas:

Yet the very idea of gender equality remains volatile in countries with strong
traditional cultures. Despite constitutional guarantees of female equality,
Zimbabwe's Supreme Court issued a unanimous ruling last year declaring
that it is in "the nature of African society that women are not equal to men.
Women should never be considered adults within the family, but only as a
junior male or teenager." In Kenya, 10 supporters of a female candidate for

---

[99] Simmons and Wright 2000.

parliament in 1992 were raped by men who opposed her, to send a message. Uganda has a long way to go too.

While the article might present Uganda as a "rights pioneer" for "traditional" Africa, it hardly provides a compelling case for emulation by the USA.

Even if many "developed" states show low levels of female representation, "developing" states are subjected to much more intense pressures for change due to being more vulnerable to the indictment of being "traditional" in two ways. First, the suspicion among global governance and development organs that there is something wrong with the culture of developing countries has returned with a vengeance. Whereas the modern status of the United States or the United Kingdom may not be seriously undermined by refusing to take affirmative action measures to increase its number of female legislators without major mobilization, the modern, democratic and women-friendly character of many developing states – indeed their very capacity to create a just society – is under constant scrutiny. Second, since the aspiration to become modern has a crucial *economic* component, the operation of financial rewards and pressures is enabled for developing states that see themselves as most desperately in need of growth. It is, after all, in the *development* organizations that the promotion of "women in decision-making" has taken root most firmly, within the UNDP, the World Bank, the regional development banks, the donor states and agencies, the development NGOs and an enormous array of "inter-donor working groups." At the risk of stating the obvious, the clients of these organs consist of developing states rather than the financial donors.

To use one forceful example of what is at stake financially in bringing about gender-balanced representation, the World Bank announced in January of 2002 the landmark decision to use "Country Gender Assessments" in its decision-making about the Bank's own assistance as well as in its support for foreign direct investments for indebted countries.[100] As UN assistant secretary-general Angela King and others have commented, "The World Bank's powerful influence with donors and recipients alike in guiding the use of funds can go a long way in sustaining more consistency and effectiveness in achieving gender

---

[100] World Bank 2002 – i.e. Integrating Gender into the World Bank's Work.

equality goals."[101] Although more time would need to pass, and additional research be conducted, to establish more precisely the operation of these partnerships and their financial role in the creation of quotas, these alliances clearly lend themselves to so-called cross-conditionality: the refusal of a member state to meet some demand of one organ can result in the deprivation of financing from other institutions.[102] To the extent that we characterize this process as one of socialization, it is socialization under conditions of palpable inequality, between states understood to be culturally and/or economically "modern" and those branded as "traditional."

Development organs are notably sensitive to the risks entailed in using financial rewards for cultural development as a strategy to bring about change in the direction of modern market economies. The World Bank therefore promotes what it refers to as "the business case" for women in politics in order to coax client countries to give up their allegedly patriarchal "cultural traditions" in favor of "growth." As a recent interview with World Bank economist Andrew Mason on the Bank's support for women in decision-making reports:

Instead of asserting that certain cultural preferences are better, which Mason believes would be counter-productive, the bank's approach focuses on reminding the countries to see the business advantages to the new strategy. "We are saying to nations with significant gender stratification, 'if you allow gender disparities to persist, it comes at a cost,'" Mason said. "If you ignore this, you ignore economically significant costs to your country."[103]

A policy paper of the UNDP for its 1999 conference "Women and Political Participation: 21st Century Challenges" in New Delhi similarly claims:

The danger in this is that in some parts of the world, there is already an over-sensitivity vis-à-vis what is perceived as "interference" in internal affairs. Where that is the case, policies concerned with accountability for the implementation of gender concerns have tended to backfire or simply be ignored. Hence the need to explore possibilities of providing "rewards" to certain countries or organizations, which need not necessarily be seen as conditions for development aid, as much as they are aspects of merit for

---

[101] King 2002. See also statements by the director of the UN Division for the Advancement of Women, Carolyn Hannan, in Moline 2002: 1.
[102] See Feinberg 1988; Biersteker 1990.   [103] Moline 2002.

performance ... This can be done, either through financial rewards – e.g. relieving part of debt burdens for a country, or increasing the chances that countries can be put on the most-favored nation trading status list, or where countries which have increased the number of women in positions of power, and who rank highly on the impact scale, could be considered for special prestige nominations ... Countries, which attain certain goals and perform particularly well, could be promoted internationally through various fora – with media coverage – and could be granted additional development co-operation funds.[104]

Conclusion

In an often cited formulation, Michel Foucault states that "the successes of history belong to those who are capable of seizing the rules, to replace those who had used them, to disguise themselves so as to pervert them, invert their meaning, and redirect them against those who had initially imposed them."[105] In the case of quotas, it is difficult to ascertain who is seizing whose rules and what, exactly, is being perverted. The custom of maintaining a political role for women in traditional Europe, traditional Africa and elsewhere, which so horrified European statesmen of the nineteenth and early twentieth centuries, has clearly been purged from the collective memory, at least in the global governance deliberations on quotas. It seems fair to say that the politically empowering role of "tradition," which was celebrated in the advocacy for NWMs and the non-Western struggles for suffrage, is presently being perverted, mis-interpreted and turned against those most closely associated with "tra-dition" in the expansion of modern market democracy.

That said, the interpretation of women in decision-making as a cultural phenomenon rather than an economic one provides an oppor-tunity for developing states to beat their developed competitors in the race to modernity. If the causal and normative claim that the status of women is indicative of general progress was indeed introduced by the "society of civilized states," then those initially colonized by that society could be said to have seized these rules to redirect them against those who initially imposed them. Indeed, there seems to be a growing sense among many Latin American, African and Asian state representatives of

---

[104] Karam 1998: 19.   [105] Foucault 1984: 85–6.

having superseded Europe and North America in bringing women into national decision-making.

The status of women has obviously been used as a site for the negotiation of international social hierarchies. Rather than being a matter of unrelated and increasingly homogeneous states, the struggles for quotas have become caught up in this great geopolitical drama between modern market democracy and "traditional" statehood, a drama that involves the simultaneously constitutive and regulative *relations* between states. Although the modern–traditional taxonomy appears set, there is an explicit fluidity in the positioning of particular states within that arrangement. That fluidity provides much of the impetus for the adoption of quotas. Indeed, the nature and significance of the quota norm lie in the power-laden re-creation of relations of similarity and difference among states. The inclusion of women as legislators is presumed to help "advance" states towards modern, market democracy and thus away from unprofitable and, to a lesser extent, unjust traditions.

Women do not only appear in this drama simply as an object of debate, a presumably cohesive category that is talked about. As in the case of suffrage and NWMs, women have emerged as central protagonists in the quests for higher levels of female legislators. It is to some women that social hierarchies speak most urgently and to whom the contradictions between the claims to be a modern democracy and the lack of female legislators are most stark. In comparison with the other measures, there seem to be some novel developments in the makeup of the lead characters in the advocacy for quotas, however. It is no longer solely or always even primarily female representatives for women's organizations, WID scholars, international organizations specializing in women, women's sections of political parties or women's legislative caucuses that promote the advancement of women. The IPU, IDEA, the World Bank, the UNDP and the regional development banks have all become crucial sites in the proliferation of quotas. In contrast with the transnational suffrage movements, the connection between the political empowerment of women and general progress now speaks to the major global governance organs. Thus, recognizing the unwieldy and contradictory nature of the category of "women," could we perhaps nonetheless toy with the idea that it is women who have most dramatically seized the rules, increasingly replaced the men who had used them, inverted their meaning, and redirected them against the sex that initially imposed them?

8 | Conclusion

The contentious politics of norms in international society

Over the past century, there have been some dramatic changes in the relations between women and the state. Women are no longer excluded from state institutions such as voting, most states have created a national agency to handle women's issues, and a large and increasing number of states are taking active steps to boost the levels of women in national legislatures. States are clearly not static beings – they embody dynamic processes with changing sets of aims and institutional forms. In pointing to changes in the relations between women and the state, this book, like many others, has attempted to show empirically that states are indeed ongoing projects that must be understood in a social context. States become engaged with and disengaged from various social forces that vary in spatial and temporal scope, some being more local and/or more shifting than others. My concern has been with the embeddedness and positioning of states within the context of international society.

What does it mean to contend that states are embedded in international society? This book uses a rather minimal conception of international society, approaching the international as a society primarily in the sense of being social: constituted by meaningful practices and inter-subjective knowledge. Like other international actors, states are discursively and relationally constituted, structured and regulated by a multiplicity of norms, values and causal claims. Claiming that states are in and of international society does not mean one has to picture that society as a socially integrated whole whose constituent parts fully share a common value system. This book has shown that state institutions such as women's suffrage have indeed been interpreted very differently around the world, being validated for diverse reasons and made into distinctive kinds of practices. Clearly, there can be multiple scripts at work in the world.

The main aim of this book has not been to make an argument about pluralism and interpretive diversity, however. Other works have already made that point very effectively. And had there been *no* shared language and practices whatsoever among the states of the world, it would make no sense to speak of them as being embedded in "international society." What I have instead attempted to show is that there have been certain shared abstract understandings about what suffrage, national women's agencies and national sex quota laws are (other than in the narrow sense of, for instance, women casting votes for political candidates). The book has tried to demonstrate that these measures are concrete instantiations of an abstract norm on state practices: "better states exhibit appropriate behavior towards women." And in the abstract, this norm appears to have informed certain state practices across the world – I have seen no evidence of rejection of the general idea that the status of women is an important standard of rank of states.

When given more specific meaning, there has been a great deal of contestation over this abstract norm, however. One of the main facets of the worldwide appearance of new state policies toward women is the contested nature of the norms at play. Such contestation does not simply take the form of opposition to a particular practice (e.g. suffrage) with a given meaning (e.g. as a Western, liberal, democratic measure), which is how much constructivist literature has conceptualized the politics of normative contestation. Normative contestation also takes the form of interpretive struggles over the rationales and motivations for engaging in certain kinds of behavior. The main issue of contention, then, is not simply determining *which* state policy is appropriate, but also *what* a particular policy is a case of, as well as *for whom* and *why* it is appropriate. And while normative contestation speaks against a notion of international society as a fully shared value system, such disputes simultaneously indicate that there is some shared terrain of meaning on the basis of which the appropriateness of a state policy can be challenged. The very notion of contestation suggests a response to some proposition, such as the appropriateness of suffrage or sex quotas.

The central aim of this book has been to draw attention to the significance of social hierarchies, both as constitutive elements of international society and as a source of change in state policy. There are conceptual reasons to link norms and social hierarchy, as norms necessarily draw upon and generate social ranking, the ordering of actors as superior and inferior. The link between norms and social ranking in turn highlights the importance of moving away from treating states as discrete and unrelated entities in the study of norms. International norms must be seen as a form of social power that draws upon and produces social relations of hierarchy among states. Normative ranking dynamics are absolutely central to the worldwide promulgation of new state policies – much of the intensity of the struggles and debates around suffrage, national machineries and sex quotas stemmed from the fact that predominant international hierarchies were challenged and redefined. What is more, the placement of particular states within those hierarchies could be called into question in the debates. This chapter will provide a more elaborate discussion of how the main conceptual arguments about norms and social ranking played out in the worldwide emergence of women's suffrage, national women's policy agencies and legislature sex quota laws.

In order to make a theoretical contribution to the study of norms within constructivist international relations (IR), the empirical analyses of this book have drawn heavily on feminist scholarship from a range of disciplines. It has done so without speaking directly to feminist theoretical themes and concerns, although it has clear implications for how we understand gender in international politics. I will thus end this chapter by picking up a theme that has received considerable attention in the feminist IR literature, namely the issue of the gendered character of states. States are often conceptualized as masculine and masculinist institutions by feminist IR scholars. What are the implications of the worldwide incorporation of women into certain political institutions for the gendered character of states? Are there reasons to believe that such developments have changed the masculine quality of states? As state practice, has the potency of feminization as a means to devalue actors and behaviors diminished with the inclusion of women? Before addressing this theme, the chapter will first turn to the main arguments that animate the book.

Western-initiated trajectories to isomorphism?

There are prevalent presumptions within the field of IR that new state behaviors develop in the European and North American "core" of international society. The study of the status of women, whose empowerment is presumably the *sine qua non* of the liberal West, does not suggest exclusively European- or North American-led change. The worldwide proliferation of these women's institutions cannot be characterized either as actively Western-initiated or as simple imitation of Western state forms.

To begin with, nineteenth-century Europe helped to standardize the practice of fully *excluding* women from political authority around the world. As we saw in Chapter 4, a new directive emerged within what was then known as the "civilized society of states": *exclude women from politics*. It was iterated time and again that as a "barbarous" practice, "[female political power] has no place in the modern world."[1] This directive was heard by Japan and China, which barred women from political participation for the first time upon formally entering the civilized society of states. Many polities subjected to colonial rule, though certainly far from all, had previously had political systems that enabled female rule. Such systems were dismantled and restructured by the colonial powers in the name of progress. Having emerged universally via the European society of states and its colonial relations in the late nineteenth and early twentieth centuries, the practice of excluding women from formal political institutions hardly warrants the label either "traditional" or "non-Western." Indeed, if we are to believe European statesmen of the turn of the century, the expulsion of women from the state polity was a modern and progressive feature of Western civilization.

If the largely European and colonizing society of civilized states helped to universalize the practice of excluding women from formal state institutions, many women and fewer men from across the world have struggled to reverse this practice. Transnational and domestic social movements, international organizations and states have all served as crucial sites for the promulgation of these measures. The mobilization around these state forms was clearly not limited to members of Western and European states. Latin American, African, Asian and East European activists and organizations have been equally (and in the case of quotas, more) active in struggling for these institutions.

The geographical trail of their activities and of the adoption of suffrage, women's machinery and quotas also called into question the interpretation of these phenomena as Western-initiated homogeneity. Suffrage is indeed the only measure that was unequivocally initiated in

[1] Parkman 1884: 10.

the West, although at its "less advanced" outskirts. As we saw in Chapter 5, the bounds of "civilization" enabled Western women to overcome the powerful pull of nationalism to form the International Women's Suffrage Alliance and other transnational organizations that fought for suffrage until the end of World War I. While they were the first, their transnationalism was not the only one important to the spread of suffrage. The international suffragism of Western women was largely limited to what they understood to be the "civilized" world and their specific role in upholding the order of that world. At least three additional waves of transnational suffragism in other states with thorny and often contentious relations with the civilized society of states were enabled by different international discourses that trans-gressed nationalism: the Socialist Women's International, which was active simultaneously with the civilized movement; the pan-American suffragism of the 1920s–50s; and the Afro-Asian solidarity movement of the 1950s–70s. The arguments by norms and world polity scholars about initial suffragist political mobilization in Europe and subsequent imitation by non-European states simply does not hold in these cases.

Rather than developing in four distinct waves, national women's machinery came to the attention of all states simultaneously, after the initial creation of the US President's Commission in the early 1960s. Although domestic women's organizations advocated for the creation of a NWM in some cases, there was no transnational movement akin to those involved in the creation of suffrage or sex quotas. Instead, as we saw in Chapter 6, elected state officials, so-called femocrats and "women in development" (WID) scholars discussed and debated the creation of such bureaucracies within the UN context. The ensuing disparate trajectory of creation does not suggest that the notion of a NWM appealed to Western states first, nor was the US commission discussed in the subsequent UN deliberations of national machinery, as a source of emulation or otherwise, as will be further elaborated below.

Finally, the route of legislature sex quotas certainly does not suggest a new measure initiated by the European West. Between the 1940s and 1980s, such quotas were deployed exclusively in communist states, emerging initially with social movement demands in China in the 1940s and then following decisions by all-male party officials in vir-tually all the remaining socialist states, in Asia, Eastern Europe, Cuba and Africa. In 1989–90, as these states abandoned the use of legislature quotas with the end of communist rule, Latin American women invented them *de novo*. As the now formerly communist states did away with their informal quota measures as an allegedly undemocratic practice, virtually every Latin American state came to adopt legislature quotas in the name of modern democratic representation. After initially being adopted all across Latin America, the measure is now implemented or under debate in countless African and Asian states. Very few Western European states have passed legislature quota laws.

The fact that the worldwide proliferation of these institutions does not support the view of an international society where new state policies and institutions necessarily emanate out of the core in turn does not unavoidably lead to alternative propositions about their general paths. Instead, these diverse trajectories underscore the need to move away from attempts to specify standard international and domestic sequences or causal paths of change in international society. International society is historically and socially constituted, and as such the identification of general causal factors and trajectories should give way to narrative forms of explanation that are concretely grounded and sensitive to context.[2]

Interpretive contestations in a homogenizing and stratifying international society

No matter where new policies first emerge, it may be tempting nevertheless to see the worldwide emergence of suffrage, women's machineries and quotas as indications of the homogenizing force of globalization, of a world of increasingly "similar actors pursuing similar goals."[3] The conceptual frameworks of most constructivist approaches do help us identify standardized inter-subjective understandings about appropriate state behavior within international society. Indeed, the study of suffrage, national machinery and quotas also suggests that some understandings have been so widely reiterated and reified that they warrant being seen as shared features of world culture.

First, as world polity scholars contend, in the spread of these practices, states have operated as rationalized vehicles for progress. To greater and lesser degrees, states around the world are oriented towards ever-receding end-functions for which they are instrumental, whether that be the promotion of national liberation, of social welfare, of

[2] Rosenberg 1994.   [3] Boli and Thomas 1999: 2.

corporate success, of individual rights or of national security. Chapter 4 discussed the fact that the unfinished and ever-receding nature of such end-functions necessarily involves the generation of new concerns that demand authoritative action by the state. Chapters 5, 6 and 7 then provided substantive evidence that the political incorporation of women has been understood in terms of some end-function of states, such as democratic justice, socialist justice, economic development or national independence. It seems safe to conclude that the reiteration of the state as a vehicle for advancement was a shared process in international society.

Second, since the nineteenth century, a shared notion that the political status of women is causally related to the success of the state in generating progress has been in effect. While the exact and concrete nature of that relation has been contested and malleable, the core abstract notion was nonetheless reproduced across the century and across the world. What is more, the status of women has sometimes been seen as so strongly indicative of the progress of the state that the level of advancement of a state has been discerned by studying the national situation of women. Again, the exact nature of the indicators varies, but the core notion has remained a surprisingly resilient component of international society.

While helpful in the identification of shared features of international society, world polity and norms scholars overlook the link between norms and social hierarchy. Along with some critical constructivists, they have not broken out of the problematic conceptualization of states as like units, something that is often puzzling to comparative scholars. In a contention typical for IR, Buzan has argued that "unless there is some sense of common identity ... society cannot exist." For the society of states, this common identity allegedly makes it difficult to imagine their "likeness as units [and a simultaneous] acceptance of a set of rules that legitimizes the differentiation of units and establishes the distribution of rights and responsibilities among functionally differentiated actors."[4]

And yet, ranking among states was a simultaneous and absolutely central feature of the worldwide emergence of these state policies and institutions. In adopting new behaviors towards women, states were in the process of becoming, and indeed often expressly sought to be, higher in standing, whether that meant being more "civilized," liberated from

---

[4] Buzan 1993: 336.

colonialism, secure from communism, safe from capitalism, economically developed or a more modern democracy. This "becoming" entailed categorical processes of differentiation and distancing from states understood to be of a less valued kind.

It is important to underscore that the twentieth century saw a great deal of contention over what *kind* of state was superior. Although social hierarchy among states was always present in some form, there were often different interpretations about what sort of social hierarchy was at stake and how different kinds of states should be positioned. The status of women has many times served as a battleground precisely to prove the point of superiority of certain kinds of states to others. Suffragism in Europe and the Americas was embedded in the hierarchical order between savage life and civilization and the "progress" of societies away from the former to the latter. Such notions also informed socialist suffragism to some extent. However, the political emancipation of women in socialism functioned more pervasively to *reject* the civilized West and to demonstrate the superiority of socialist to bourgeois Western states. The quest away from the European West also infused the suffragists of the Afro-Asian solidarity movements, who argued that their political empowerment was an essential step in liberating the colonies and Afro-Asian women from Europe. Whereas the kind of social hierarchy at stake may have been debated, the presence of *some form* of social ranking was nevertheless a general feature present in suffrage deliberations across the world. In the operation of international suffrage norms, similarity among some states indeed rested on differentiation from and superiority to others.

The ranking character of norms was a pivotal force in the proliferation of the subsequent institutions as well. Chapter 6 demonstrated that the creation of national women's machinery entailed ordering along two broad dimensions. On the one hand, the socialist East was differentiated from the capitalist West, with socialist states largely exempt from creating NWMs because they had allegedly already resolved the woman question. And socialist states were upheld as models within the UN even though the first NWM, the US President's Commission, had been created to show the achievements of the leader of the "free world" with regard to women's liberation. Western capitalist democracies in general fell short with respect to the advancement of women, and there was thus a perceived need for and expectation of the establishment of a national women's agency.

In addition to the East–West distinction, the NWM norm simultaneously differentiated between developed and developing states. And
again, Western capitalist democracies fell short with respect to the
advancement of women. In the discussions of the need for establishing
NWMs among developing states, Western capitalist modernization was
identified not as an ideal to be emulated but as a primary source of the
oppression of women. Pre-modern "tradition" in the non-European
world was understood to have empowered women in many ways. The
initial creation of women's policy agencies among "developing" states
was thus not part of a general movement to become like the developed
West. Instead, once again, the state institution for the advancement of
women was often a mechanism for release from the West and underscored the superiority of non-Western traditions for the status of
women.

The contemporary proliferation of sex quota laws for national legislatures seems to rest on no such challenges to the presumed superiority
of Western modernity. In the advocacy for sex quotas, states are called
upon to become modern, market democracies. Whereas the appeal of
the norm in Latin America placed the emphasis on market *democracy*,
the subsequent advocacy by major global governance organs clearly
places the weight on quotas as a measure of modern *market* democracies. In either case, there is now a clear differentiation and deprecation
of practices indicative of "traditional" statehood, a presumably oppressive condition that quotas help to remedy. Even in cases where norms
call on all states to take on the same form, social ranking remains an
important dynamic component.

Radically divergent interpretations of the nature of the problem
within which suffrage, machineries and quotas have appeared as feasible solutions have abounded. Not only has the interpretation of what
women *are* differed dramatically, but so has the understanding of the
nature of international hierarchy and the relation of women to the
categorization and rank of states in that order. Rather than offering a
single vision of the world of states shared by all, the debates and
mobilization around each measure have given rise to critical examina-
tions and contestations around the very nature of the hierarchies of
international society. Continuous interpretive struggles about the
essence and character of the problem itself rendered what may appear
as a single norm – e.g. suffrage – a contextually different phenomenon.
However, *some form of social ranking among states was nevertheless*

always part and parcel of the contested politics of international norms. Norms thus need to be conceptualized in conjunction with social hierarchy.

The link between norms and social ranking persists whether those norms concern the status of women or some other state behavior. To briefly discuss another development in state behavior, an international norm of multicultural statehood (expecting complex internal structures that empower ethnic minorities) has emerged in the past decade or so. This norm positions multicultural states as "modern," contrasted with unitary homogeneous states as "traditional" and a throwback to the nineteenth century.[5] Reactions in Europe to the election of Barack Obama as US president in 2008 provide a good illustration of the ranking dynamics in emerging expectations about political representation of minorities. A 2008 *New York Times* article argued that "Mr. Obama's victory seemed to underscore how much farther behind Europe is" in this regard.[6] Obama's success was deemed "a great and concrete provocation to European society and European politics," an Italian member of parliament proclaimed.[7] A French political analyst likewise contended that "we realize we are late, and America has regained the torch of a moral revolution."[8] Like all standards of behavior, multiculturalism also operates as a criterion to rank states. Until the link between norms and social ranking has been examined comparatively with a number of other standards, however, focusing in particular on the intensity of interest and effect surrounding the standard, it is difficult to know whether policies targeting women are particularly potent in drawing on and producing social hierarchies among states.

Sexual inequality – also a form of social differentiation and ranking – is simultaneously implicated in the hierarchies among states. It is no coincidence that those who advocated for change in state behavior were overwhelmingly women. The sexual normative order spoke most loudly to some women about the necessity for change, and it was almost exclusively women who struggled for transformations in relations between women and the state. These women sometimes argued against the immobile nature of certain aspects of sexual differentiation, whereas allegedly biologically given sexual characteristics served as justifications for inclusion for others.

[5] Kymlicka 2007: 42–3.   [6] Erlanger 2008: A13.   [7] Ibid.   [8] Ibid.

In each case, the empowerment of women as political equals necessarily rested on their simultaneous articulation as a category, generally as different from men. Substantiating Joan Scott's well-known paradox with regard to liberal feminism – the need both to accept *and* to refuse sexual difference as the constitutive condition of such feminism – the previous chapters have pointed to some of the contextually and historically changing interpretations of sex/gender differences that were central to the debates and creation of suffrage, machineries and quotas.[9] Never did suffrage, national machinery and quotas eradicate male/female distinctions or other demarcations that made women appear as a category distinctive from men. The presumption in previous constructivist literature that the spread of measures such as suffrage is indication of the "individualization" of humanity, the de-gendering of human beings as individual citizens, is misguided. Instead, these measures helped reinterpret sex/gender differences and the implications of these in terms of incorporation into the state.

Discursive tensions and social hierarchy

The invoking and producing of social hierarchy as norms are brought into play are in turn a crucial and overlooked source of normative dynamism, productive of change in state policy. First, social ranking helps us better understand where, among what states, new policies initially emerge. States that are not well positioned in a social hierarchy may be the first to adopt a new policy. On the one hand, pressures to rise in standing within an accepted social order may lead to the adoption of new behavior. On the other, a new policy may develop in an attempt to reject the very order within which a state is poorly ranked. Either way, new state behavior may emerge "from below."

Second, in the presumed causal relations between the political status of women and the social ranking of a state, strains and apparent contradictions can and do emerge. Such contradictions have consistently allowed new political possibilities, and they thus provide additional insights about norms, social hierarchy and the change in state behavior worldwide. Connell has argued persuasively that "crisis tendencies develop in the gender order, which allow new political possibilities."[10] This is certainly true in the case of the worldwide emergence of suffrage,

[9] J. W. Scott 1996.   [10] Connell 1990: 532.

women's policy agencies and sex quotas. Crises, or at least strains, in the legitimation of state institutions as exclusively male spheres have developed time and again around the presumed causal relations between male political rule/exclusion of women from politics and a state's advancement.

When women were first barred from any formally political role in Europe, this was justified by reference to scientific evidence demonstrating the detrimental effects of female rule. Female involvement in the affairs of state would jeopardize general progress, the advancement of the very civilization that presumably ensured women's own welfare and liberty. Was it not savage societies, after all, that provided a political role for women? To enjoy its benefits, women could clearly not be entrusted with managing the state-led advancement of civilization. Emerging in this context, European and North American suffragists pointed to apparent inconsistencies in the causal logic: if male rule ensured progress, then why was Europe engulfed in such destructive warfare? Why was civilization not providing the protection of women that it had promised?

The destructive effects of women on the progress of socialism were similarly an accepted fact within socialist transnational organizations in the nineteenth century, even by many women. The advances of bourgeois suffragists in organizing women turned this presumption into an apparent contradiction: unless the vote was advocated for working women, their exclusion from politics would undermine socialism rather than advance it by luring working women into bourgeois organization. The inconsistencies that emerged within socialism thereby differed from those speaking to the women of "European civilization."

The proliferation of suffrage legislation in Europe was initially not interpreted as entirely relevant among many Latin American women's organizations. As nationals of states of "less advanced" civilization, it was feared that such measures were too radical for a continent whose women were presumed to be culturally backward. International social hierarchy thus initially worked against the adoption of suffrage among Latin American states, as the prohibition of women's voting rights seemed consistent with the allegedly less advanced character of these states. In this context, many Latin American suffragists argued that *some* women, the cultured strata, were indeed civilized enough to merit the vote. Denying them suffrage was inconsistent with the quest for national progress towards more advanced civilization, they contended. In most cases, however, the view even of elite women as politically backward and conservative would ultimately win them the vote, as this construal of elite women became compatible with shoring up Latin America against communism.

The creation of national women's machinery pivoted not around civilization but around modernization, which was identified as a source detrimental for the status of women around the world. And again, discursive tensions and contradictions appeared in the presumed causal relations between the status of women and the standing of a state. In the developed world, the advocates of NWM pointed to the contradictions between the allegedly advanced and just nature of modern states and the ongoing oppression of women. In the developing world, it was not simply inevitable modernization processes but specifically *Western and colonial* modernization that was identified as exploitative and oppressive to women. Third World woman emerged as a powerful symbol of the abuses of colonialism and the Western development establishment.

Gender and state-making in international society

Gender – discourses differentiating between male and female, masculine and feminine in relational and mutually constitutive ways – is a major force in the ongoing constitution of states. While clearly not the only force, gender has been a central element of modern state-formation, a process essential to what states are and do.[11] The study of gender is thus not peripheral to the study of states and it is certainly not solely "about women." Instead, studying gender helps to reveal and explain central aspects of the changing form, character and behavior of states. Gender and state-making are intimately connected.

One way this book addresses the link between gender and state-making in international politics is of course by drawing attention to how the status of women operates as a standard of rank among states. Social hierarchies among states, what states are made to be and the behaviors they adopt while being positioned in relation to one another, rest on gender. I have necessarily had to ask what "women" – as contrasted with "men" – are being made to be, and with what capacities for action. What are "women" (as differentiated from men) that they

[11] E.g. Connell 1990; Pateman 1990; Peterson 1992c.

should or should not be allowed to vote, be subject to a national policy agency or be included in national legislatures in larger numbers? How does the inclusion of "women" conceptualized in a particular way advance the standing of a state? Over the course of the past century and across the world, women have been made into all kinds of beings as they were integrated into state institutions. The empirical chapters thus underscore a common contention in feminist scholarship: gender is not fixed but a process of ongoing constitution. Femininity and masculinity, what men and women are made to be, are not given as natural facts. Nor are understandings of gender monolithic. Instead, gender is a context-bound process of differentiation and one that is highly contested.

A second way to think about the link between gender and state-making focuses on the gendered character of states. State institutions and policies have been crafted from materials that invariably involved masculinity as contrasted with femininity and with devalued forms of masculinity. Drawing on a large body of existing feminist scholarship, Chapter 4 showed that the nineteenth-century liberal-constitutional state in Europe rested on conceptualizations of gender that necessitated the preclusion of women from state affairs. The state became a masculine construction that depended upon keeping out and ruling over not just feminine traits but the whole collective of women. State institutions became masculinized in ways that strongly privileged certain forms of manhood and male participation. Particular understandings of masculinity and statehood in fact became so closely intertwined that it appeared reasonable and proper to keep women out of its formal institutions altogether. Given what the state and women were made to be, women were simply not understood to possess the qualities appropriate for taking on official functions of the state, whether as voters, elected officials, civil servants or military personnel.

Women are no longer fully excluded from formal state affairs, however. The practice of adding women to states around the world speaks to questions that have long been of concern to feminist students of the state, IR ones included: What does this suggest about the gendered nature of states? Do states remain masculine constructions in largely the same terms as in late nineteenth-century Europe? Alternatively, have states been feminized along with the inclusion of women? If so, what are the implications for the effectiveness and potency of feminization as a means to devalue actors and behaviors in international politics? These are not the questions the book set out to address. A satisfying attempt to speak to these issues would clearly demand much more careful and contextual analyses than I can offer here. Let me nevertheless put forward some thoughts on the possible implications of my analysis for the feminist IR treatment of gendered states, beginning with a brief recapitulation of that literature.

Feminist IR scholars have largely focused on the masculine character of states and on international politics as "a world of traditionally masculine pursuits."[12] This in some part seems to be an effect of the focus on concepts and practices that lie at the center of IR as an academic discipline: warfare, the military, coercive power, sovereignty, and so on. Institutions such as the military and the police have clearly been primarily in the hands of men, although always relying on women to fulfill vital but subordinated functions presumably necessary for the operation of these institutions (e.g. providing sexual services or sewing uniforms for the military).[13] State institutions and policies have simultaneously been central in forming what "men" (and "women") are. The coercive institutions and practices of states entail scripts of masculinity that strongly inform and shape the behavior of state institutions as well as of individuals acting as representatives of states.

Generally noting that there are multiple masculinities,[14] the IR literature has primarily focused on certain predominant understandings of masculinity and manhood – those bound up with violence, sexual prowess and domination. Many aspects of masculinity have in fact been forged in the nexus of the state and war, where these traits have been operative for some time.[15] Scholars have highlighted that the state and men alike are seen as having a monopoly on the legitimate use of violence, legitimized partially with the stated goal of protecting women as the weak and physically defenseless sex. Soldiers, as state agents, are expected to be just and heroic males, partially fighting for the protection of female noncombatants.[16] States similarly operate with reference to the protection of nations, collectivities whose symbolic figuration relies heavily on presumably feminine and familial traits of love, devotion and

---

[12] Hooper 2001: 12.   [13] E.g. Enloe 1990; Yuval-Davis 1997.

[14] On multiple masculinities and hegemonic masculinity, see e.g. Alison 2007; Neumann 2008; Zalewski and Parpart 1998.

[15] See e.g. Alison 2007; Cohn 1998; Dudink and Goldstein 2001: 251–331; Hagemann 2004; Johnson 1997; Keen 1991; Niva 1998.

[16] E.g. Elshtain 1995; Kinsella 2005; Ruddick 1993.

cultural reproduction.[17] The security-seeking and violent behavior of states thus becomes legitimated by appeals to masculinity, a function in part of what states are made to be as gendered institutions.[18]

Sexual prowess and strong, sometimes uncontrollable sexual needs are also characteristics consistently associated with masculinity and state policy. Setting up systems to enable masculinist and heterosexual sexual relations for troops have indeed been the express policy of a number of states, including the USA and Japan.[19] Male sexuality sometimes becomes construed as very closely interlinked with violence and domination, so much so that masculinity becomes centered on violent sexual conquest and sexual subordination of others. This form of masculinity manifests in multiple ways in state practice. Strategic discourse may rely on the feminization of the enemy and military objectives in quite sexual terms as a means to devalue adversaries and legitimate their conquest.[20] With such scripts of masculinity operative in the military, soldiers may emerge as sexual conquerors who engage in rape and sexual humiliation of the enemy, male or female. State interrogations and torture of men have frequently relied on sexual denigration intended to humiliate by "treating men as women" – forced to be naked, exposed, and the vulnerable sexual objects of male domination.[21] Wartime sexual violence has then functioned as a way of expressing state power and masculinity, serving to subjugate a feminized enemy.[22]

Judging from the recent literature, there seems to be little evidence of substantial changes in these kinds of masculine constructions of the state. The character of the abuses during recent decades in places ranging from the former Yugoslavia to Abu Ghraib and Guantánamo indeed point to a surprising endurance of certain scripts of masculinity at work in the military. The forms of inclusion of women into the state that were the subject of this book do not appear to have significantly altered the gendered character of coercive state apparatuses in this respect. Elshtain may thus be correct in contending that although much has changed about the social identities and proper spheres for men and women over the past century, it is mistaken to assume that the changes have "undercut received webs of social meaning as these

[17] E.g. Yuval-Davis 1997; Yuval-Davis and Anthias 1989.
[18] E.g. Milliken and Sylvan 1996; Tickner 2001: 49.
[19] E.g. Enloe 1993; Moon 1997; Yoshimi and O'Brien 2000.
[20] E.g. Campbell 1992; Cohn 1987; Hooper 2001.
[21] E.g. Alison 2007; Eisenstein 2007; Enloe 2004.   [22] E.g. Alison 2007.

revolve around men, women, and war."[23] Even with a growing number
of women in the military, the masculine and masculinist character of
those institutions seems to persist. Women are not primarily brought
in as "feminine," which would necessitate some change in the masculine character of the institution. As Eisenstein argues, instead "the
uniform remains the same. Male or female can be a masculinized
commander."[24]

There are clearly reasons to continue to treat states as masculinized
coercive institutions. But this is not the only thing states have been and
are presently made to be. There are also reasons to argue that adding
women has disrupted some of the prior masculinist foundations of the
state by inserting presumably female traits. This book has shown that
women were indeed brought into the state partly as beings distinctive
from men, believed to be sharing certain "female" characteristics and
values. Adding "that which constitutes femininity" to previously masculine constructions has involved transformations of the gendered quality of states.[25] Indeed, some alteration must take place in order to
accommodate the inclusion of women-as-feminine.

The struggles for inclusion of women as voters, legislators and the
objects of a national policy agency have in many cases been struggles to
bring female elements and traits to the state, as this book has shown.
Again, precisely what "female" traits were understood to be has varied
over time and across context. To highlight but one example, suffragists
in the European West argued that women would help to transform the
state and save society from the competitive, destructive and war-prone
apparatus it had turned into in the hands of men. Their participation
would mean adding female qualities and functions to the state, they
contended, such as giving voice to peaceful and cooperative ways of
being and bringing values of compassion, care and selflessness into the
public arena. This resonates with an argument made by a number of
comparative welfare state scholars, who contend that the introduction
of an ethical duty to care for citizens was (and remains) understood as
"adding 'female' functions to the more clearly masculine protector role"

---

[23] Elshtain 1995: 6.
[24] Eisenstein 2004. Noting the continuities, I would nevertheless hesitate to
overstate the claim about the stability of the masculine character of the coercive
institutions of state. See e.g. Niva 1998 and Stensöta 2004.
[25] On this point, see Peterson 1992b: 17.

of the state.[26] States have taken on roles and practices expressly seen as female and mired in gendered metaphors, such as caring for children, the elderly and the infirm. And not only have women been central in reconfiguring the gender of states, but the feminization of states has simultaneously prompted the inclusion of women as "female expertise."

While continuing to operate as masculine constructions in certain ways, states have also been feminized: talked about in feminine terms, performing tasks considered female, and incorporating women to perform those tasks. The emergence of suffrage, national women's agencies and sex quota laws have all in part rested on claims that female elements (and women-as-female) were necessary for the advancement of the state. And since exhibiting involvement of women in public affairs is now widely seen as indicative of some form of progress, feminization does not necessarily function as a means to devalue actors and behaviors. For instance, having a certain share of female legislators is presently celebrated among global governance institutions as bringing female virtues of honesty and selflessness into the state. Female traits are sometimes elevated in international politics; in other words, they are used to exalt rather than diminish the standing of a state. What this in turn suggests is that state institutions are gendered in much more complex ways than any unified notion of a "male state" would suggest. Although warfare and the military may continue to be homelands of masculinity, it is far from clear that the formal "political" institutions that are the subject of this book persist only as such.

[26] Sawer 1996b: 119. See also Anttonen 1990; Dahlerup 1988; Hernes 1987; Koven and Michel 1993; Stensöta 2004.

Primary sources, by chapter

When a text is used as an object of analysis for the empirical chapters, it is listed as a primary source. When the findings of a text are used to support the empirical argument, that text is listed in the Bibliography, along with scholarship used for the discussions on previous constructivist literature and my theoretical approach.

Where primary sources are listed as reproduced or collected in secondary sources, full details of those secondary sources will be found in the Bibliography.

1 Introduction

López, Clemencia, 1902. "Women of the Philippines," address at the Annual Meeting of the New England Woman Suffrage Association, May 29, 1902, in *The Women's Journal*: June 7, 1902.

4 Excluding women in the society of civilized states

Aimé-Martin, Louis, 1843. *The Education of Mothers: or the Civilization of Mankind by Women*. Philadelphia: Lea and Blanchard.

Campbell, Charles, 1892. "A Journey through North Korea through the Ch'ang-pai shan." *Proceedings of the Royal Geographical Society and Monthly Record of Geography* 14(3):141–61.

Darwin, Charles, 1873/1936. *The Origin of Species by Means of Natural Selection; or, the Preservation of Favored Races in the Struggle for Life and the Descent of Man and Selection in Relation to Sex*. New York: Modern Library Edition.

Engels, Frederick, 1884/1972. *The Origin of the Family, Private Property and the State in the Light of the Researches of Lewis H. Morgan*. New York: International Publishers.

Fullom, Stephen Watson, 1855. *The History of Woman, and her Connexion with Religion, Civilization, & Domestic Manners from the Earliest Period*. London: Routledge & Co.

Gamble, Eliza, 1894. *The Evolution of Woman: An Inquiry into the Dogma of her Inferiority to Man*. New York: G. P. Putnam's Sons.

Hobbes, Thomas, 1651/1968. *Leviathan, or The Matter, Forme & Power of a Common-Wealth Ecclesiasticall and Civill.* Harmondsworth: Penguin Books.

Lewis, Sarah, 1840. *Woman's Mission.* London: John W. Parker, West Strand.

Livingstone, David, 1858. *Missionary Travels and Researches in South Africa Including a Sketch of Sixteen Years Residence in the Interior of South Africa, and a Journey from the Cape of Good Hope to Loanda on the West Coast; Thence Across the Continent Down the River Zambesi, to the Eastern Ocean.* New York: Harper & Brothers.

Malthus, Thomas, 1798/1926. *First Essay on Population,* at www.faculty.rsu.edu/~felwell/Theorists/Malthus/essay2.htm, accessed September 5, 2008.

Man, Edward H., 1883/1932. *The Andamanese Islanders.* London: Bibling & Sons Ltd.

Mason, Otis Tufton, 1895. *Woman's Share in Primitive Culture.* London: Macmillan and Co.

Millar, John, 1806. *The Origin of the Distinction of Ranks; or, An Inquiry into the Circumstances which Give Rise to Influence and Authority in the Different Members of Society.* Edinburgh: William Blackwood.

Morgan Lewis, 1877. *Ancient Society, or Researches in the Lines of Human Progress from Savagery through Barbarism.* London: Macmillan and Co.

Parkman, Francis, 1884. *Some of the Reasons against Woman Suffrage.* Boston.

Pike, Warburton, 1892. *Journeys to the Barren Grounds of Northern Canada Through the Subarctic Forests.* London: Macmillan.

Reuterskiöld, Carl Axel, 1911. *Politisk rösträtt för kvinnor: utredning anbefalld genom nådigt beslut den 30 april 1909, I: Om utvecklingen och tillämpningen i utlandet af idéen om kvinnans politiska rösträtt.* Uppsala: Almqvist & Wiksell.

Sigourney, Lydia Howard, 1835. *Letters to Young Ladies.* Hartford: W. Watson.

Im Thurn, Everard, 1883. *Among the Indians of Guiana.* London: Kegan Paul.

Young, Samuel, 1837. "Suggestions on the Best Mode of Promoting Civilization and Improvement; or, the Influence of Woman on the Social State," lecture delivered before the Young Men's Association for Mutual Improvement in Albany, NY. Albany: Hoffman & White.

Zetkin, Clara, 1906. "Woman Suffrage," speech delivered at Mannheim Socialist Women's Conference. London: Twentieth Century Press.

5 Women's suffrage and the standards of civilization

Alvarado Rivera, María Jesús, 1910. "El feminismo," paper presented at the First International Feminine Congress, Buenos Aires, stencil. Biblioteca Nacional del Perú.

1912. "El feminismo," talk given at the Sociedad Geográfica de Lima, October 28, 1911. Lima: Imprenta de la Escuela de Ingenieros.

Anaya de Urquidi, Mercedes, 1936. "La mujer y sus reivindicaciones justas," in Macedonio Urquidi 1937: 105–9.

Bebel, August, 1885. *Woman in the Past, Present and Future*. London: the Modern Press.

1879/1910. *Woman and Socialism*. New York: Socialist Literature.

Bukharin, Nikolai, 1919. "The Communist International and the Colonies." *Pravda*, March 6, 1919, reproduced in Riddell 1987, 307–8.

Cáceres, Zoila Aurora, 1924. *Programa de Principios del Feminismo Peruano*. Lima: La Prensa.

1944. Radio transmission on "America Today," in Cáceres 1946.

1946. *Labor de armonía interamericana en los Estados Unidos de Norte América 1940–1945*. Lima: n.p.

Catt, Carrie Chapman, 1918. *Do You Know?* New York: National American Woman Suffrage Association.

Ch'en Yün, 1939. "How to be a Communist Party Member," in Brandt *et al.* 1952: 322–36.

Chinese Communist Party, 1922. "First Manifesto of the CCP on the Current Situation," in Brandt *et al.* 1952: 54–63.

1928. "Resolution of the Sixth National Congress [of the CCP] on the Peasant Movement," September, in Brandt *et al.* 1952: 156–65.

1929. "Resolution and Spirit of the Second Plenum of the Central Committee," July 9, in Brandt *et al.* 1952: 166–79.

1931. "Constitution of the Soviet Republic [of China]," November 7, in Brandt *et al.* 1952: 220–4.

Feminismo Peruano, 1931. "El voto femenino," *La Prensa*, June 15.

First International Working Women's Conference, 1920. "To the Working Women of the World," appeal adopted by the International Conference of Communist Women, Moscow, July 30–August 2, 1920, in Riddell 1991: II, 972–6.

Fourier, Charles, 1846. *Œuvres Complètes*, I, 145–50, at http://irw.rutgers. edu/research/ugresearch/international/fourier.html, accessed October 10, 2003.

Illinois Association Opposed to the Extension of Suffrage to Women, 1900. *Address to the Voters of the Middle West*. Chicago.

Inter-American Commission of Women (IACW), 1954. *Derechos civiles y políticos de la mujer de América*, Primera Parte: *Derechos políticos*. Report presented to the Tenth Interamerican Conference. Washington DC: Panamerican Union.

1965. *Historical Review on the Recognition of the Political Rights of American Women*. Washington DC: Panamerican Union.

Inter-Parliamentary Union (IPU) 2000. *Participation of Women in Political Life: An Assessment of Developments in National Parliaments, Political Parties, Governments and the Inter-Parliamentary Union, Five Years after the Fourth World Conference on Women.* Geneva: IPU.

Kollontai, Alexandra, 1909. "The Struggle for Political Rights," in *The Social Basis of the Woman Question,* reproduced in Kollontai 1977: 58–74.

———. 1919. "Working Women's Day and the Third International." *Pravda,* March 7, 1919, reproduced in Riddell 1987: 308–10.

Lenin, Vladimir, 1918. "Speech at the First All-Russian Congress of Women Workers, November 19, 1918," in *Lenin's Collected Works,* XXVIII. Moscow: Progress Publishers, 1974: 180–2.

———. 1919. "Soviet Power and the Status of Women," in *Lenin's Collected Works,* XXX. Moscow: Progress Publishers, 1965: 120–3.

———. 1921. "International Working Women's Day," in *Lenin's Collected Works,* XXXII. Moscow: Progress Publishers, 1965: 161–3.

Luna Arroyo, Antonio, 1936. *La mujer mexicana en la lucha social.* Mexico City.

Lutz, Bertha, 1918. "Women's Letters," *Revista da Semana,* December 23, 1918, reproduced in Hahner 1990: 22–4.

Marx, Karl, and Friedrich Engels, 1845/1956. *The Holy Family: or, Critique of Critical Critique.* New York: International Publishers.

Merino Carvallo, Nelly, 1936. "Mi opinión sobre derechos femeninos," in Macedonio Urquidi 1937: 111–12.

Morgan Lewis, 1877. *Ancient Society, or Researches in the Lines of Human Progress from Savagery through Barbarism.* London: Macmillan and Co.

National Council of Women of the United States, 1933. *Our Common Cause, Civilization,* report of the International Congress of Women. New York: National Council of Women.

Pan American Union, 1945. *Final Act of the Inter-American Conference on Problems of War and Peace.* Washington DC: Pan American Union.

Peruvian Constituent Congress, 1931. *Diario de los debates del Congreso Constituyente de 1931.* Lima (Publicación Oficial).

Portal, Magda, 1933. *El aprismo y la mujer.* Lima: Editorial Cooperativa Aprist "Atahualpa."

Reuterskiöld, Carl Axel, 1911. *Politisk rösträtt för kvinnor: utredning anbefalld genom nådigt beslut den 30 april 1909, I: Om utvecklingen och tillämpningen i utlandet af idéen om kvinnans politiska rösträtt.* Uppsala: Almqvist & Wiksell.

Roosevelt, Eleanor, 1953. "UN Deliberations on Draft Convention on the Political Rights of Women," *Department of State Bulletin,* January 5, 29–32.

Sirola, Yrjö, 1919. "The White Terror," in Riddell 1987: 235–8.

Trotsky, Leon, 1945. "Speech Delivered at the Second World Conference of
    Communist Women, July 15, 1921," in Leo Trotsky, *The First Five Years
    of the Communist International*, I. New York: Pioneer Publishers, 153–7.
Zetkin, Clara, 1889. "For the Liberation of Women," speech at the
    International Worker's Congress, Paris, July 19, in Zetkin 1984: 45–50.
    1895. "Concerning the Women's Rights Petition," *Vorwärts*, January 24,
    in Zetkin 1984: 60–71.
    1896. "Only in Conjunction with the Proletarian Woman will Socialism be
    Victorious," speech at the Party Congress of the Social Democratic Party
    of Germany, Gotha, October 16, in Zetkin 1984: 72–83.
    1906. "Woman Suffrage," speech delivered at Mannheim Socialist
    Women's Conference. London: Twentieth Century Press.
    1910. "International Women's Day," from a proposal to the Second
    International Women's Conference at Copenhagen, August 27, in
    Zetkin 1984: 108–9.
    (ed.), 1920. "Theses for the Communist Women's Movement," resolution
    adopted by the Comintern Executive Committee in 1920, in Riddell
    1991: I, 977–98.

No author

El Comercio, 1938. "Consejo Nacional de Mujeres del Perú," July 17.
Documents from the International Conference of Socialist Women at Berne,
    March 26–8, 1915, in Gankin and Fisher 1940: 286–301.
Informal Socialist Women's Conference at Stockholm, "Official Report of the
    Sessions, September 14–15, 1917," in Olga and Fisher 1940: 688–91.
Proceedings of the First Afro-Asian Women's Conference, Cairo, January 14–23,
    1961. Cairo: Amalgamated Press of Egypt.
Proceedings of the First Asian–African Conference of Women, Colombo,
    Ceylon, February 15–24, 1958. Bombay: Mouj Printing Bureau.

6 National women's policy bureaus and the standards of development

Boserup, Esther, 1970. *Women's Role in Economic Development*. New York:
    St. Martin's Press.
Bunch, Charlotte, and Shirley Castley (eds.), 1980. *Developing Strategies for
    the Future: Feminist Perspectives. Report of the International
    Workshops in Stony Point, NY, 1980 and in Bangkok, Thailand,
    1979*. New York: International Women's Tribune Centre.
Comisión Nacional de la Mujer Peruana 1975a. "La problemática de la mujer
    en el Perú," working paper. Lima: Centro de Estudios de Participación
    Popular – SINAMOS.

1975b. "Sintesis informativa y anexos de la conferencia mundial del Año Internacional de la Mujer, 19 Junio-2 Julio 1975," Lima: n.p.

1976. "Analisis de la legislación vigente, relacionada con la situación de la mujer," working paper. Lima: CONAMUP.

Gilmore, Marguerite, and Mary M. Cannon, 1968. "Commissions on the Status of Women in Foreign Countries – 1963–1968," report of the US Women's Bureau, mimeograph.

International Labor Office, 1953. *The ILO and Women*. Geneva: International Labor Office.

Kennedy, John F., 1961. *Executive Order 10980. Establishing the President's Commission on the Status of Women*. December 14, at www.lib.umich.edu/govdocs/jfkeo/eo/10980.htm, accessed October 10, 2008.

Lewis, W. Arthur, 1955. *The Theory of Economic Growth*. London: Allen & Unwin.

Oficina de la Mujer (Ministry of Justice, Peru), 1984. *Situación de la mujer en el Perú: estudio demográfico*. Lima: Ministry of Justice.

1986. "Informe," internal document. Lima: Ministry of Justice.

1987. "Evaluación de las actividades realizadas por la Oficina de la Mujer durante el año 1986," internal document, February 24. Lima: Ministry of Justice.

Rogers, Barbara, 1975. "Female Forms of Power and the Myth of Male Dominance: A Model of Female–Male Interaction in a Peasant Society," *American Ethnologist* 2(4): 727–56.

1980. *The Domestication of Women: Discrimination in Developing Societies*. London: Kogan Page.

Roosevelt, Eleanor, 1995. *What I Hope to Leave Behind: The Essential Essays of Eleanor Roosevelt*. Brooklyn: Carlson Publishers.

Rosaldo, Michele, and Louise Lamphere (eds.), 1974. *Women, Culture and Society*. Stanford: Stanford University Press.

Sandberg, Elisabet, 1975. *Equality is the Goal: A Swedish Report*. Stockholm: Advisory Council to the Prime Minister on Equality Between Men and Women.

Sandlund, Maj-Britt, 1968. *The Status of Women in Sweden: Report to the United Nations 1968*. Stockholm: Swedish Institute.

Staudt, Kathleen, 1978. "Agricultural Productivity Gaps: A Case Study of Male Preference in Government Policy Implementation," *Development and Change*, 9(3): 439–57.

1982. "Bureaucratic Resistance to Women's Programs: The Case of Women in Development," in Ellen Boneparth (ed.), *Women, Power and Policy*. New York: Pergamon Press, 263–81.

Tinker, Irene, 1976. "The Adverse Impact of Development on Women," in Irene Tinker and Michele Bo Bramsen (eds.), *Women and World Development*. Washington DC: Overseas Development Council, 22–34.

Tinker, Irene, and Michele Bo Bramsen, 1976. "Proceedings of the Seminar on Women in Development," in Irene Tinker and Michele Bo Bramsen (eds.), *Women and World Development*. Washington DC: Overseas Development Council, 141–77.

Tinker, Irene, and Jane Jaquette, 1987. "UN Decade for Women: Its Impact and Legacy," *World Development* 15(3): 419–27.

UNICEF (Oficina Regional Para las Américas), 1976. *Servicios de apoyo: mecanismos para la incorporación de la mujer al desarrollo*. La Paz, Bolivia: UNICEF.

United Nations, 1963. *Yearbook of the United Nations 1963*. New York: Columbia University Press.

United Nations Branch for the Advancement of Women 1987. *Women 2000*, no. 3. Vienna: Branch for the Advancement of Women.

United Nations Department of Economic and Social Affairs, 1973. *Report of the Interregional Meeting of Experts on the Integration of Women in Development*. New York: United Nations. ST/SOA/120.

  1974a. *Interregional Seminar on the Family in a Changing Society: Problems and Responsibilities of its Members*. Report from the seminar held in London, July 18–31, 1973. New York: United Nations. ST/ESA/SER.B/3.

  1974b. *Plan of Action*. From the Regional Consultation for Asia and the Far East on Integration of Women in Development with Special Reference to Population Factors, Bangkok, Thailand, May 13–17, 1974. New York: United Nations. ST/ESA/SER.B/6/Add.1.

  1975a. *Interregional Seminar on National Machinery to Accelerate the Integration of Women in Development and to Eliminate Discrimination on Grounds of Sex*. Report from the Seminar held in Ottawa, September 4–17, 1974. New York: United Nations. ST/ESA/SER.B/7.

  1975b. *Report of the Regional Seminar for Africa on the Integration of Women in Development, with Special Reference to Population Factors*. Addis Ababa, Ethiopia, June 3–7, 1974. New York: United Nations. ST/ESA/SER.B/6.

  1975c. *Plan of Action*. From the Regional Seminar for Africa on the Integration of Women in Development, with Special Reference to Population Factors, Addis Ababa, Ethiopia, June 3–7, 1974. New York: United Nations. ST/ESA/SER.B/6.Add.1.

1977. *Report of the United Nations Regional Seminar on the Participation of Women in Political, Economic and Social Development, with Special Emphasis on the Machinery to Accelerate the Integration of Women in Development.* Kathmandu, Nepal, February, 15–22, 1977. New York: United Nations. ST/ESA/SER.B/10.

1980a. *Report of the World Conference of the United Nations Decade for Women: Equality, Development and Peace.* New York: United Nations. A/CONF.94.

1980b. *Review and Evaluation of Progress Achieved in the Implementation of the World Plan of Action National Machinery and Legislation.* Prepared for the World Conference of the United Nations Decade for Women: Equality, Development and Peace. New York: United Nations. A/CONF.94.11.

United Nations Economic Commission for Africa (Human Resources Development Division), 1972. "Women: the Neglected Human Resource for African Development," *Canadian Journal of African Studies* 6(2): 359–70.

United Nations Economic and Social Council (ECOSOC), 1965. Resolution 1068 D(XXXIX) of July 1965.

1967. Resolution 1209 (XLII) of May 1967.

1972. Resolution 1682 (LII) of June 1972.

United Nations Secretary General, 1968. *National Commissions on the Status of Women: Report by the Secretary General to the 21st Session of the Commission on the Status of Women.* E/CN.6/494.

US President's Commission on the Status of Women, 1963. *American Women.* Washington: US Government Printing Office.

7 Legislature sex quotas and cultural rank

Abdela, Lesley, 2001. "Women Lose Ground: Quotas Are the Only Way to Ensure an Adequate Number of Female MPs," *Guardian*, May 8, 2001.

Annan, Kofi, 1997. "Inaugural Address" given at the United Nations International Conference on Governance for Sustainable Growth and Equity. New York, July 28–30, 1997.

Asplund, Bo (UNDP Resident Representative), 2003. "Statement at the Public Discussion 'Indonesian Women Welcoming the General Elections 2004: Preparedness and Strategy' and Launch of UNDP's Publication Women's Political Participation and Good Governance: 21st Century Challenges," Jakarta, March 6, at www.undp.or.id/statements/20030307_rrspeech. asp, accessed October 15, 2003.

Center for Legislative Development, 2000. "The Quota System: Women's Boon or Bane?" *Women Around the World* 1(3), at www.cld.org/waw 5. htm, accessed April 3, 2006.

2002. "A Policy Paper on Promoting Gender Balance in Political Representation," March 22, 2002.

Chandhoke, Neera, 2000. "Some Thought on Women's Quota Bill," *The Hindu*, December 6, 2000.

Congress of Peru, 1997. "Debate del texto sustitutorio del proyecto de Ley General de Elecciones," Segunda Legislatura Ordinaria de 1996. 24a sesión, miércoles, 18 de junio de 1997, 2519–21.

Desai, Lord, 1997. "Keynote Address," given at the United Nations International Conference on Governance for Sustainable Growth and Equity. New York, July 28–30, 1997.

Dollar, David, Raymond Fisman and Roberta Gatti, 1999. "Are Women Really the 'Fairer' Sex? Corruption and Women in Government," *World Bank Policy Research Report on Gender and Development*, Working Paper Series, no. 4.

Favoreu, Louis, 1996. "Principe d'égalité et représentation politique des femmes: la France et les exemples étrangers," report of the French Council of State, no. 48.

Frey Nakonz, Regula, 1999. "Genderdimension von Korruption," Paper written for Bread for All, December 1999.

Inter-American Commission of Women, 1994. "Strategic Plan of Action of the Inter-American Commission of Women (CIM)," 27th Assembly of Delegates of the Inter-American Commission of Women. Washington DC: Organization of American States.

1998–2002 (annual). "Annual Report of the Inter-American Commission of Women to the [29th–33rd] Regular Session of the General Assembly of the Organization of American States," Washington DC: Organization of American States.

1999. "Plan of Action of the CIM on Women's Participation in Power and Decision Making Structures," CIM/Ser.L./II.8.1.

Inter-Parliamentary Union, 1995a. "Parliamentary Action for Women's Access to and Participation in Decision-Making Structures Aimed at Achieving True Equality for Women," resolution adopted by the 93rd Inter-Parliamentary Conference, Madrid, April 1.

1995b. "Beijing Parliamentary Declaration," adopted by the participants in Parliamentarians' Day at the Fourth World Conference on Women, Beijing, September 7.

1995c. *Women in Parliaments 1945–1995*. Geneva: IPU.

1997a. "Specialized Conference in New Delhi," in *Gender Partnership: What the IPU is Doing*, at www.ipu.org/wmn-e/nd-conf.htm, accessed August 4, 2003.

1997b. "Concluding Statement by the President on the Outcome of the Conference" ("New Delhi Declaration"), in *Specialized Inter-Parliamentary*

Conference "Towards Partnership Between Men and Women in Politics," at www.ipu.org/splz-e/Ndelhi97.htm, accessed September 28, 2008.

1997c. *Men and Women in Politics: Democracy Still in the Making.* Geneva: IPU.

1997d. "Women Make up Less than 12 Percent of World's Parliaments, Less than 11 Percent of Party Leaders," press release no. 62, February 13, 1997.

1997e. *Towards Partnership Between Men and Women in Politics: New Delhi, 14–18 February 1997.* "Reports and Documents" series, no. 29. Geneva: Inter Parliamentary Union.

2000. *Participation of Women in Political Life: An Assessment of Developments in National Parliaments, Political Parties, Governments and the Inter-Parliamentary Union, Five Years after the Fourth World Conference on Women.* Geneva: IPU.

2000. "Tripartite Consultation on 'Democracy Through Partnership Between Men and Women',," organized with the UN Division for the Advancement of Women on the occasion of the Beijing + 5 Special Session of the UN General Assembly, at www.ipu.org/splz-e/bjn5.htm, accessed September 30, 2008.

2003. "Political Will Indispensable for Steady Progress in Women's Participation in Parliament," press release no. 155, March 5, 2003.

Karam, Azza, 1998. "Beijing + 5: Women's Political Participation: Review of Strategies and Trends," background paper no. 1 for the UNDP Meeting on Women and Political Participation: 21st Century Challenges, March 24–6, 1999, New Delhi, India.

King, Angela, 2002. "Statement at the Panel Session: Working Together Toward Gender Equality in the Context of the Millennium Development Goal," at the Launch of the Publication of the World Bank's Gender Mainstreaming Strategy, Washington DC, January 15.

Lowe Morna, Colleen, 2000. "Towards Sustainable Democratic Institutions in Southern Africa," paper prepared for the International SADC-IDEAS Conference on Women's Political Participation in SADC, May.

Lubertino Beltrán, M. José, 1992. "Historia de la 'Ley de Cuotas'," in *Cuotas minima de participación de mujeres: el debate in Argentina.* Fundación Friedrich Ebert, 9–43.

Matland, Richard, 1998. "Box 1. The Effect of Development and Culture on Women's Representation," in Azza Karam (ed.), *International IDEA Handbook on Women in Parliament: Beyond Numbers.* Stockholm: Idea, 65–90, at www.idea.int/women/parl/ch2_box1.htm, accessed December 3, 2003.

Mehlomakhulu, Sandra, 1999. "Creating New Structures of a Chapter: Gender and Corruption. Transparency International Zimbabwe (TIZ)," paper presented at the Annual Meeting of TI in November 1999.

Mujer y Sociedad 1986."Cuotas femeninas," 6(2):11.

Organization of American States, 2001. *Inter-American Democratic Charter*, Twenty-Eighth Special Session of the General Assembly, September 11. OEA/Ser.P AG/RES. 1 (XXVIII-E/01).

Stückelberger, Christoph, 2003. *Continue Fighting Corruption: Experiences and Tasks of Churches and Development Agencies.* Geneva: Bread for All.

Summit of the Americas, 1994. *Plan of Action*, at www.summit-americas.org/miamiplan.htm, accessed November 14, 2008.

   1998. *Plan of Action*, at www.summit-americas.org/chileplan.htm, accessed November 14, 2008.

   2001. *Plan of Action*, at www.state.gov/p/wha/rls/59664.htm, accessed November 14, 2008.

Swamy, Anand, Stephen Knack, Young Lee and Omar Azfar, 2001. "Gender and Corruption," *Journal of Development Economics* 64: 25–55.

United Nations, 2001. *Beijing to Beijing; Review and Appraisal of the Implementation of the Beijing Platform for Action: Report of the Secretary General.* New York: UN Publications.

United Nations Commission on the Status of Women. 1990. *Report of the Commission on the Status of Women on its Thirty-Fourth Session.* Supplement 5.

   1992. *Report of the Commission on the Status of Women on its Thirty-Sixth Session.* E/CN.6/1992/13.

   1997. *Report of the Forty-First Session.* E/1997/27 CSW.

United Nations Development Fund for Women, 2000. *Progress of the World's Women 2000.* New York: UNIFEM.

United Nations Development Programme (UNDP), 1995. *Human Development Report.* New York: Oxford University Press.

   1997. *Governance for Sustainable Growth and Equity.* New York: UN Publications.

   1999a. "Women Call for Transformation of Political Process: Recommendations from 'Women & Politics Meeting'," *UNDP India News.*

   1999b. "Women and Political Participation: 21st Century Challenges," draft aide-memoire, March 24–6, 1999, New Delhi.

   2000. *Women's Political Participation and Good Governance: 21st Century Challenges.* New York: UN Publications.

United Nations Division for the Advancement of Women, 1990. "Equality: Equality in Political Participation and Decision-Making," annex, para. 22, E/CN.6/1990/2.

2000. "Women in Power and Decision-Making," Fact Sheet No. 7.

United Nations Economic and Social Council (ECOSOC) Resolution 1990/4: "Equality in Political Participation and Decision-Making."

United Nations Economic Commission for Africa (UN ECA) 1998. "AFR-FEM Working Group: Summary Three (4/04–4/11)," of the conference African Women and Economic Development: Investing in Our Future, held in Addis Ababa, Ethiopia, April 28–May 1, 1998.

United Nations Economic Commission on Eastern Europe, 2001. "Regional Workshop on Gender and Labour Markets in Transition Countries," held in Warsaw, January 15–17, 2001. Geneva: United Nations.

United Nations General Assembly, 2001. *Road Map Towards the Implementation of the United Nations Millennium Declaration*, Report of the Secretary-General to the fifty-sixth session of the General Assembly. A/56/326.

United Nations Office at Vienna, 1992. *Women in Politics and Decision-Making in the Late Twentieth Century: A United Nations Study*. Dordrecht: Martinus Nijhoff Publishers.

Women's Environment and Development Organization (WEDO), 2003a. "50/50 Campaign," at www.wedo.org, accessed October 25, 2003.

2003b. "The 50/50 Campaign: Get the Balance Right!" at www.wedo.org, accessed October 25, 2003.

World Bank (WB), 2000. *Reforming Public Institutions and Strengthening Governance*. Washington: World Bank.

2001. *Engendering Development – Through Gender Equality in Rights, Resources and Voice*. Oxford: Oxford University Press.

2002. *Integrating Gender into the World Bank's Work: A Strategy for Action*. Washington: World Bank.

Bibliography

Acsády, Judit, 1999. "Remarks on the History of Hungarian Feminism," *Hungarian Studies Review* 26(1–2): 59–64.

Adler, Emanuel, 1997. "Seizing the Middle Ground: Constructivism in World Politics," *European Journal of International Relations* 3(3): 319–63.

Aguilar, Carmencita, 1992. "The Role of Women in Public Life and Decision-Making in the Philippines," *Journal of Asian and African Affairs* 3(2): 89–122.

Ahmed Al Amin, Nafisa and Ahmed Abdel Magied, 2001. "A History of Sudanese Women Organizations and the Strife for Liberation and Empowerment," *Ahfad Journal* 18(1): 2–24.

Alderson, Kai, 2001. "Making Sense of State Socialization," *Review of International Studies* 27: 415–33.

Alison, Miranda, 2007. "Wartime Sexual Violence: Women's Human Rights and Questions of Masculinity," *Review of International Studies* 33(1): 75–90.

Alstadt, Audrey, "Azerbaijan's First and Second Republics: The Problem of National Consciousness," at http://en.baybek.com/azerbaijan%E2%80% 99s-first-and-second-republics-the-problem-of-national-consciousness-audrey-l-alstadt.azr, accessed November 20, 2008.

Aminova, R. Kh., 1977. *The October Revolution and Women's Liberation in Uzbekistan*. Moscow: Nauka Publishing House.

Anderson, Jeanine, 1992. "Instancias nacionales para la promoción de la igualdad de las mujeres trabajadores en América Latina," Documento Informativo del OIT, *Coloquio Regional Sobre el Fomento de la Igualdad en el Empleo para la Mujer en América Latina*, São Paolo, August 31–September 4, 1992. Geneva: ILO.

Anttonen, Anneli, 1990. "The Feminization of the Scandinavian Welfare State," in Leila Simonen (ed.), *Finnish Debates on Women's Studies*. University of Tampere: Research Institute for Social Science, 197–216.

Arat, Yesim, 2000. "From Emancipation to Liberation: The Changing Role of Women in Turkey's Public Realm," *Journal of International Affairs* 54 (1): 107–23.

214

Åseskog, Birgitta, 1998. "National Machinery for Gender Equality in Sweden and Other Nordic Countries," draft paper for the Expert Group Meeting on National Machineries for Gender Equality, Santiago de Chile, August 31–September 4, 1998. Stockholm: Ministry of Industry.

Ashley, Richard, 1987a. "Foreign Policy as Political Performance," *International Studies Notes* 13: 51–4.

1987b. "Living on Borderlines: Man, Poststructuralism, and War," in James Der Derian, and Michael Shapiro (eds.), *International/ Intertextual Relations*. Washington DC: Lexington Books, 259–322.

Asian Development Bank 1998. "Chapter 5. National Policy on Women and National WID Machinery," in *Women in Malaysia: Country Briefing Paper*, 33–41, at www.adb.org/documents/books/country_briefing_papers/women_in_malaysia/women_malaysia.pdf, accessed October 14, 2008.

Axton, Marie, 1977. *The Queen's Two Bodies*. London: Royal Historical Society.

el-Bakri, Zeinab, Fahima Zahir, Belghis Badri, Tamadur Khalid and Madiha el-Sanusi, 1987. "Sudanese Sub-Project: Women in Sudan in the Twentieth Century," in Saskia Wieringa (ed.), *Women's Movement and Organizations in Historical Perspective*. The Hague: Institute of Social Studies, 175–85.

Barnett, Michael, 1993. "Institutions, Roles, and Disorder: The Case of the Arab States System." *International Studies Quarterly* 37: 271–96.

Barnett, Michael, and Raymond Duvall, 2005. "Power in International Politics," *International Organization* 59(1): 39–75.

Barrig, Maruja, 1990. "Qué es lo femenino en política?" *Viva!* 5(19): 44–5.

Bartelson, Jens, 1995. *A Genealogy of Sovereignty*. Cambridge: Cambridge University Press.

1998. "Second Natures: Is the State Identical with Itself?" *European Journal of International Relations* 4(3): 295–326.

Berger, Peter and Thomas Luckmann, 1966. *The Social Construction of Reality*. New York: Anchor Books.

Bergqvist, Christina, 1994. *Mäns makt och kvinnors intressen*. Uppsala: Statsvetenskapliga föreningen.

Berkovitch, Nitza, 1994. *From Motherhood to Citizenship: The Worldwide Incorporation of Women into the Public Sphere in the Twentieth Century*. PhD dissertation, Department of Sociology, Stanford University.

1999a. "The Emergence and Transformation of the International Women's Movement," in Boli and Thomas 1999: 100–26.

1999b. *From Motherhood to Citizenship: Women's Rights and International Organizations*. Baltimore: Johns Hopkins University Press.

Bier, Laura, 2004. "Modernity and the Other Woman: Gender and National Identity in the Egyptian Women's Press: 1952–1967," *Gender & History* 16(1): 99–112.

Biersteker, Thomas, 1990. "Reducing the Role of the State in the Economy: A Conceptual Exploration of IMF and World Bank Prescriptions," *International Studies Quarterly* 34(4): 477–92.

Biswas, Shampa, 2001. "'Nuclear Apartheid': Race as a Postcolonial Resource?" *Alternatives* 26(4): 485–522.

Blackburn, Susan, 1999. "Winning the Vote for Women in Indonesia," *Australian Feminist Studies* 14(29): 207–18.

Blondet, Cecilia, 1997. "La emergencia de las mujeres en el poder: hay cambios en el Perú?" *Perfiles Latinoamericanos* 11(6): 91–112.

Blumenberg, Hans, 1983. *The Legitimacy of the Modern Age*. Cambridge, MA: MIT Press.

Bock, Gisela, 2002. *Women in European History*. Oxford: Blackwell.

Boli, John, and George M. Thomas, 1997. "World Culture in the World Polity: A Century of International Non-Governmental Organization," *American Sociological Review* 62: 171–90.

  (eds.) 1999. *Constructing World Culture: International Non-Governmental Organizations since 1875*. Stanford: Stanford University Press.

Booth, Karen M., 1998. "National Mother, Global Whore and Transnational Femocrats: The Politics of AIDS and the Construction of Women at the World Health Organization," *Feminist Studies* 24: 115–39.

Bosch, Mineke, 1999. "Colonial Dimensions of Dutch Women's Suffrage: Aletta Jacobs's Travel Letters from Africa and Asia, 1911–1912," *Journal of Women's History* 11(2): 8–34.

Botman, Selma, 1999. *Engendering Citizenship in Egypt*. New York: Columbia University Press.

Bourque, Susan C., 1989 "Gender and the State: Perspectives from Latin America," in Sue Charlton, Jana Everett and Kathleen Staudt (eds.), *Women, the State, and Development*. Albany: State University of New York Press, 114–29.

Boyle, Elizabeth Heger, Barbara J. McMorris and Mayra Gómez, 2002. "Local Conformity to International Norms: The Case of Female Genital Cutting," *International Sociology* 17(1): 5–33.

Boyle, Elizabeth Heger, Fortunata Songoro and Gail Foss, 2001. "International Discourse and Local Politics: Anti-Female-Genital-Cutting Laws in Egypt, Tanzania, and the United States," *Social Forces* 48(4): 524–44.

Brandt, Conrad, Benjamin Schwartz and John K. Fairbank (eds.), 1952. *A Documentary History of Chinese Communism*. Cambridge, MA: Harvard University Press.

Brill, Alida (ed.), 1995. *A Rising Public Voice: Women in Politics Worldwide.* New York: Feminist Press.

Brown, Chris, 1994. "'Turtles All the Way Down': Anti-Foundationalism, Critical Theory and International Relations," *Millennium* 23(2): 213–36.

Browning, Genia, 1985. "Soviet Politics – Where Are the Women?" in Barbara Holland (ed.), *Soviet Sisterhood: British Feminists on Women in the USSR.* London: Fourth Estate, 207–36.

Buckley, Mary, 1985. "Soviet Interpretations of the Woman Question," in Barbara Holland (ed.). *Soviet Sisterhood: British Feminists on Women in the USSR.* London: Fourth Estate, 24–53.

Bull, Hedley, and Adam Watson, 1977. *The Anarchical Society: A Study of Order in World Politics.* London: Macmillan.

(eds.) 1984. *The Expansion of International Society.* Oxford University Press.

Bunch, Charlotte, 1990. "Women's Rights as Human Rights: Toward a Revision of Human Rights," *Human Rights Quarterly* 12: 486–98.

Bunch, Charlotte, and Niahm Reilly, 1994. *Demanding Accountability: The Global Campaign and Vienna Tribunal for Women's Human Rights.* New York: Center for Women's Global Leadership.

Burton, Antoinette, 1994. *Burdens of History: British Feminists, Indian Women and Imperial Culture, 1865–1915.* Chapel Hill: University of North Carolina Press.

Buttel, Frederick H., 2000. "World Society, the Nation State, and Environmental Protection. Comment on Frank, Hironaka, and Schofer," *American Sociological Review* 65: 117–21.

Buzan, Barry, 1993. "From International System to International Society: Structural Realism and Regime Theory Meet the English School," *International Organization* 47(3): 327–52.

Campbell, David, 1992/1998. *Writing Security: United States Foreign Policy and the Politics of Identity.* Minneapolis: University of Minnesota Press.

Cancian, Francesca, 1975. *What Are Norms? A Study of Beliefs and Action in a Maya Community.* New York: Cambridge University Press.

Cannon, Mary, 1943. "Women's Organizations in Ecuador, Paraguay and Peru," *Bulletin of the Pan American Union* 77(11): 601–7.

Carr, Edward Hallett, 1939. *The Twenty Years' Crisis, 1919–1939.* New York: Harper & Row.

Center for Women's Global Leadership, 1993. *International Campaign for Women's Human Rights, 1992–1993 Report.* New Brunswick: Rutgers University.

Chaney, Elsa, 1979. *Supermadre: Women in Politics in Latin America.* Austin: University of Texas Press.

Chase, Robert, Emily Hill and Paul Kennedy, 1996. "Pivotal States and US Strategy," *Foreign Affairs* (January/February): 33–51.

Checkel, Jeffrey, 1998. "The Constructivist Turn in International Relations Theory," *World Politics* 50: 324–48.

  1999. "Norms, Institutions and National Identity in Contemporary Europe," *International Studies Quarterly* 43: 83–114.

  2001. "Why Comply? Social Learning and European Identity Change," *International Organization* 55(3): 553–88.

Chesterman, Simon, 1998. "Human Rights as Subjectivity: The Age of Rights and the Politics of Culture," *Millennium* 27(1): 97–118.

Chin, Hue-Ping, 1995. *Refiguring Women: Discourse on Gender in China, 1880–1919*. PhD dissertation, Department of History, University of Iowa.

Chodorow, Nancy, 1995. "Gender as a Personal and Cultural Construction," *Signs: Journal of Women in Culture and Society* 20(3): 516–44.

Clements, Barbara Evans, 1979. *Bolshevik Feminist: The Life of Aleksandra Kollontai*. Bloomington: Indiana University Press.

Cohn, Carol, 1987. "Sex and Death in the Rational World of Defense Intellectuals," *Signs: Journal of Women in Culture and Society* 12(4): 687–718.

  1998. "Gays in the Military: Texts and Subtexts," in Zalewski and Parpart 1998: 129–49.

Colley, Linda, 1986. "Whose Nation? Class and National Consciousness in Britain 1750–1830," *Past and Present* 113: 97–117.

  1992. *Britons: Forging the Nation 1707–1837*. New Haven: Yale University Press.

Connell, R. W., 1990. "The State, Gender, and Sexual Politics: Theory and Appraisal," *Theory and Society* 19: 507–44.

Connolly, William, 1991. *Identity/Difference*. University of Minnesota Press.

Cooper, Charlotte, 2001. *Manly States: Masculinities, International Relations, and Gender Politics*. New York: Columbia University Press.

Cosandey, Fanny, 1997. "De Lance en Quenouille: La place de la reine dans l'état moderne (14e–17e siècles)," *Annales: Histoire, Sciences Sociales* 52(4): 799–820.

Cortell, Andrew, and James Davis, Jr., 1996. "How Do Institutions Matter? The Domestic Impact of International Rules and Norms," *International Studies Quarterly* 40: 451–78.

  2000. "Understanding the Domestic Impact of International Norms: A Research Agenda," *International Studies Review* 2(1): 65–87.

Crawford, Neta, 2002. *Argument and Change in World Politics*. Cambridge: Cambridge University Press.

Crawford, Neta, and Audie Klotz (eds.), 1999. *How Sanctions Work: Lessons from South Africa*. New York: St. Martin's Press.

Croll, Elisabeth, 1978. *Feminism and Socialism in China*. London: Routledge & Kegan Paul.

Cuénin, Micheline, 1984. "Les femmes aux affaires (1598–1661)," *Dix-Septième Siècle* 36(6): 203–9.

Dahlerup, Drude, 1988. "From a Small to a Large Minority: Women in Scandinavian Politics," *Scandinavian Political Studies* 11(4): 275–98.

　　2002. "Using Quotas to Increase Women's Political Representation," updated version of chapter originally published in International IDEA's handbook *Women in Parliament: Beyond Numbers*. Stockholm: IDEA, 1998; at www.idea.int, accessed December 3, 2003.

　　2003. "Comparative Studies of Electoral Gender Quotas," paper presented at the International IDEA workshop "The Implementation of Quotas: Latin American Experiences" held in Lima, Peru, February 23–4, 2003.

　　(ed.), 2006. *Women, Quotas and Politics*. London: Routledge.

Dahrendorf, Ralf, 1968. *Essays in the Theory of Society*. Stanford: Stanford University Press.

Dalziel, Raeqyn, 1994. "Presenting the Enfranchisement of New Zealand Women," in Caroline Daley and Melanie Nolan (eds.), *Suffrage and Beyond: International Feminist Perspectives*. New York: New York University Press.

de la Cadena, Marisol, 1995. "Women Are More Indian: Gender and Ethnicity in a Community in Cuzco," in Larson Brooke and Olivia Harris (eds.), *Ethnicity, Markets, and Migration in the Andes: At the Crossroads of History and Anthropology*. Durham, NC: Duke University Press, 329–48.

Delaney, Carol, 1995. "Father State, Motherland, and the Birth of Modern Turkey," in Sylvia Yanagisako and Carol Delaney, *Naturalizing Power: Essays in Feminist Cultural Analysis*. New York: Routledge, 177–99.

Diamond, Irene, and Nancy Hartsock, 1998. "Beyond Interests in Politics: A Comment on Virginia Sapiro's 'When Are Women's Interests Interesting?'" in Anne Phillips (ed.), *Feminism and Politics*. Oxford: Oxford University Press, 193–203.

Diez, Thomas, 2004. "Europe's Others and the Return of Geopolitics," *Cambridge Review of International Affairs* 17(2): 319–35.

DiMaggio, Paul, 1988. "Interest and Agency in Institutional Theory," in Lynne G. Zucker (ed.), *Institutional Patterns and Organizations: Culture and Environment*. Cambridge, MA: Ballinger, 3–21.

Dollar, David, Raymond Fisman and Roberta Gatti, 2001. "Are Women Really the 'Fairer' Sex? Corruption and Women in Government," *Journal of Economic Behavior and Organization* 46(4): 423–9.

Doty, Roxanne, 1996. *Imperial Encounters: The Politics of Representation in North–South Relations*. Minneapolis: University of Minnesota Press.

DuBois, Ellen, 1975. "The Radicalism of the Woman Suffrage Movement: Notes Toward the Reconstruction of Nineteenth-Century Feminism," *Feminist Studies* 3(1/2): 63–71.

1991. "Woman Suffrage and the Left: An International Socialist-Feminist Perspective," *New Left Review* 186: 20–45.

1994. "Woman Suffrage Around the World: Three Phases of Suffragist Internationalism," in Caroline Daley and Melanie Nolan (eds.), *Suffrage and Beyond: International Feminist Perspectives*. New York: New York University Press, 252–74.

Dudink, Stefan, and Karen Hagemann, 2004. "Masculinity in Politics and War in the Age of Democratic Revolutions, 1750–1850," in Stefan Dudink, Karen Hagemann and John Tosh (eds.), *Masculinities in Politics and War*. Manchester: Manchester University Press, 3–21.

Duerst-Lahti, Georgia, 1989. "The Government's Role in Building the Women's Movement," *Political Science Quarterly* 104(2): 249–68.

Dunne, Timothy, 1995. "The Social Construction of International Society," *European Journal of International Relations* 1(3): 367–89.

Duverger, Maurice, 1955. *The Political Role of Women*. Paris: UNESCO.

Edmondson, Linda, 1992. "Women's Rights, Civil Rights and the Debate over Citizenship in the 1905 Revolution," in Linda Edmondson (ed.), *Women and Society in Russia and the Soviet Union*. Cambridge: Cambridge University Press, 77–100.

Edwards, Louise, 2000. "Women's Suffrage in China: Challenging Scholarly Conventions," *Pacific Historical Review* 69(4): 617–38.

Edwards, Louise, and Mina Roces, 2004. "Introduction: Orienting the Global Women's Suffrage Movement," in Louise Edwards and Mina Roces (eds.), *Women's Suffrage in Asia: Gender, Nationalism and Democracy*. New York: RoutledgeCurzon, 1–23.

Eisenstein, Zillah, 2004. "Sexual Humiliation, Gender Confusion and the Horrors at Abu Ghraib," at www.iiav.nl/ezines/web/WHRnet/2004/July.pdf, accessed December 15, 2008.

2007. *Sexual Decoys: Gender, Race and War in Imperial Democracy*. New York: Palgrave.

Elshtain, Jean Bethke, 1974. "Moral Woman and Immoral Man: A Consideration of the Public Private Split and its Political Ramifications," *Politics and Society* 4: 453–61.

1981. *Public Man, Private Woman: Women in Social and Political Thought*. Princeton: Princeton University Press.

1992. "Sovereignty, Identity, Sacrifice," in Peterson 1992a: 141–54.

1995. *Women and War*. Chicago: University of Chicago Press.

Enloe, Cynthia, 1990. *Bananas, Beaches and Bases: Making Feminist Sense of International Politics*. Berkeley: University of California Press.

   1993. *The Morning After: Sexual Politics at the End of the Cold War*. Berkeley: University of California Press.

   2000. *Maneuvers: The International Politics of Militarizing Women's Lives*. Berkeley: University of California Press.

   2004. "Wielding Masculinity Inside Abu Ghraib: Making Feminist Sense of an American Military Scandal," *Asian Journal of Women's Studies* 10(3): 89–102.

Erlanger, Steven, 2008. "After US Breakthrough, Europe Looks in Mirror," *New York Times*, CLVIII, no. 54,492 (November 12, 2008): A1 and A13.

Escobar, Arturo, 1984. "Discourse and Power in Development: Michel Foucault and the Relevance of His Work to the Third World," *Alternatives* X: 377–400.

   1995. *Encountering Development: The Making and Unmaking of the Third World*. Princeton: Princeton University Press.

Evangelista, Matthew, 1995. "The Paradox of State Strength: Transnational Relations, Domestic Structures, and Security Policy in Russia and the Soviet Union," *International Organization* 49(1): 1–38.

Evans, Richard J., 1979. *The Feminists: Women's Emancipation Movements in Europe, America and Australasia 1840–1920*. London: Croom Helm.

Eyre, Dana, and Mark Suchman, 1996. "Status, Norms, and the Proliferation of Conventional Weapons: An Institutional Theory Approach," in Katzenstein 1996: 79–113.

Fauré, Christine, 1991. *Democracy Without Women*. Bloomington: Indiana University Press.

Fearon, James, and Alexander Wendt, 2002. "Rationalism v. Constructivism: A Skeptical View," in Walter Carlsnaes, Thomas Risse and Beth Simmons (eds.), *Handbook of International Relations*. London: Sage, 52–72.

Feinberg, Richard E., 1988. "The Changing Relationship Between the World Bank and the International Monetary Fund," *International Organization* 42(3): 545–60.

Feliciano, Myrna, 1990–1. "Political Rights of Women in Philippine Context," *Review of Women's Rights* 1(2): 34–49.

Ferguson, James, 1990. *The Anti-Politics Machine: "Development", Depoliticization, and Bureaucratic Power in Lesotho*. Cambridge: Cambridge University Press.

Fierke, Karin, 2000. "Logics of Force and Dialogue: The Iraq/UNSCOM as Social Interaction," *European Journal of International Relations* 6(3): 335–71.

Finnemore, Martha, 1993. "International Organizations as Teachers of Norms: The United Nations Educational, Scientific, and Cultural Organization and Science Policy," *International Organization* 47(4): 565–97.

　　1996a. "Studies of the Modern World-System," *International Organization* 50(2): 325–47.

　　1996b. *National Interests in International Society.* Ithaca: Cornell University Press.

　　1996c. "Constructing Norms of Humanitarian Intervention," in Katzenstein 1996: 153–85.

Finnemore, Martha, and Kathryn Sikkink, 1999. "International Norm Dynamics and Political Change," in Peter Katzenstein, Robert Keohane and Stephen Krasner (eds.), *Exploration and Contestation in the Study of World Politics.* Cambridge, MA: MIT Press, 247–78.

Florini, Ann, 1996. "The Evolution of International Norms," *International Studies Quarterly* 40(3): 363–89.

Flowers, Petrice, 2009. *Refugees, Women and Weapons: International Norm Adoption and Compliance in Japan.* Stanford: Stanford University Press.

Foner, Philip, 1984. "Introduction," in Philip Foner (ed.), *Clara Zetkin: Selected Writings.* New York: International Publishers, 17–42.

Foucault, Michel, 1975/1977. *Discipline and Punish: The Birth of the Prison.* New York: Vintage.

　　1984. "Nietzsche, Genealogy, History," in Paul Rabinow (ed.), *The Foucault Reader.* New York: Pantheon, 76–100.

Franck, Thomas, 1990. *The Power of Legitimacy Among Nations.* Oxford University Press.

Frank, Björn, and Günther Schulze, 1998. "How Tempting is Corruption? More Bad News About Economists," in *Diskussionsbeiträge aus dem Institut für Volkswirtschaftslehre,* no. 164/1998. Universität Hohenheim, Stuttgart, at www.icgg.org/downloads/contribution03_frank.pdf, accessed October 12, 2008.

Frank, David John, and Elizabeth McEneaney, 1999. "The Individualization of Society and the Liberalization of State Policies on Same-Sex Sexual Relations, 1984–1995," *Social Forces* 77(3): 911–44.

Fraser, Arvonne S., 1987. *The UN Decade for Women: Documents and Dialogue.* Boulder: Westview.

Freedom House, 2007. "Women's Rights in the Middle East and North Africa: Citizenship and Justice," Special Report. New York: Freedom House.

Friedman, Elisabeth, 1994. "Women's Human Rights: The Emergence of a Movement," in Julie Peters and Andrea Wolper (eds.), *Women and Human Rights: An Agenda for Change.* New York: Routledge.

Friedman, Susan Stanford, 1995. "Beyond White and Other: Relationality and Narratives of Race in Feminist Discourse," *Signs: Journal of Women in Culture and Society* 21(1): 1–41.

Friedman, Thomas, 1999. *The Lexus and the Olive Tree.* New York: Farrar, Star Giroux.

Fukuyama, Francis, 1992. *The End of History and the Last Man.* London: Hamish Hamilton.

Galey, Margaret, 1979. "Promoting Nondiscrimination Against Women: The UN Commission on the Status of Women," *International Studies Quarterly* 23(2): 273–302.

Gankin, Olga, and H. H. Fisher, 1940. *The Bolsheviks and the World War: The Origin of the Third International.* Stanford: Stanford University Press.

Geertz, Clifford, 1979. "'From the Native's Point of View': On the Nature of Anthropological Understanding," in Paul Rabinow and W. M. Sullivan (eds.), *Interpretive Social Science.* Berkeley: University of California Press, 225–41.

Gentile, Carmen, 1999. "Searching for Freedom from the Taliban," *Middle East Times,* May 9, 1999, at www.rawa.org/metimes.htm, accessed July 15, 2008.

Geraci, Robert, 2001. *Window on the East: National and Imperial Identities in Late Tsarist Russia.* Ithaca: Cornell University Press.

Giddens, Anthony, 1979. *Central Problems in Social Theory: Action, Structure and Contradiction in Social Analysis.* Berkeley: University of California Press.

Gilmartin, Christina K., 1995. *Engendering the Chinese Revolution: Radical Women, Communist Politics and Mass Movements in the 1920s.* Berkeley: University of California Press.

Goertz, Gary, and Paul F. Diehl, 1992. "Toward a Theory of International Norms: Some Conceptual and Measurement Issues," *Journal of Conflict Resolution* 36(4): 634–55.

Goetz, Anne Marie, (ed.), 1997. *Getting Institutions Right for Women in Development.* London: Zed Press.

Goetz, Anne Marie, 2003. "National Women's Machinery: State-Based Institutions to Advocate for Gender Equality," in Rai 2003: 69–95.

Goldstein, Joshua, 2001. *War and Gender: How Gender Shapes the War System and Vice Versa.* Cambridge: Cambridge University Press.

Gong, Gerrit, 1984. *The Standard of "Civilization" in International Society.* Oxford: Oxford University Press.

Gonzalez, Charity Coker, 2000. "Agitating for Their Rights: The Colombian Women's Movement 1930–1957," *Pacific Historical Review* 69(4): 689–711.

Gordon, Linda (ed.), 1990. *Women, the State and Welfare*. Madison: University of Wisconsin Press.

Gordon, Shirley (ed.), 1984. *Ladies in Limbo: The Fate of Women's Bureaus: Six Case Studies From the Caribbean*. London: Women and Development Programme, Commonwealth Secretariat, Marlborough House.

Greenblatt, Stephen, 1986. "Fiction and Friction," in Thomas Heller, Morton Sosna and David Wellbery (eds.), *Reconstructing Individualism: Autonomy, Individuality, and the Self in Western Thought*. Stanford: Stanford University Press, 32–50.

Grewal, Inderpal, 1996. *Home and Harem: Nation, Gender, Empire, and the Cultures of Travel*. Durham, NC: Duke University Press.

Gruberg, Martin, 1973. "Official Commissions on the Status of Women: A Worldwide Movement," *International Review of Education*, 19(1): 140–7.

Gurowitz, Amy, 1999. "Mobilizing International Norms: Domestic Actors, Immigrants and the Japanese State," *World Politics* 51(3): 413–45.

2000. "Migrant Rights and Activism in Malaysia: Opportunities and Constraints," *Journal of Asian Studies*, 59(4): 863–88.

Hahner, June, 1990. *Emancipating the Female Sex: The Struggle for Women's Rights in Brazil, 1850–1940*. Durham, NC: Duke University Press.

Hale, Sondra, 1996. *Gender Politics in Sudan: Islamism, Socialism, and the State*. Boulder: Westview.

Halliday, Fred, 1992. "International Society as Homogeneity: Burke, Marx, Fukuyama," *Millennium* 21(3): 435–61.

Hanley, Sarah, 1997. "Mapping Rulership in the French Body Politics: Political Identity, Public Law and the King's One Body," *Historical Reflections / Réflexions Historiques* 23(2): 129–49.

Harrison, Cynthia, 1980. "A 'New Frontier' for Women: The Public Policy of the Kennedy Administration," *The Journal of American History* 67(3): 630–46.

Hauch, Gabriella, 2001. "Women's Spaces in the Men's Revolution of 1848," in Dieter Dowe, Heinz-Gerhard Haupt and Dieter Langewiesche (eds.), *Europe in 1848: Revolution and Reform*. New York: Berghahn Books, 639–82.

Haupt, Heinz-Gerhard, and Dieter Langewiesche, 2001. "The European Revolution of 1848: Its Political and Social Reforms, its Politics of Nationalism, and its Short- and Long-Term Consequences," in Dieter Dowe, Heinz-Gerhard Haupt and Dieter Langewiesche (eds.), *Europe in 1848: Revolution and Reform*. New York: Berghahn Books, 1–24.

Hawkins, Darren, 1997. "Domestic Responses to International Pressure: Human Rights in Authoritarian Chile," *European Journal of International Relations* 3(4): 403–34.

Hayden, Carole Eubanks, 1976. "The Zhenotdel and the Bolshevik Party," *Russian History* 3(2): 150–73.

Healey, Robert, 1994. "Waiting for Deborah: John Knox and Four Ruling Queens," *Sixteenth Century Journal* 25(2): 371–86.

Henderson, Katherine Usher, and Barbara McManus, 1985. *Half Humankind: Contexts and Texts of the Controversy about Women in England 1540–1640*. Urbana: University of Illinois Press.

Hernes, Helga, 1987. *Welfare State and Women Power*. Oslo: Norwegian University Press.

Hidalgo Lim, Pilar, 1967. "Women's Suffrage Since 1937," *Unitas* 40(3): 414–22.

Hinsley, Francis H., 1966. *Sovereignty*. London: C. A. Watts.

2001. *Manly States: Masculinities, International Relations, and Gender Politics*. New York: Columbia University Press.

Honeycutt, Karen, 1975. *Clara Zetkin: A Left-Wing Socialist and Feminist in Wilhelmian Germany*. PhD dissertation, Department of History, Columbia University.

1976. "Clara Zetkin: A Socialist Approach to the Problem of Woman's Oppression," *Feminist Studies* 3(3/4): 131–44.

Hooper, Charlotte, 1998. "Masculinist Practices and Gender Politics: The Operation of Multiple Masculinities in International Relations," in Zalewski and Parpart 1998: 28–53.

Htun, Mala, 1998. "Women's Political Participation, Representation and Leadership in Latin America," *Women's Leadership Conference of the Americas Issue Brief*. Inter-American Dialogue, September 1998.

Htun, Mala, and Mark Jones, 2002. "Engendering the Right to Participate in Decision-Making: Electoral Quotas and Women's Leadership in Latin America," in Nikki Craske and Maxine Molyneux (eds.), *Gender and the Politics of Rights and Democracy in Latin America*. New York: Palgrave, 32–56.

Hubbard, Ruth, 1983. "Have Only Men Evolved?" in Sandra Harding and Merrill B. Hintikka (eds.), *Discovering Reality: Feminist Perspectives on Epistemology, Metaphysics, Methodology and Philosophy of Science*. Boston: D. Reidel, 45–69.

Hurrell, Andrew, and Ngaire Woods, 1995. "Globalisation and Inequality," *Millennium* 24(3): 447–70.

IDEA 2008. "Data Grouped by Quota Type," *Global Database of Quotas for Women*, at www.quotaproject.org/system.cfm, accessed September 14, 2008.

Ikenberry, G. John, and Charles A. Kupchan, 1990. "Socialization and Hegemonic Power," *International Organization* 44(3): 283–315.

Inayatullah, Naeem, and David L. Blaney, 1996. "Knowing Encounters: Beyond Parochialism in International Relations Theory," in Yosef Lapid and Friedrich Kratochwil (eds.), *The Return of Culture and Identity in IR Theory*. Boulder: Lynne Rienner Publishers, 65–84.

Inglehart, Ronald, and Pippa Norris, 2003. "The True Clash of Civilizations," *Foreign Policy* 135: 62–70.

INSTRAW, 2000. *Engendering the Political Agenda: The Role of the State, Women's Organizations and the International Community*. Santo Domingo, Dominican Republic: United Nations. INSTRAW/SER.B/54.

Jackson, Robert, 1993. "The Weight of Ideas in Decolonization: Normative Change in International Relations," in Judith Goldstein and Robert Keohane (eds.), *Ideas and Foreign Policy: Beliefs, Institutions and Political Change*. Ithaca: Cornell University Press, 111–38.

Jancar, Barbara, 1978. *Women under Communism*. Baltimore: Johns Hopkins University Press.

Jaquette, Jane, 1982. "Women and Modernization Theory: A Decade of Feminist Criticism," *World Politics* 34: 267–84.

Johnson, Allan, 1997. *The Gender Knot: Unraveling Our Patriarchal Legacy*. Philadelphia: Temple University Press.

Johnson-Odim, Cheryl, and Nina Mba, 1997. *For Women and the Nation: Funmilayo Ransome-Kuti of Nigeria*. Urbana: University of Illinois Press.

Jónasdóttir, Anna, 1994. *Why Women Are Oppressed*. Philadelphia: Temple University Press.

Junzuo, Zhang, 1992. "Gender and Political Participation in Rural China," in Shirin Rai, Hilary Pilkington and Annie Phizacklea (eds.), *Women in the Face of Change: The Soviet Union, Eastern Europe and China*. London: Routledge, 41–56.

Kabeer, Naila, 1994. *Reversed Realities: Gender Hierarchies in Development Thought*. London: Verso.

Kandiyoti, Deniz, 1989. "Women and the Turkish State: Political Actors or Symbolic Pawns," in Yuval-Davis and Anthias 1989: 126–49.

Katzenstein, Peter (ed.), 1996. *The Culture of National Security: Norms and Identity in World Politics*. New York: Columbia University Press.

Kavka, Frantisek, 1963. *An Outline of Czechoslovak History*. Prague: Orbis.

Keck, Margaret, and Kathryn Sikkink, 1998. *Activists Beyond Borders: Advocacy Networks in International Politics*. Ithaca: Cornell University Press.

Keen, Sam, 1991. *Fire in the Belly: On Being a Man*. New York: Bantam.

Kinsella, Helen, 2003. "The Image Before the Weapon: A Genealogy of the 'Civilian' in International Law and Politics." PhD dissertation, University of Minnesota.

    2005. "Discourses of Difference: Civilians, Combatants, and Compliance with the Laws of War," *Review of International Studies* 31(S1): 163–85.

Klotz, Audie, 1995a. *Norms in International Politics: The Struggle Against Apartheid*. Ithaca: Cornell University Press.

    1995b. "Norms Reconstituting Interests: Global Racial Equality and US Sanctions Against South Africa," *International Organization* 49(3): 451–78.

    1996. "Norms and Sanctions: Lessons from the Socialization of South Africa," *Review of International Studies* 22: 173–90.

    2002. "Transnational Activism and Global Transformations: The Anti-Apartheid and Abolitionist Experiences," *European Journal of International Relations* 8(1): 49–76.

Koikari, Mire, 2002. "Exporting Democracy? American Women, 'Feminist Reforms', and Politics of Imperialism in the US Occupation of Japan, 1945–1952," *Frontiers: A Journal of Women's Studies* 18(1): 23–45.

Kollontai, Alexandra, 1977. *Selected Writings*, ed. Alix Holt. London: Allison & Busby.

Kováks, Maria, 1996. "Ambiguities of Emancipation: Women and the Ethnic Question in Hungary," *Women's History Review* 5(4): 487–95.

Koven, Seth, and Sonya Michel (eds.), 1993. *Mothers of a New World: Maternalist Politics and the Origins of the Welfare State*. London: Routledge.

Kraditor, Aileen, 1971. *The Ideas of the Woman Suffrage Movement 1890–1920*. New York: Anchor Books.

Kramer, Jane, 2000. "Liberty, Equality, Sorority: French Women Demand Their Share," *The New Yorker*, May 29: 112–23.

Krasner, Stephen, 1993. "Westphalia and All That," in Judith Goldstein and Robert Keohane (eds.), *Ideas and Foreign Policy: Beliefs, Institutions and Political Change*. Ithaca: Cornell University Press, 235–64.

Kratochwil, Friedrich, 1986. "Of Systems, Boundaries, and Territory: An Inquiry into the Formation of the State System," *World Politics* 39: 27–52.

    1988. "Regimes, Interpretation and the 'Science' of Politics: A Reappraisal," *Millennium* 17(2): 263–84.

    1989. *Rules, Norms, and Decisions: On the Conditions of Practical and Legal Reasoning in International Relations and Domestic Affairs*. New York: Cambridge University Press.

    2000. "Constructing a New Orthodoxy? Wendt's 'Social Theory of International Politics' and the Constructivist Challenge," *Millennium* 29(1): 73–101.

Kratochwil, Friedrich, and John Gerard Ruggie, 1986. "International Organization: A State of the Art on an Art of the State," *International Organization* 40(4): 753–75.

Krook, Mona Lena, 2006. "Reforming Representation: The Diffusion of Candidate Gender Quotas Worldwide," *Gender & Politics* 2, 303–27.

2009. *Quotas for Women in Politics: Gender and Candidate Selection Reform Worldwide*. Oxford University Press.

Kvale, Steinar, 1995. "The Social Construction of Validity," *Qualitative Inquiry* 1(1): 19–40.

1996. *InterViews: An Introduction to Qualitative Research Interviewing*. Thousand Oaks: Sage.

Kymlicka, Will, 2007. *Multicultural Odysseys: Navigating the New International Politics of Diversity*. Oxford: Oxford University Press.

Laffey, Mark, 2000. "Locating Identity: Performativity, Foreign Policy and State Action," *Review of International Studies* 26: 429–44.

Laffey, Mark, and Jutta Weldes, 1997. "Beyond Belief: Ideas and Symbolic Technologies in the Study of International Relations," *European Journal of International Relations* 3(1): 1–45.

Lambsdorff, Johann Graf, 1999. "Corruption in Empirical Research – A Review," Paper presented at the 9th International Anti-Corruption Conference, Durban, South Africa, December 10–15, 1999, at www1.worldbank.org/publicsector/anticorrupt/d2ws1_jglambsdorff.pdf, accessed October 14, 2008.

Lange, Lynda, 1983. "Woman is not a Rational Animal: On Aristotle's Biology of Reproduction," in Sandra Harding and Merrill B. Hintikka (eds.), *Discovering Reality: Feminist Perspectives on Epistemology, Metaphysics, Methodology and Philosophy of Science*. Boston: D. Reidel, 1–15.

Lapidus, Gail, 1978. *Women in Soviet Society: Equality, Development, and Social Change*. Berkeley: University of California Press.

Laqueur, Thomas, 1990. *Making Sex: Body and Gender from the Greeks to Freud*. Cambridge, MA: Harvard University Press.

Lavrin, Asunción, 1994. "Suffrage in South America: Arguing a Difficult Case," in Caroline Daley and Melanie Nolan (eds.), *Suffrage and Beyond: International Feminist Perspectives*. New York: New York University Press, 184–209.

1995. *Women, Feminism, and Social Change in Argentina, Chile and Uruguay, 1890–1940*. Lincoln, NE: Nebraska University Press.

Leacock, Eleanor, 1972. "Introduction," in Frederick Engels, *The Origin of the Family, Private Property and the State in the Light of the Researches of Lewis H. Morgan*. New York: International Publishers, 7–68.

1978. "Women's Status in Egalitarian Societies: Implications for Social Evolution," *Current Anthropology* 19(2): 247–55.

Legro, Jeff, 1997. "Which Norms Matter? Revisiting the 'Failure' of Internationalism," *International Organization* 51(1): 31–63.

Lenoir, Noëlle, 2001. "The Representation of Women in Politics: From Quotas to Parity in Election," *International and Comparative Law Quarterly* 50: 217–47.

Lightman, Harriet, 1981. "Queens and Minor Kings in French Constitutional Law," *Proceedings of the Annual Meeting of the Western Society for French History* 9: 26–36.

Linklater, Andrew, 1998. *The Transformation of Political Community: Ethical Foundations of the Post-Westphalian Era*. Columbia: University of South Carolina Press.

Löfgren, Orvar, 1993. "Nationella Arenor," in Billy Ehn, Jonas Frykman and Orvar Löfgren, *Försvenskningen av Sverige: Det nationellas förvandlingar*. Stockholm: Natur och Kultur.

Loos, Tamara, 2004. "The Politics of Women's Suffrage in Thailand," in Louise Edwards, and Mina Roces (eds.), *Women's Suffrage in Asia: Gender, Nationalism and Democracy*. New York: Routledge Curzon, 170–94.

Lovenduski, Joni, 2005. *Feminizing Politics*. Cambridge: Polity Press.

Macedonio Urquidi, José, 1937. *La Condición jurídica o situación legal de la mujer en Bolivia*. Cochabamba: La Aurora.

McCarthy, Thomas, 1992. "The Critique of Impure Reason: Foucault and the Frankfurt School," in Thomas Wartenberg (ed.), *Rethinking Power*. Albany: State University of New York Press, 121–47.

McDermott, Jeremy, 1999. "Women Police Ride in on a Ticket of Honesty," *Daily Telegraph*, July 31.

MacIntyre, Alasdair, 1981/1984. *After Virtue: A Study in Moral Theory*. Notre Dame: University of Notre Dame Press.

Mackie, Vera, 1997. *Creating Socialist Women in Japan: Gender, Labor, and Activism, 1900–1937*. New York: Routledge.

Mahoney, Maureen, and Barbara Yngvesson, 1992. "The Construction of Subjectivity and the Paradox of Resistance: Reintegrating Feminist Anthropology and Psychology," *Signs: a Journal of Women in Culture and Society* 18(1): 44–73.

Mair, Lucille, 1986. "Women: A Decade is Time Enough," *Third World Quarterly* 8(2): 583–93.

Manning, C. A. W., 1962. *The Nature of International Society*. London: LSE.

March, James G., and Johan P. Olsen, 1989. *Rediscovering Institutions: The Organizational Basis of Politics*. New York: Free Press.

1998. "The Institutional Dynamics of International Political Orders," *International Organization* 52(4): 729–57.

Marchand, Marianne, 1996. "Reconceptualising 'Gender and Development' in an era of 'Globalization'," *Millennium* 25(3): 577–603.

Markoff, John, 2003. "Margins, Centers, and Democracy: The Paradigmatic History of Women's Suffrage," *Signs: Journal of Women in Culture and Society* 29(1): 85–116.

Matsukawa, Yukiko, and Kaoru Tachi, 1994. "Women's Suffrage and Gender Politics in Japan," in Caroline Daley and Melanie Nolan, *Suffrage and Beyond: International Feminist Perspectives*. New York University Press, 171–83.

Mayall, James, 1990. *Nationalism and International Society*. Cambridge: Cambridge University Press.

Meehan-Waters, Brenda, 1975. "Catherine the Great and the Problem of Female Rule," *Russian Review* 34(4): 293–307.

Meyer, John, 1980. "The World Polity and the Authority of the Nation-State," in W. Richard Scott and John W. Meyer (eds.), *Institutional Environments and Organizations*. Newbury Park, CA: Sage, 28–54.

Meyer, John, John Boli, George M. Thomas and Francisco O. Ramrez, 1997. "World Society and the Nation-State," *American Journal of Sociology* 103(1): 144–82.

Meyer, Mary K., 1999. "Negotiating International Norms: The Inter-American Commission of Women and the Convention on Violence against Women," in Mary K. Meyer and Elisabeth Prugl (eds.), *Gender Politics in Global Governance*. Lanham, MD: Rowman & Littlefield Publishers, 58–71.

Miller, Francesca, 1986. "The International Relations of Women of the Americas 1890–1928," *The Americas* 43(2): 171–82.

1991. *Latin American Women and the Search for Social Justice*. London: University Press of New England.

Milliken, Jennifer, 1999a. "Intervention and Identity: Reconstructing the West in Korea," in Weldes *et al.* 1999: 91–118.

1999b. "The Study of Discourse in International Relations: A Critique of Research and Methods," *European Journal of International Relations* 5(2): 225–54.

Milliken, Jennifer, and David Sylvan, 1996. "Soft Bodies, Hard Targets and Chic Theories: US Bombing Policy in Indochina," *Millennium* 25(2): 321–59.

Mohanty, Chandra Talpade, 1988. "Under Western Eyes: Feminist Scholarship and Colonial Discourses," *Feminist Review* 30: 61–88.

Moline, Ann, 2002. "World Bank to Rate All Projects for Gender Impact," *Women's E-News*, April 4, at www.womensenews.org/article.cfm/dyn/ aid/866/context/archive, accessed December 2, 2003.

Moon, Katharine, 1997. *Sex Among Allies: Military Prostitution in US–Korea Relations*. New York: Columbia University Press.

Moore, Molly, 1999. "Mexico City's Stop Sign to Bribery; to Halt Corruption, Women Traffic Cops Replace Men," *Washington Post*, July 31.

Moravcsik, Andrew, 1993. "Liberalism and International Relations Theory: A Social Scientific Assessment," Working Paper Series, Center for International Affairs, Harvard University.

Muppidi, Himadeep, 1999. "Postcoloniality and the Production of International Insecurity: The Persistent Puzzle of US–Indian Relations," in Weldes *et al.* 1999: 119–46.

Murphy, George, 1966. *Soviet Mongolia: A Study of the Oldest Political Satellite*. Berkeley: University of California Press.

Mutume, Gumisai, 2001. "Gender Discrimination Not Good for Growth," *One World*, March 7, at www.twnside.org.sg/title/gender.htm, accessed October 14, 2008.

NACLA, 1974. "Feminismo Beleguerista: A Strategy of the Right," *NACLA Latin America and Empire Report* 8(4): 28–31.

Nadelman, Ethan, 1990. "Global Prohibition Regimes: The Evolution of Norms in International Society," *International Organization* 44: 479–526.

Nandy, Ashis, 1983. *The Intimate Enemy: Loss and Recovery of Self Under Colonialism*. Oxford: Oxford University Press.

Nelson, Barbara, and Najma Chowdury, (eds.), 1994. *Women and Politics Worldwide*. New Haven: Yale University Press.

Neufeld, Mark, 1993. "Interpretation and the 'Science' of International Relations," *Review of International Studies* 19: 39–61.

Neumann, Iver B., 1996a. *Russia and the Idea of Europe. A Study in Identity and International Relations*. London: Routledge.

1996b. "Self and Other in International Relations," *European Journal of International Relations* 2(2): 139–74.

1998. "European Identity, EU Expansion, and the Integration/ Exclusion Nexus," *Alternatives* 23(3): 397–416.

1999. *Uses of the Other. 'The East' in European Identity Formation*. Minneapolis: University of Minnesota Press.

2001. "From Meta to Method: The Materiality of Discourse." Paper presented at the International Studies Association, Chicago, February 2001.

2003. *Mening, Materialiet, Makt: En Introduktion till Diskursanalys*. Lund: Studentlitteratur.

2008. "The Body of the Diplomat," *European Journal of International Relations* 14(4): 671–95.

Neumann, Iver B., and Jennifer M. Welsh, 1991. "The Other in European Self-Definition: An Addendum to the Literature on International Society," *Review of International Studies* 17(4): 327–48.

Newman, Louise, 1999. *White Women's Rights: The Racial Origins of Feminism in the United States.* Oxford: Oxford University Press.

Nimtz, August, 2000. *Marx and Engels: Their Contribution to the Democratic Breakthrough.* New York: State University of New York Press.

Niva, Steve, 1998. "Tough and Tender: New World Order Masculinity and the Gulf War," in Zalewski and Parpart 1998: 109–28.

1999. "Contested Sovereignties and Postcolonial Insecurities in the Middle East," in Weldes *et al.* (eds.), 147–72.

Norton, Barbara, 1992. "Laying the Foundations of Democracy in Russia: E.D. Kuskova's contribution, February-October 1917," in Linda Edmondson (ed.), *Women and Society in Russia and the Soviet Union.* Cambridge: Cambridge University Press, 101–23.

Ohlander, Ann-Sofie, 2000. *Staten var en man: om kvinnor och män i statens tjänst i historien.* Stockholm: Utvecklingsrådet.

Okin, Susan Moller, 1979. *Woman in Western Political Thought.* Princeton University Press.

(with respondents), 1999. *Is Multiculturalism Bad for Women?* Princeton: Princeton University Press.

Okonjo, Kamene, 1994. "Women and the Evolution of a Ghanaian Political Synthesis," in Nelson and Chowdhury 1994: *Women and Politics Worldwide.* New Haven: Yale University Press, 285–97.

Ortner, Sherry B., 1972. "Is Female to Male as Nature is to Culture?" *Feminist Studies* 1(2): 5–31.

Parkman, Francis, 1884. *Some of the Reasons against Woman Suffrage.* Boston.

Parsons, Talcott, 1951. *The Social System.* New York: Free Press.

Pateman, Carole, 1989. *The Disorder of Women. Democracy, Feminism and Political Theory.* Stanford University Press.

Perman, Dagmar, 1962. *The Shaping of the Czechoslovak State.* Leiden: E.J. Brill.

Pernet, Corinne, 2000. "Chilean Feminists, the International Women's Movement, and Suffrage, 1915–1950," *Pacific Historical Review* 69(4): 663–88.

Peterson, V. Spike (ed.), 1992a. *Gendered States: Feminist (Re)Visions of International Relations Theory.* Boulder: Lynne Rienner Publishers.

1992b. "Introduction," in Peterson 1992a: 1–29.

1992c. "Security and Sovereign States: What Is at Stake in Taking Feminism Seriously?" in Peterson 1992a: 31–64.

Phillips, Anne, 1991. *Engendering Democracy*. Cambridge: Polity Press.

Pietilä, Hilkka, and Jeanne Vickers, 1994. *Making Women Matter. The Role of the United Nations*. London: Zed Books.

Poggi, Gianfranco, 1978. *The Development of the Modern State*. Stanford University Press.

Price, Richard, 1995. "A Genealogy of the Chemical Weapons Taboo," *International Organization* 49(1): 73–103.

1997. *The Chemical Weapons Taboo*. Ithaca: Cornell University Press.

1998. "Reversing the Gun Sights: Transnational Civil Society Targets Land Mines," *International Organization* 52(3): 613–45.

Price, Richard, and Christian Reus-Smit, 1998. "Dangerous Liaisons? Critical International Theory and Constructivism," *European Journal of International Relations* 4(3): 259–94.

Puchala, Donald, and Raymond Hopkins, 1983. "International Regimes: Lessons from Inductive Analysis," in Stephen Krasner (ed.), *International Regimes*. Ithaca: Cornell University Press, 61–92.

Raaum, Nina C., 1999. "Women in Parliamentary Politics: Historical Lines of Development," in Christina Bergqvist, Anette Borchorst and Ann Dorte Christensen (eds.), *Equal Democracies? Gender and Politics in the Nordic Countries*. Oslo: Scandinavian University Press, 27–47.

Rai, Shirin, (ed.), 2003. *Mainstreaming Gender, Democratizing the State? Institutional Mechanisms for the Advancement of Women*. Manchester University Press.

Ramirez, Francisco, and Elizabeth McEneaney, 1997. "From Women's Suffrage to Reproduction Rights? Cross-national Considerations," *International Journal of Comparative Sociology* 38(1–2): 6–35.

Ramirez, Francisco, Yasemin Soysal and Suzanne Shanahan, 1997. "The Changing Logic of Political Citizenship: Cross-National Acquisition of Women's Suffrage Rights, 1890–1990," *American Sociological Review* 62(5): 736–47.

Ramirez, Francisco, and Jane Weiss, 1979. "The Political Incorporation of Women," in John W. Meyer and Michael Hannan (eds.), *National Development and the World System*. Chicago: University of Chicago Press, 238–49.

Rank, David J., Ann Hironaka and Evan Schofer, 2000. "The Nation-State and the Natural Environment over the Twentieth Century," *American Sociological Review* 65: 96–116.

Rendall, Jane, 1994. "Citizenship, Culture and Civilization: The Languages of British Suffragists, 1866–1874," in Caroline Daley and Melanie Nola (eds.), *Suffrage and Beyond: International Feminist Perspectives.* New York University Press, 126–50.

Reus-Smit, Christian, 1997. "The Constitutional Structure of International Society and the Nature of Fundamental Institutions," *International Organization* 51(4): 555–89.

Richards, Judith M., 1997. "'To Promote a Woman to Beare Rule': Talking of Queens in Mid-Tudor England," *Sixteenth Century Journal* 28(1): 101–21.

Riddell, John (ed.), 1987. *Founding the Communist International: Proceedings and Documents of the First Congress, March 1919.* New York: Pathfinder.

  1991. *Workers of the World and Oppressed Peoples, Unite! Proceedings and Documents of the Second Congress, 1920.* Vols. I and II. New York: Pathfinder.

Riley, Denise, 1988. *"Am I That Name?" Feminism and the Category of "Women" in History.* Basingstoke: MacMillan.

Ringmar, Erik, 1996. *Identity, Interest and Action: A Cultural Explanation of Sweden's Intervention in the Thirty Years War.* Cambridge: Cambridge University Press.

Risse, Thomas, 2000. "Let's Argue! Persuasion and Deliberation in International Relations," *International Organization* 54(1): 1–39.

Risse, Thomas, Stephen C. Ropp and Kathryn Sikkink (eds.), 1999. *The Power of Human Rights: International Norms and Domestic Change.* Cambridge: Cambridge University Press.

Risse, Thomas, and Kathryn Sikkink, 1999. "The Socialization of International Human Rights Norms into Domestic Practices: Introduction," in Risse, Ropp and Sikkink 1999: 1–38.

Risse-Kappen, Thomas, 1994. "Ideas do not Float Freely: Transnational Coalitions, Domestic Structures and the End of the Cold War," *International Organization* 48(2): 185–214.

Robertson, Roland, 1987. "Globalization Theory and Civilization Analysis," *Comparative Civilization Review* 17: 31–59.

  1992. *Globalization: Social Theory and Global Culture.* London: Sage.

  1995. "Globalization: Time-Space and Homogeneity-Heterogeneity," in Mike Featherstone, Scott Lash and Roland Robertson (eds.), *Global Modernities.* London: Sage, 27–44.

Rosenberg, Justin, 1994. "The International Imagination: IR Theory and 'Classical Social Analysis'," *Millennium* 23(1): 85–108.

Ruddick, Sara, 1993. "Notes Toward a Feminist Peace Politics," in Miriam Cooke and Angela Woollacott (eds.), *Gendering War Talk.* Princeton University Press, 109–27.

Rueschemeyer, Dietrich, Evelyne Huber Stephens and John Stephens 1992. *Capitalist Development and Democracy.* Chicago: Chicago University Press.

Ruggie, John, 1989. "International Structure and International Trans-formation: Space, Time, and Method," in Ernst Otto Czempiel and James Rosenau (eds.), *Global Changes and Theoretical Challenges*. Washington DC: Lexington Books, 21–35.

Rumelili, Bahar, 2003. "Liminality and Perpetuation of Conflicts: Turkish–Greek Relations in the Context of Community-Building by the EU," *European Journal of International Relations* 9(2): 213–48.

2004. "Constructing Identity and Relating to Difference: Understanding EU's Mode of Differentiation," *Review of International Studies* 30: 27–47.

Rupp, Leila, 1997. *Worlds of Women: The Making of an International Women's Movement*. Princeton: Princeton University Press.

Sacks, Karen, 1982. "An Overview of Women and Power in Africa," in Jean O'Barr (ed.), *Perspectives on Power: Women in Africa, Asia and Latin America*. Durham, NC: Duke University, Center for International Studies, 1–10.

SADC, 1999. "Thirty Percent Women in Power by 2005," *SADC Gender Monitor*, at www.sardc.net/Widsaa/sgm/1999/sgm_ch3.html, accessed September 16, 2008.

Said, Edward, 1979. *Orientalism*. New York: Vintage.

Sainsbury, Diane, 1993. "The Politics of Increased Women's Representation: The Swedish Case," in Joni Lovenduski and Pippa Norris (eds.), *Gender and Party Politics*. London: Sage, 263–90.

(ed.) 1999, *Gender and Welfare State Regimes*. Oxford: Oxford University Press.

Salvador, Riosang, 1995. "Non Governmental Organizations Address Beijing World Women's Conference at Conclusion of General Exchange of Views," press release of Fourth United Nations World Conference of Women. WOM/BEI/32 (am) September 14, 1995.

Sapiro, Virginia, 1998. "When Are Interests Interesting? The Problem of Political Representation of Women," in Anne Phillips (ed.), *Feminism and Politics*. Oxford: Oxford University Press, 161–92.

Sassoon, Anne Showstack, 1987. *Women and the State: The Shifting Boundaries of Public and Private*. London: Hutchinson.

Sawer, Marian, 1996a. "Femocrats and Ecorats: Women's Policy Machinery in Australia, Canada and New Zealand," Occasional Paper Series, Fourth World Conference on Women. Geneva: United Nations Research Institute for Social Development.

1996b. "Gender, Metaphor and the State," *Feminist Review* 52 (Spring): 118–34.

Schirmacher, Kaethe, 1912. *The Modern Woman's Rights Movement: A Historical Survey*. New York: Macmillan.

Scott, Catherine, 1995. *Gender and Development: Rethinking Modernization and Dependency Theory*. Boulder: Lynne Rienner Publishers.

Scott, James, 1931. *The International Conferences of American States, 1889–1928: A Collection of the Conventions, Recommendations, Resolutions, Reports, and Motions Adopted by the First Six International Conferences of American States, and Documents Relating to the Organization of the Conferences*. New York: Oxford University Press.

Scott, Joan W., 1992. "Experience," in Judith Butler and Joan W. Scott (eds.), *Feminists Theorize the Political*. New York: Routledge, 22–40.

1988/1999. *Gender and the Politics of History*. New York: Columbia University Press.

1996. *Only Paradoxes to Offer. French Feminists and the Rights of Man*. Cambridge, MA: Harvard University Press.

Sgier, Lea, 2001. "Gender Quotas and Institutionalised Conceptions of Citizenship: France and Switzerland," paper presented at the Eighth Annual Conference of the International Political Science Association, Copenhagen, Denmark, August 23–5, 2001.

Shapiro, Michael J., 1988. "The Constitution of the Central American Other: The Case of 'Guatemala'," in Michael Shapiro (ed.), *The Politics of Representation: Writing Practices in Biography, Photography and Policy Analysis*. Madison: University of Wisconsin Press, 89–123.

Sikkink, Kathryn, 1993a. "The Power of Principled Ideas: Human Rights Policies in the United States and Western Europe," in Judith Goldstein and Robert Keohane (eds.), *Ideas and Foreign Policy: Beliefs, Institutions, and Political Change*. Ithaca: Cornell University Press, 139–72.

1993b. "Human Rights, Principled Issue-Networks and Sovereignty in Latin America," *International Organization* 47(3): 411–41.

2004. *Mixed Messages: US Human Rights Policy and Latin America*. Ithaca: Cornell University Press.

Silberman, Bernard, 1993. *Cages of Reason: The Rise of the Rational State in France, Japan, the United States, and Great Britain*. Chicago: University of Chicago Press.

Silverblatt, Irene, 1987. *Moon, Sun and Witches: Gender Ideologies and Class in Inca and Colonial Peru*. Princeton: Princeton University Press.

Simmons, Ann, and Robin Wright, 2000. "Gender Quota Puts Uganda in Role of Pioneer," *Los Angeles Times*, February 23.

Skocpol, Theda, and Margaret Somers, 1980. "The Uses of Comparative History in Macrosocial Inquiry," *Comparative Studies of Society and History* 22(2): 174–97.

Smith, Hilda, 1982. *Reason's Disciples: Seventeenth-Century English Feminists*. Urbana: University of Illinois Press.

Smith, Jeremy, 1999. *The Bolsheviks and the National Question, 1917–1923*. New York: St. Martin's Press.

Somers, Margaret, 1992. "Narrativity, Narrative Identity, and Social Action: Rethinking English Working-Class Formation," *Social Science History* 16(4): 591–630.

Squires, Judith, 2000. "Group Representation, Deliberation and the Displacement of Dichotomies," in Michael Saward (ed.), *Democratic Innovation: Deliberation, Representation and Association*. London: Routledge, 93–105.

Status of Women. Canada, 2000. "Institutional Mechanisms for the Advancement of Women," fact sheet for the United Nations General Assembly, Special Session, Beijing +5, at www.swc-cfc.gc.ca/pubs/b5_factsheets/b5_factsheets_e.html, accessed September 24, 2008.

Staudt, Kathleen (ed.), 1990. *Women, International Development and Politics: The Bureaucratic Mire*. Philadelphia: Temple University Press.

Steinberg, Marc, 1995. "'The Great End of All Government ...': Working People's Construction of Citizenship Claims in Early Nineteenth-Century England and the Matter of Class," *International Review of Social History* 40, Supplement 3, 19–50.

Stensöta, Helena, 2004. *Den Empatiska Staten: Jämställdhetens Inverkan på Daghem och Polis 1950–2000*. Göteborg Studies in Politics 85.

Stephenson, Carolyn, 1995. "Women's International NGOs at the United Nations," in Winslow 1995: 135–54.

Stetson, Dorothy McBride, and Amy Mazur (eds.), 1995. *Comparative State Feminism*. London: Sage.

Stienstra, Deborah, 1994. "Organizing for Change: International Women's Movements and World Politics," in Francine D'Amico and Peter Beckman (eds.), *Women in World Politics*. Westport, CT: Bergin & Garvey, 143–54.

Stites, Richard, 1976. "Zhenotdel: Bolshevism and Russian Women, 1917–1930," *Russian History* 3(2): 174–93.

1978. *The Women's Liberation Movement in Russia: Feminism, Nihilism, and Bolshevism 1860–1930*. Princeton: Princeton University Press.

Stoler, Ann Laura, 1996. "Carnal Knowledge and Imperial Power: Gender, Race and Morality in Colonial Asia," in Joan Scott (ed.), *Feminism and History*. Oxford: Oxford University Press, 209–66.

Strang, David, and John W. Meyer, 1993. "Institutional Conditions for Diffusion," *Theory and Society* 22: 487–511.

Straw, Jack 2002. "Rebuilding Afghanistan," *Financial Times*, March 21.

Styrkársdóttir, Audur, 1998. *From Feminism to Class Politics: The Rise and Decline of Women's Politics in Reykjavik, 1908–1922*. Umeå universitet: Statsvetenskapliga institutionen.

Subtelny, Orest, 2000. *Ukraine: A History.* Toronto: University of Toronto Press.

Sveriges Riksdag, Utredningstjänsten 2000. "Jämställdhetsenheten inom Regeringskansliet," PM 2000-08-10. Dnr 2000:1687. Stockholm.

Szayna, Thomas S., Daniel Byman, Steven C. Bankes, Derek Eaton, Seth G. Jones, Roberts Mullins, Ian O. Lesser and William Rosenau, 2001. *The Emergence of Peer Competitors: A Framework for Analysis.* Santa Monica: Rand Publications.

Therborn, Goran, 1977. "The Rule of Capital and the Rise of Capitalism," *New Left Review* 103: 3–41.

Thomas, Daniel, 2001. *The Helsinki Effect: International Norms, Human Rights, and the Demise of Communism.* Princeton: Princeton University Press.

Thomas, George, Francisco O. Ramirez, John Boli and John Meyer, 1987. *Institutional Structure: Constituting the State, Society and the Individual.* Newbury Park: Sage.

Thompson, Elizabeth, 2000. *Colonial Citizen: Republican Rights, Paternal Privilege, and Gender in French Syria and Lebanon.* New York: Columbia University Press.

Thomson, Janice, 1990. "State Practices, International Norms, and the Decline of Mercenarism," *International Studies Quarterly* 34(1): 23–47.

Tickner, J. Ann, 2001. *Gendering World Politics.* New York: Columbia University Press.

Tilly, Charles, 1975. "Reflections on the History of European State Making," in Charles Tilly (ed.), *The Formation of National States in Western Europe.* Princeton: Princeton University Press, 3–83.

1994. *European Revolutions, 1492–1992.* Oxford: Blackwell.

Tinker, Irene, and Jane Jaquette, 1987. "UN Decade for Women: Its Impact and Legacy," *World Development* 15(3): 419–27.

Todorov, Tzvetan, 1984. *The Conquest of America: The Question of the Other.* New York: Harper & Row.

Togeby, Lise, 1994. *Fra tilskuere til deltagare.* Aarhus: Politica.

Tolbert, Pamela, and Lynne G. Zucker, 1983. "Institutional Sources of Change in the Formal Structure of Organizations: The Diffusion of Civil Service Reform, 1880–1935," *Administrative Sciences Quarterly* 28: 22–39.

Torstendahl, Rolf, 1991. *Bureaucratisation in Northwestern Europe, 1880–1985.* London: Routledge.

Towns, Ann, 2002. "Paradoxes of (In)Equality: Something is Rotten in the Gender Equal State of Sweden," *Cooperation and Conflict* 37(2): 157–79.

2003. "Understanding the Effects of Larger Ratios of Women in National Legislatures: Proportions and Gender Differentiation in Sweden and Norway," *Women and Politics* 25(1–2): 1–29.

2004. "Norms and Inequality: Global Politics of Women and The State." PhD dissertation, University of Minnesota.

2008. "Inevitable Inequalities? Approaching Gender Equality and Multiculturalism," in Richard Price (ed.). *Moral Limit and Possibility in World Politics*. Cambridge: Cambridge University Press, 225–52.

2009. "The Status of Women as a Standard of 'Civilization'," *European Journal of International Relations* 15(4): 681–706.

Triandis, Harry, 1994. *Culture and Social Behavior*. New York: McGraw-Hill.

Tripp, Aili Mari, 2000. *Women and Politics in Uganda*. Madison: University of Wisconsin Press.

2001. "The New Political Activism in Africa," *Journal of Democracy* 12 (3): 141–55.

True, Jacqui, and Michael Mintrom, 2001. "Transnational Networks and Policy Diffusion: The Case of Gender Mainstreaming," *International Studies Quarterly* 45(1): 27–57.

Tsikata, Dzodzi, 2001. "National Machineries for the Advancement of Women in Africa: Are They Transforming Gender Relations?" *Social Watch*, 73–4, at www.socialwatch.org/en/informesTematicos/29.html, accessed October 8, 2008.

Turner, Brian, Paul Abercrombie and Stephen Hill, 1981. *The Dominant Ideology Thesis*. London: Allen & Unwin.

United Nations, Department of Economic and Social Affairs, 1955. *The Convention on the Political Rights of Women: History and Commentary*. New York: UN Publications.

Ünlüdag, Tânia, 2002. "Bourgeois Mentality and Socialist Ideology as Exemplified by Clara Zetkin's Constructs of Femininity," *International Review of Social History* 47: 33–58.

Vernon, James, 1993. *Politics and the People: A Study in English Political Culture c. 1815–1867*. Cambridge: Cambridge University Press.

1994. "Who's Afraid of the Linguistic Turn?: The Politics of Social History and Its Discontents," *Social History* 19: 81–7.

Vincent, John, 1986. *Human Rights and International Relations*. Cambridge: Cambridge University Press.

Waever, Ole, 1992. "International Society – Theoretical Promises Unfulfilled?" *Cooperation and Conflict* 27, 97–128.

Walker, R. B. J., 1989. "History and Structure in the Theory of International Relations," *Millennium* 28(2): 163–83.

1993. *Inside/Outside: International Relations as Political Theory*. Cambridge: Cambridge University Press.

Walker, R. B. J., and Saul Mendlovitz (eds.), 1990. *Contending Sovereignties: Redefining Political Community*. Boulder: Lynne Rienner Publishers.

Walt, Stephen M., 1991. "The Renaissance of Security Studies," *International Studies Quarterly* 35: 211–39.

Waltz, Kenneth, 1979. *Theory of International Politics*. Boston: Addison-Wesley.

1986. "Reflections on *Theory of International Politics*: A Response to my Critics," in Robert Keohane (ed.), *Neorealism and its Critics*. New York: Columbia University Press.

2004. "Neorealism: Confusions and Criticisms," *Journal of Politics and Society* 15: 2–6.

Ward, Kathryn, 1984. *Women in the World System*. New York: Praeger.

Wartenberg, Thomas, 1992. *Rethinking Power*. Albany: State University of New York Press.

Waters, Elizabeth, 1989. "In the Shadow of the Comintern: The Communist Women's Movement, 1920–43," in Sonia Kruks, Rayna Rapp and Marilyn B. Young (ed.), *Promissory Notes: Women in the Transition to Socialism*. New York: Monthly Review Press, 29–56.

Watson, Adam, 1984. "New States in the Americas," in Bull and Watson 1984: 127–41.

1987. "Hedley Bull, State Systems, and International Studies," *Review of International Studies* 13, 146–53.

1992. *The Evolution of International Society: A Comparative Historical Analysis*. New York: Routledge.

Waylen, Georgina, 1997. "Women's Movements, the State and Democratization in Chile: The Establishment of SERNAM," in Goetz 1997: 90–103.

Weber, Cynthia, 1995. *Simulating Sovereignty: Intervention, the State and Symbolic Exchange*. Cambridge: Cambridge University Press.

Weber, Max, 1947. *The Theory of Social and Economic Organization*. London: W. Hodge.

Weibull, Jörgen, 1997. *Swedish History in Outline*. Stockholm: Svenska Institutet.

Weldes, Jutta, 1999. "The Cultural Production of Crises: US Identity and Missiles in Cuba," in Weldes *et al.* 1999: 35–62.

Weldes, Jutta, Mark Laffey, Hugh Gusterson and Raymond Duvall (eds.), 1999. *Cultures of Insecurity: States, Communities, and the Production of Danger*. Minneapolis: University of Minnesota Press.

Wendt, Alexander, 1992. "Anarchy is What States Make of It: The Social Construction of Power Politics," *International Organizations* 46(2): 391–425.

1994. "Collective Identity Formation and the International State," *American Political Science Review* 88(2): 384–96.

1998. "On Constitution and Causation in International Relations," *Review of International Studies* 24: 101–17.

1999. *Social Theory of International Politics*. Cambridge: Cambridge University Press.

White, Stephen, 1980. "The USSR Supreme Soviet: A Developmental Perspective," *Legislative Studies Quarterly* 5(2): 247–74.

Whittick, Arnold, 1979. *Woman into Citizen*. London: Athenaeum.

Wight, Martin, 1966. "Western Values in International Relations," in Herbert Butterfield and Martin Wight (eds.), *Diplomatic Investigations*. London: Allen & Unwin, 89–131.

Wikander, Ulla, Alice Kessler-Harris and Jane Lewis (eds.), 1995. *Protecting Women: Labor Legislation in Europe, the United States and Australia, 1880–1920*. Urbana: University of Illinois Press.

Winslow, Anne (ed.), 1995. *Women, Politics and the United Nations*. Westport, CT: Greenwood Press.

Wolchik, Sharon, 1982. "Demography, Political Reform and Women's Issues in Czechoslovakia," in Margherita Rendel, (ed.), *Women, Power and Political Systems*. New York: St. Martin's Press, 135–50.

    1998. "Czechoslovakia" in Sabrina Ramet (ed.), *Eastern Europe: Politics, Culture and Society since 1939*. Bloomington: Indiana University Press, 35–70.

Wood, Elizabeth, 1997. *The Baba and the Comrade: Gender and Politics in Revolutionary Russia*. Indianapolis: Indiana University Press.

Yee, Albert, 1997. "Thick Rationality and the Missing 'Brute Fact': The Limits of Rationalist Incorporation of Norms and Ideas," *Journal of Politics* 59(4): 1001–39.

Yoshimi, Yoshiaki, and Suzanne O'Brien, 2000. *Comfort Women: Sexual Slavery in the Japanese Military During World War II*. New York: Columbia University Press.

Young, Iris Marion, 1990. *Justice and the Politics of Difference*. Princeton: Princeton University Press.

    1994. "Gender as Seriality: Thinking about Women as a Social Collective," *Signs: Journal of Women in Culture and Society* 19(3): 713–38.

Yuval-Davis, Nira, 1997. *Gender and Nation*. London: Sage.

Yuval-Davis, Nira, and Floya Anthias, 1989. *Woman – Nation – State*. New York: St. Martin's Press.

Zalewski, Marysia, and Jane Parpart (eds.), 1998. *The "Man" Question in International Relations*. Boulder: Westview.

Zaremba, Maciej, 1999. *De rena och de andra: om tvångssteriliseringar, rashygien och arvsynd*. Stockholm: Bokförlaget DN.

Zetkin, Clara, 1895. "Concerning the Women's Rights Petition," *Vorwärts*, January 24, reproduced in Foner 1984: 60–71.

    1984. *Selected Writings*, ed. Philip Foner. New York: International Publishers.

Zheng, Wang, 1999. *Women in the Chinese Enlightenment: Oral and Textual Histories*. Berkeley: University of Berkeley Press.

Index

absolutist state 59, 62, 63
affirmative action 153, 154, 156, 160, 180
Afghanistan 3, 9
Africa 2, 8, 14, 69, 79, 89, 116, 117, 118, 119, 138, 140, 142, 151, 182, 187, 188
African states 3, 157, 179, 182
African-Asian Solidarity Organization 8
Afro-Asian Solidarity Movement 117, 188, 191
Afro-Asian Women's Conference (1961) 117
Al Saied, Amina 8
Algeria 116, 176
Álvarez, Sayan 109
America 103, 107, 115, 118, 119
Central 114
American Women (report of US President's Commission on the Status of Women) 135
Americas 83, 90, 191; *see also* pan-American context
Andaman Islands 73
Anglo-European states 14, 90, 119
Angola 2, 116
Annan, Kofi 162
Arab Women's Union 8
Argentina 3, 33, 90, 105, 107, 114, 115, 154, 164
Armenia 101
Arroyo, Luna 114
Ashley, Richard 36
Asia 2, 3, 8, 13, 14, 79, 89, 90, 107, 116, 117, 118, 119, 138, 140, 151, 152, 157, 182, 187, 188
Asian-African Conference of Women (1958) 117
Ataturk, Kemal 95
Australia 2, 3, 83, 90, 93, 108, 131

Austria 59, 78, 95
Awe, Bolanle 142
Azerbaijan 101

Bahamas 116
Bahrain 116
el-Bakri, Zeinab 79
"barbarous" societies 7, 33, 67–80; *see also* "savage" society
Bartelson, Jens 67
Bebel, August 97
Beijing Platform for Action 155
Belarus 101
Belgium 3, 59, 95, 116, 177
Berkovitch, Nitza 146
Berlin Act of 1885 69
Bolivia 110, 111
Bolshevik Party, Bolsheviks 97, 100–2, 125
Brasil, José Fransisco Assis 107
Brazil 107
Bukharin, Nikolai 102
Bull, Hedley 25
bureaucracy 19, 61, 137, 146
bureaucrats, *see* civil servants
Bush, George W. 149

Cáceres, Aurora 111
Cambodia 116
Campbell, Charles 73
Campbell, David 35, 36
Canada 95, 131
Canadian Committee for Equality of Women 131
Cape Verde 116
capitalism 98–9, 112, 135, 142, 158–73
capitalist states 98–100, 102–3, 112–15, 134–7
capitalist West 134–7, 147, 191
Catherine the Great 64

masculinized states, *see* gendered states
Mason, Otis Tufton 74
Mauritania 116
Mexican Institutional Revolutionary
    Party 109
Mexico 109, 113, 114, 115
Meyer, John 21, 23, 24, 25
Mill, J. S. 92
Millar, John 70
Milliken, Jennifer 16, 39
mobilization of shame 176
modern democracies, *see* democracy
"modern" states 19, 151–2, 158–83,
    169–82, 193
modernization 138–48, 165, 192, 196
    theory 22, 164
Mongolia 102
Morgan, Lewis 68, 97
Morocco 3, 116, 176
Mozambique 2, 116
multiculturalism 193
Mussolini, Benito 113

Napoleonic Code 108
national legislature sex quota laws, *see*
    legislature sex quotas
national women's machinery
    (NWM), *see* national women's
    policy bureaus
national women's policy bureaus, or
    national women's machinery
    (NWM) Ch 6: 6, 8, 122–48, 151,
    159, 162, 182, 183, 191–2
    adoption trajectory 2–3, 13, 122,
        123, 124, 129, 137, 146, 188
    and developing states 192
    and development 133, 137–45, 192
    and ECOSOC 129
    and modernization 192, 196
    and UN Decade for Women 132
    and Western, capitalist states 191
Nepal 3, 149, 154, 179
Netherlands 59, 78, 95, 116, 153, 177
Neumann, Iver B. 37
New England Woman Suffrage
    Association 7, 9
New Zealand 2, 83, 93, 108
Nicaragua 114
Nigeria 116, 117
non-alignment movement 117

non-governmental organizations
    (NGOs) 20, 28, 145, 146, 152,
    153, 180
norm entrepreneurs 28
norms 24–34, 42–52, 185–6
    and change 19–24, 28–33, 48–54
    and contestation 46, 185, 189–94
    definition 42
    and "entrepreneurs" 28
    and homogeneity 6, 18–19, 27–8,
        189–90
    and identity 31–3, 35–7, 42–4
    and mimicry 20, 120
    and social hierarchy / ranking 48,
        185–6
    and socialization 29–30, 181
    See also Katzenstein, Peter
norms approach, *see* liberal
    constructivism
Norris, Pippa 5
North America 2, 3, 5, 13, 91, 104, 114,
    151, 157, 183, 186
Norway 2, 59, 83, 108, 153, 154, 177

Odría, Manuel 115
Okin, Susan 5

Pakistan 3
Palestine 91
Pan American Association for the
    Advancement of Women
    (PAAW) 106
Pan-American Conference in Santiago
    (1923) 106
Pan-American Conference of Women
    (1922) 106
Pan-American context, or Pan-
    Americanism 82, 83, 104–15,
    188
Pan-American Union 106, 113
Panama 112, 115
Paraguay 115, 154
parity law (France) 176, 177–9
Parkman, Francis 73
Partido Socialista Obrero Español 153
patriarchy 47, 121, 140, 164
    "traditional" 143
Peru 107, 109, 110, 115, 154
    National Women's Council of Peru
        108

CPSIA information can be obtained
at www.ICGtesting.com
Printed in the USA
FFOW04n2045200715
15287FF